Serving *All* Urban Consumers

Serving *All* Urban Consumers

A marketing approach to water services in low and middle-income countries

Book 2: Guidance notes for managers

Kevin Sansom, Richard Franceys, Cyrus Njiru,
Sam Kayaga, Sue Coates and Srinivas Chary

Water, Engineering and Development Centre
Loughborough University
2004

Water, Engineering and Development Centre,
Loughborough University,
Leicestershire, LE11 3TU, UK

Institute of Water and Environment
Cranfield University
Silsoe, Bedford
MK45 4DT UK

Produced as part of a WEDC/IWE partnership

© Water, Engineering and Development Centre; 2004

ISBN 13 Paperback: 978 1 84380 055 2
ISBN Ebook: 9781788533492
Book DOI: http://dx.doi.org/10.3362/9781788533492

A catalogue record for this book is available from the British Library.

A reference copy of this publication is also available online at:
http://www.lboro.ac.uk/wedc/publications/sftup.htm

Sansom, K., Franceys, R., Njiru, C., Kayaga. S., Coates, S. and Chary, S. (2004) Serving All Urban Consumers - A marketing approach to water services in low and middle-income countries. Book 2: Guidance notes for managers.
WEDC, Loughborough University, UK.

WEDC (The Water, Engineering and Development Centre) at Loughborough University in the UK is one of the world's leading institutions concerned with education, training, research and consultancy for the planning, provision and management of physical infrastructure for development in low- and middleincome countries.

This edition is reprinted and distributed by Practical Action Publishing.
Since 1974, Practical Action Publishing has published and disseminated books and information in support of international development work throughout the world. Practical Action Publishing trades only in support of its parent charity objectives and any profits are covenanted back to Practical Action (Charity Reg. No. 247257, Group VAT Registration No. 880 9924 76).

This document is an output from a project funded by the UK
Department for International Development (DFID)
for the benefit of low-income countries.
The views expressed are not necessarily those of DFID.

Acknowledgements

The financial support of the Department for International Development of the British Government is gratefully acknowledged. The valuable assistance and contributions of engineers, managers and consultants in our field research cities is much appreciated by the authors. Key people include: A. Narender in Guntor, India, G. Bhattarai in various small towns in Nepal, S.K. Gupta, Agra, India and Ms A. Kamalie for the Lesotho report. Many other utility, NGO and college staff provided valuable assistance in our fieldwork in the main research locations: Mombasa, Kampala, Durban and Guntor for which we are most grateful.

The advice and review work of Dennis Mwanza, Alison Wedgwood, Kimberly Clarke and Guy Howard is also appreciated.

How to use this series of books

This book is the second in a series of three on marketing approaches to water services. The main target audience of this book is utility managers in low and middle-income countries who are interested in innovative ways of serving more of their consumers. It is also designed to be of value to government staff, to policymakers and regulators who have responsibilities for the sector, as well as to donors.

A key question that is considered is how best can commercial/marketing approaches to utility management be adapted to serve low-income areas so that sustainable services are achieved? This issue is addressed in this series of three books titled: 'Serving All Urban Consumers'.

Included in this publication (Book 2) are many examples of applying different and useful marketing approaches for the urban water sector, which has made it a relatively long document. It is intended as a sourcebook for readers to refer to as and when it is convenient, using the table of contents to navigate around the text, together with the notes on the document structure at the beginning of Parts I, II and III.

There are two other publications in this series. Book 1 provides guidance for government's enabling role in using marketing approaches and moving towards serving all consumers. Book 3 gives a detailed explanation of the PREPP methodology to facilitate utility consultation with low-income communities.

List of boxes

Box 1.1.   Estimated urban water and sanitation service levels in India 7
Box 1.2.   Importance of marketing orientation 17
Box 2.1.   GIS at Durban Metro Water 36
Box 2.2.   High vendor prices in East Africa 52
Box 3.1.   Roof catchments in low-income shanties in Tegucigalpa, Hondurash 79
Box 3.2.   Payment option preferences in Kampala 82
Box 3.3.   Shared management of water services in Haiti (Part 1) 84
Box 3.4.   Shared management of water services in Haiti (Part 2) 85
Box 4.1.   The history of informal settlements in Durban, South 94
Box 4.2.   Success factors of small-scale independent providers (SSIPs) 101
Box 4.3.   Co-operative management of water distribution in Kibera, Nairobi 102
Box 4.4.   Performance contract for the NWSC water utility in Uganda 104
Box 4.5.   Incentives offered by Durban Metro Water to ground tank users 105
Box 6.1.   The water kiosks of Kibera, Nairobi 122
Box 6.2.   Typical PEST factors to consider 133
Box 6.3.   Categories for subjective performance descriptions 133
Box 6.4.   Examples of items to be assessed using a SWOT analysis 136
Box 7.1.   Utility mission statements 142
Box 7.2.   Potential utility objectives 142
Box 7.3.   Developing tariff policies using the 'AESCE' principles 143
Box 7.4.   Block tariffs to subsidize the poor? 144
Box 7.5.   Estimation of water treatment plant costs 148
Box 7.6.   Estimation for transmission mains 148
Box 7.7.   Estimate of construction costs of concrete reservoir tanks 149
Box 7.8.   Matching tariffs with projected costs and willingness to pay 159
Box 7.9.   Example financial projections for investments in Kampala 163
Box 8.1.   Community mobilisation at Durban Metro Water 166
Box 8.2.   External education services unit of Umgeni water, S. Africa 167
Box 8.3.   Marketing Sanitation in Rural India 167
Box 8.4.   Durban Metro Water's promotion of service options 170
Box 8.5.   Hyderabad Metro Water Board's Customer Care Initiatives 172
Box 8.6.   Durban Metro Water Department Mission Statement 174
Box 8.7.   Simplifying procedures in Chennai to improve CRM 175
Box 8.8.   Investing in technology in order to improve CRM 175
Box 8.9.   Computer billing systems 179
Box 8.10.   Lusaka's evolving policy on water and sanitation in peri-urban areas ... 181
Box 8.12.   Customer orientation at Chennai Metro Water, India 182
Box 8.11.   Change management and customer orientation in NWSC, Uganda 182
Box 8.13.   Establishment of a peri-urban unit in Lusaka 184

List of figures

Figure 1.1.   Service options offered by Durban Metro Water 10
Figure 1.2.   The customer value chain 19
Figure 1.3.   Key stages of the Strategic Marketing Framework 20
Figure 1.4.   Strategic marketing activities for improving water services (Part A) 21
Figure 1.5.   Strategic marketing activities for improving water services (Part B) 22
Figure 2.1.   Arusha sample market segmentation plan 33
Figure 2.2.   Social map of La Paz and El Alto, Bolivia 35
Figure 2.3.   Outline market survey process 38
Figure 2.4.   Relating questions to the research purpose 40
Figure 2.5.   Total cash income earned per family per year 45
Figure 2.6.   Preferences for utility connections 47
Figure 3.1.   Individual, in-house connections 61
Figure 3.2.   Individual house connections - flexible pipes to meter/valve clusters 62
Figure 3.3.   Individual house connections - daily filled overhead tank 63
Figure 3.4.   Individual yard connections/taps 65
Figure 3.5.   Individual yard connection with ground tank 66
Figure 3.6.   Communal or shared yard connections/taps 67
Figure 3.7.   Communal yard connections with raised or ground tank 68
Figure 3.8.   Public standpost - staffed (kiosk) 69
Figure 3.9.   Public standpost with water storage - staffed (kiosk) 71
Figure 3.10. Public standpost - pre-paid with tokens 72
Figure 3.11. Public standpost 73
Figure 3.12. Private vendors, price regulated 74
Figure 3.13. Public or private street tank/water tankers 76
Figure 3.14. Public handpump in urban or peri-urban areas 77
Figure 3.15. Water services in Port-Au-Prince shanty towns 85
Figure 3.16. Outline process for developing new service/payment options 87
Figure 3.17. Typical contingent valuation process (Part A) 89
Figure 3.18. Typical contingent valuation process (Part B) 90
Figure 3.19. Mombasa example WTP survey results 91
Figure 5.1.   Strategic marketing activities for improving water services (Part A) 110
Figure 5.2.   Strategic marketing activities for improving water services (Part B) 111
Figure 6.1.   Average numbers of water supply hours in Mombasa 118
Figure 6.2.   General steps in performance measurement 127
Figure 6.3.   Three stages of PEST analysis 132
Figure 7.1.   Outline investment planning process 140
Figure 8.1.   Marketing mix issues for water utilities 168
Figure 8.2.   Typical steps towards a purchase and the communication tools 170
Figure 8.3.   The positive effect of customer satisfactions 173
Figure 8.4.   Towards a customer orientated organization 183
Figure 8.5.   Strategic marketing and service improvement 185
Figure 8.6.   Steps leading to risk management 186
Figure 8.7.   A learning cycle incorporating experience 191

List of tables

Table 1.1.   Service levels of watsan utilities in selected African cities 6
Table 1.2.   Percentage of households with pipe connections in Asian cities 7
Table 1.3.   Wastewater and sanitation technologies 23
Table 1.4.   Utility-managed or supported sanitation options 24
Table 2.1.   Socio-economic index variables for water quality zoning in Kampala 32
Table 2.2.   Average household income by market segment in Guntur, India 34
Table 2.3.   Key socio-demographic data for urban population in Uganda 46
Table 2.4.   Coping costs for water users in Dehra Dun, India 49
Table 2.5.   Opportunity cost of time spent collecting water 50
Table 2.6.   Expenses on boiled/mineral water (as a percentage of income) 50
Table 2.7.   Total annual capital expenditure (TACE) as a percentage of income 51
Table 2.8.   Coping costs as percentage of income 51
Table 2.9.   Small-scale providers' market share in 10 African cities 52
Table 2.10.   Water Price Range in Kampala poor communities 53
Table 2.11.   PREPP - The basic steps 55
Table 2.12.   Potential outputs from PREPP surveys 56
Table 3.1.   Examples of existing and improved water options in informal settlements 58
Table 3.2.   Water service options for selected variables in urban areas 60
Table 3.3.   Alternative water sources in Guntur 79
Table 3.4.   Coping strategies of new middle-income residents in Kampala 80
Table 3.5.   Payment option summary 83
Table 4.1.   Implications of status of land for extension of water services 96
Table 4.2.   Examples of small water enterprises 101
Table 6.1.   Mombasa summary of existing services in each market segment 117
Table 6.2.   Methods of water storage in Guntur, India 118
Table 6.3.   Lesotho water consumption per district 119
Table 6.4.   Guntur preferences for existing water options 120
Table 6.5.   Guntur preferences for proposed water options 121
Table 6.6.   Key elements of institutional development 124
Table 6.7.   Urban watsan services responsibilities in Maharashtra 126
Table 6.8.   Financial indicator and ratio examples 128
Table 6.9.   Performance indicator and ratio examples 129
Table 6.10.   Service levels indicators from consumer surveys 130
Table 6.11.   Subjective performance indicators for NWSC 136
Table 6.12.   SWOT analysis of NWSC, Kampala 137
Table 7.1.   Key issues for setting tariffs 145
Table 7.2.   Balancing service option tariffs with income 146
Table 7.5.   Service options offered in low-income areas in Kampala 150
Table 7.3.   Service options offered for 1 to 3-roomed dwellings in Mombasa 150
Table 7.4.   Service options offered to people in informal settlements in Mombasa .150
Table 7.6.   WTP results for people in 1,2 or 3-roomed dwellings in Mombasa 151
Table 7.7.   WTP results for people in informal settlements in Mombasa 152
Table 7.8.   Individual ranking of options in Mombasa informal settlements 153
Table 7.9.   Take-up of service options by Market segment in Mombasa 155
Table 7.10.   Water service levels and health concerns 156
Table 7.11.   Estimated water consumption for service options in Mombasa 157
Table 7.12.   Proposed tariff structure for Mombasa 160
Table 7.13.   Projected revenues in Mombasa 161
Table 8.1.   Estimation of Risk: magnitude of consequence and probabilities 187
Table 8.2.   Water supply frequency by market segment in Mombasa 190
Table 11.1.   Scenario 1: AIC calculation based on high level of management

efficiency (15% UFW and 90% bill collection efficiency) 233

Table 11.2.   Scenario 2: AIC calculation based on high level of management
efficiency (15% UFW and 90% bill collection efficiency) 235

Contents

Acknowledgements v
How to use this series of books v
List of boxes vi
List of figures vii
List of tables viii

Part I Overview

Structure of this document 1

Chapter 1 2

Introduction and overview

1.1   Introduction 2

1.2   Who is this document for? 5

1.3   Water and sanitation services for the urban poor 5
        Typical service coverage 5
        The effects of inadequate utility services on poor communities 8
        Pricing and service differentiation to serve the poor 8

1.4   Examples of innovative approaches to serve the poor 9
        Approaches at Durban Metro Water 9
        Approaches in Manila 10
        Approaches in Guntur and Rajhamundry 12
        Approaches in Buenos Aires 12
        Approaches in El Alto 14

1.5   Conventional 'predict and provide' approaches 15

1.6   The marketing approach 16

1.7   The strategic marketing framework 20

1.8   Marketing for sanitation 23

Part II Marketing water services to low-income consumers

Chapter 2 28

Knowing and understanding all consumer groups

2.1   Introduction 28

2.2   Market segmentation overview 28
        Types of building as a criterion for market segmentation 30
        Socio-economic criteria for water sector market segmentation 31
        Using segmentation plans and data 32

2.3   **Use of GIS** **35**

2.4   **Overview of consumer survey techniques** **36**

     Communicating with different consumer groups *39*

     Questionnaire surveys *40*

     Potential aspects to be researched for the water sector *41*

     Sampling *42*

     Pilot testing *42*

     Managing the survey and analysing the results *43*

     Surveys and gender *44*

     Presenting the consumer survey results *44*

2.5   **Triangulating and cross-checking results** **45**

2.6   **Understanding water consumer's willingness to pay** **47**

2.7   **Revealed preferences: Coping strategies and costs** **48**

2.8   **Revealed preferences: Small scale providers and informal market** **51**

2.9   **Focus group discussions and the 'PREPP' approach** **54**

     PREPP methodology outline *54*

     Potential PREPP benefits and outputs *55*

Chapter 3 .... **57**

Targeting low-income water consumers

3.1   **Introduction and summary** **57**

3.2   **The need for innovation** **57**

3.3   **Service options** **58**

     Examples of service options that utilities can provide or support *60*

     Consumer-organized service options *78*

     Unprotected or unauthorized water options *80*

3.4   **Payment options** **81**

3.5   **Shared management options** **82**

3.6   **Processes for option development** **86**

3.7   **Demand assessment - the Contingent Valuation Method** **87**

     Outline of CVM *88*

     Benefits and potential drawbacks of CVM *91*

3.8   **Selecting priority areas** **92**

Chapter 4 .... **93**

Selling to and providing services for low-income customers

4.1   **Introduction** **93**

4.2   **Overcoming barriers to serving informal settlements** **93**

Land tenure issues 94
Connection fees, procedures and costs 97
Staff attitudes to serving informal settlements 97
The 'spaghetti' problem 98
Culture of free or cheap water 98
Differing priorities for men and women 99

4.3   Utility projects for serving low-income areas **99**

4.4   Partners for improving services to the poor **100**
Potential partners 100
Developing partnerships to serve low-income areas 103

4.5   Incentives and policies for serving the poor **103**
Policy level initiatives 103
Potential utility initiatives and incentives for serving the poor 105

4.6   Piloting and scaling up **106**

Part III Strategic marketing for all consumers

Chapter 5 .... **108**

What is a good strategic marketing process?

5.1   Overview **108**

5.2   Strategic marketing plans **109**
Stage 1 - Where are we now? 112
Stage 2 - Where do we want to be? 112
Stage 3 - How might we get there? 113
Stage 4 - How do we ensure success? 114

Chapter 6 .... **115**

Stage 1: 'Where are we now'?

6.1   Key consumer data **116**
6.2   Perceptions and preferences of low-income groups **120**
6.3   Alternative water service providers **122**
6.4   Institutional appraisal and development overview **123**
Key elements of institutional analysis and development 123
Tools for appraisal 125
Activity and responsibility analyses 125
Performance measurement 125
Utility performance indicators and ratios 127
Potential indicators for serving all consumer groups 128
Rationale for proposed service level indicators 131
PEST analysis 132
Subjective institutional performance descriptions 132
Swot analysis and assessment report 135

Chapter 7 .... **139**

Stage 2: 'Where do we want to be?'

7.1	**Overview**	**139**
7.2	**Review priorities and objectives**	**141**
7.3	**Proposed tariff policies**	**142**
	General principles	*143*
	Agreeing tariffs for different service levels	*145*
7.4	**Projected costs**	**147**
	Cost concepts	*147*
	Estimates of costs for water supply components	*148*
	Determination of Average Incremental Cost (AIC)	*149*
7.5	**Selecting water service options**	**149**
7.6	**Willingness to pay for selected options**	**151**
	The contingent valuation method	*151*
	Alternative methods of demand assessment	*152*
7.7	**Population projections**	**154**
7.8	**Estimates for service option take- up**	**154**
7.9	**Estimating water consumption**	**155**
	Water consumption and health risks	*156*
	Estimating consumption	*157*
7.10	**Infrastructure improvements**	**158**
7.11	**Agreeing tariff levels**	**159**
7.12	**Projected revenue**	**160**
7.13	**Financial projections and investment scenarios**	**161**

Chapter 8 .... **165**

Stage 3: 'How we might get there?'

8.1	**Product positioning**	**165**
8.2	**The marketing mix - the seven P's**	**167**
	Products or options	*168*
	Price	*169*
	Promotion	*169*
	Place	*169*
	People	*169*
	Processes	*171*
	Presence	*171*
8.3	**Improved Customer Relations Management**	**173**
	Developing CRM strategies	*173*
	The internal customer and interdepartmental collaboration	*175*

        Customer charters *177*

8.4   **Supporting service, payment and management options** **177**
        General Support *177*
        Support for Service Options *178*
        Support for Payment Options *178*
        Support for shared management options *180*

8.5   **Utility institutional improvements** **180**

8.6   **Evaluation of benefits and risks** **184**
        Evaluation of Financial Benefits *184*

8.7   **PPP options and serving the poor** **188**

8.8   **Strategic marketing or investment plans** **190**

8.9   **Ensuring success** **190**

Chapter 9 .... **193**

Glossary

Chapter 10 .... **197**

References and Bibliography

Chapter 11 .... **203**

Annexes

11.1   **Annex 1: Example consumer survey format** **204**
11.2   **Annex 2: Example WTP survey form**
        Opening statement to the bidding game **216**
11.3   **Annex 3: Calculations for Average Incremental Cost (AIC)** ... **230**
11.4   **Annex 4: Example financial projections for Kampala** **236**
11.5   **Annex 5: Short questionnaire for water services in infomal**
        settlements **237**

Part I Overview

Structure of this document

Part I of this publication provides an introduction to, followed by an overview of, the water and sanitation service experiences in developing countries of different consumer groups, including the poor. Examples of innovative marketing approaches using price and service differentiation in the water sector are provided from Asia, Africa and Latin America. The problems with the conventional 'predict and provide' approaches are outlined, followed by an overview of marketing definitions and how marketing philosophies relate to the urban water sector. Finally, marketing for sanitation is briefly discussed at the end of Chapter 1.

Part II focuses on marketing water services to low-income consumers, including how to gather key information on all consumer groups, using the *customer value chain* as a framework Utilities are encouraged to pilot marketing approaches for serving low-income consumers in selected locations, before scaling up to larger areas.

Part III focuses on strategic marketing approaches that can enable the effective scaling up of the piloted approaches and thus move towards serving all consumer groups across a city or town, in a reliable and sustainable manner.

Chapter 1

Introduction and overview

1.1 Introduction

The purpose of this document is to demonstrate how water utilities can meet the needs of the unserved urban poor for water and sanitation by developing an understanding of the needs and wants of *all* consumers and by adopting a marketing approach.

Many governments in developing countries have adopted policies for providing better services to the poor, including water supply, often with limited success. How can urban water utilities provide better services for more of their expanding populations, including low-income communities, while improving the financial viability and credit-worthiness of the utility?

The people without adequate water supply and sanitation services live in the unplanned, informal, and often illegal slums and shanties, the low-income settlements of the metropolitan and secondary cities. The task of filling this service gap is further compounded by the rapid growth of population in the urban areas of low-income countries.

The Water Supply and Sanitation Collaborative Council estimates that there is a need to provide an improved water supply for an extra one billion urban dwellers by the year 2015, 1.9 billion by the year 2025. The challenge is even greater with sanitation services, where 1.1 billion and 2.1 billion extra urban dwellers need to gain access to urban sanitation services by the years 2015 and 2025 respectively (WHO/UNICEF, 2000).

The title of this document, *Serving All Urban Consumers*, is intended to be a challenge to network utilities. Much of the urban population in Africa and Asia has to use alternative service providers, other than the recognized utilities or municipalities, in order to obtain their daily supply. People living in informal settlements often pay high prices to water vendors or incur high coping costs in terms of time spent on collecting water or providing their own borewells.

Network utilities are well placed to provide cheaper and more convenient piped water supplies, compared with alternative providers such as vendors. The difficulties arise in planning, justifying and implementing service expansion in a sustainable manner. If the utilities, with their potential economies of scale, were able to capture a larger share of the 'water markets' in their cities and towns, at a fair price for each group of customers, they should be able to reduce the price presently paid by the poor to vendors, dramatically improving services, whilst ensuring the utilities' long-term financial viability.

The present situation is that utilities tend to price their water below cost, a subsidy which is then absorbed by the middle and higher income groups who already have household water connections. The poor then have to pay more for a limited supply of poorer quality of water often delivered less conveniently by the vendors. However, capturing a larger share of the water market cannot be achieved by perpetuating the conventional 'one size fits all' approach. Reputedly it was Henry Ford who decreed of his customers that they could have any colour of car they liked as long as it was black. Water suppliers appear to have taken a similar approach over household connections. Traditionally utilities have offered consumers a conventional, full-pressure, buried-pipe household connection only if they live in 'legal' areas and pay a large connection fee. This is an approach which automatically excludes half the population in many cities.

Water services providers and the governments who support and potentially regulate them generally have two key objectives:

- To improve water services and increase service coverage, so that all consumers, including the poor, have adequate provision

- To ensure utilities are financially sustainable and therefore creditworthy to enable additional investment to improve further.

To meet the needs of the poor, whilst remaining financially viable, water utilities have to learn to differentiate their technology and price of service provision. Only by this approach can they hope to meet the needs of their present and potential customers *where they are*, not where the utility would like them to be. This approach means adopting and adapting the techniques which the consumer goods and service industries have long had to use to ensure their commercial survival in a competitive market. The automobile market has developed a long way since Henry Ford and have learned to adapt the design of their vehicles to meet the various interests of customers. The water industry, being a monopoly supplier in its conventional role, has assumed that a supply-driven 'predict and provide' approach to meeting the needs of consumers is sufficient. Such an assumption is no longer acceptable as it fails to meet the needs of the poorest who can benefit most from clean water and sanitation, from a public health as well as a direct poverty alleviation viewpoint.

An illustration of the value of the marketing approach in public health, pricing and service differentiation for the poor has also been demonstrated in the new public-private partnerships, for example in the case of hand-washing in Ghana.

'The health experts are bowled over by the marketing prowess that the companies are bringing to the project. Together they have, for instance, understood that Ghanaians prefer liquid to solid soap for hand-washing and are more likely to wash their hands before eating if the soap does not smell too strong. They have learnt when and how often to show advertisements to have maximum impact. And they have realized that small families may want to buy soap in very small quantities - perhaps like a sweet wrapped in paper - because some dislike sharing toilet soap and others cannot afford to buy big bars' (Economist, 2002).

A similar, consumer-sensitive approach to water and sanitation, going beyond the recognized ideals of social marketing, can bring similar benefits.

This researched-based document is intended for both public and private water utilities. It is about the adaptation of marketing techniques which any service provider, public or private, must use. However, we do recognize the value of partnerships, and that particularly where utilities cannot provide services directly to certain areas for whatever reason, there is the potential to form partnerships as part of shared management arrangements with either small water enterprises such as vendors or with community-based organizations. In addition, in unserved areas that are far from pipe networks, a utility can provide information to potential customers about how to seek alternative water supply options such as borewells and rainwater harvesting, until the utility is able to serve those areas. The utility could also provide useful information to potential partners on the nature of the consumer base and likelihood of success for partner schemes. By such means the utility is improving its reputation as a consumer-focused organization and developing trust amongst existing and potential customers.

There is evidence that utilities can do far more directly to serve the unplanned, perhaps illegal, low-income areas that have traditionally been ignored. In recent years there have been a number of utilities that have demonstrated that it is possible to differentiate service and prices to meet the needs of the poor. As part of the research that forms the basis for this book, and through complementary research, we have investigated those suppliers, public and private, which have apparently been most successful at differentiating their services and prices to serve low-income customers, wherever they live. The examples described come from public utilities in South Africa and India as well as from private operators in Argentina, Bolivia and the Philippines.

However, the research also demonstrates that service to low-income customers cannot be sustainable unless they are considered in the context of a long-term and city-wide strategy. It is not possible to give every customer exactly what they want at the price they want to pay. There has to be a balancing of services and prices so that overall the utility earns sufficient revenue to pay the costs of delivery to all consumers. Returning to the automobile industry example, car manufacturers find that if they try to produce too many different vehicles in too many different colours, to try and match too exactly the different groups of customer demands, the resulting inefficiencies lead to vehicles that are too expensive to make profitably. In our desire to serve low-income consumers in the best possible way at the lowest price we also have to be aware of the overall impact on utility efficiency and sustainability.

Therefore we have also included in this document an introduction to the strategic marketing approach that is necessary to ensure overall viability of service to all consumers, the necessity for which is included in the title. Serving the lowest income consumers also demands an efficient utility selling water to higher income customers at a cost-reflective price. Strategic marketing enables 'serving the poor' to be integrated into city-wide planning and provision. Our international research partners have tested this methodology in six urban areas with varying degrees of detail: Kampala, Uganda (S. Kayaga); Mombasa, Kenya (C. Njiru); Lesotho (A. Kamalie); Guntur, India (A. Narender and V.S. Chary); Agra, India SK Gupta; and various small towns in Nepal (G Bhattarai). The results suggest that in most situations it is possible to create a financially viable marketing plan that would enable a city to serve the needs of *all* consumers.

1.2   Who is this document for?

These guidelines are intended for use by water sector managers in low and middle-income countries. They are also designed to be of value to government staff, to policymakers and to regulators who have responsibility for the sector, as well as to donors.

The authors developed detailed research-based strategic marketing plans to prove the concepts, these guidelines are designed as a simplified version that will give sufficient accuracy to be implemented immediately. The goal is for 'good enough' marketing and business plans that encourage early achievement of the universal service obligation. Part II of this document focuses on the development of pilot programmes in a few specific low-income areas using the value chain concept of *know, target, sell and service* as a framework. Part III then discusses the use of strategic marketing in more depth - to move towards providing financially sustainable services for *all* consumers.

We hope that these guidelines will also assist civil society organizations, whether water consumer organizations or CBOs and NGOs, acting on behalf of the unserved poor, by detailing what can reasonably be expected as good practice from utilities in the sector. We trust that civil society will use them to challenge the networked utilities to raise their performance.

This document is complemented by the shorter Book 1 which provides guidance for government's enabling role in using marketing approaches and moving towards serving all consumers. Book 3 gives a detailed explanation of the PREPP methodology to facilitate utility consultation with low-income communities.

1.3   Water and sanitation services for the urban poor

Typical service coverage

In low and middle-income countries many water utilities and municipalities fail to serve as many as 50 to 80 per cent of the people living in their urban areas. Many existing customers also rely on other water sources for part of their water supply. Such alternative non-utility water sources may be supplied through water vendors or neighbours to whom poor consumers usually pay high prices. In addition other water sources such as wells, springs, and rivers, though often contaminated, may also have to be used. The situation is exacerbated by high urban population growth rates of up to seven per cent per year. Where sustained this rate of population growth means a doubling of the urban population in just ten years. Many, often the majority, of these new urban dwellers live in the informal, unplanned areas - often termed 'illegal' by government planning officials - creating an even greater challenge.

This challenge of improving urban water and sanitation services in developing countries therefore has two main aspects:

- improvement of current service levels for all consumer groups; and

- providing for the rapid increase in the urban population.

In terms of current service levels, data compiled by the Water Supply and Sanitation Collaborative Council in 2000 revealed a large service gap in low-income countries. In Africa, for example, a continent with an estimated population of 784 million people in the year 2002, only 62 per cent had access to 'improved' water supply, while 60 per cent were served by 'improved' sanitation (WHO/UNICEF 2000 'Improved' water supply was described as one of the following service options: household connections, public standpipes, bore-holes, protected dug wells, protected springs, or rainwater collection.

Typical service levels in African cities are set out in Table 1.1, which shows that only 17 to 31 per cent of households in many Africa cities have in-home connections.

Table 1.1. Service levels of watsan utilities in selected African cities[1]

Common service levels	Kampala (Uganda)	Dar Es Salaam (Tanzania)	Conakry (Guinea)	Nouakchott (Mauritania)	Continuo (Benin)	Ouagadougou (Burkina Faso)	Bamako (Mali)
Source of water for household use (percentage of households)							
• In-home connection	36	31	29	19	27	23	17
• Standpipe water fetched by household	5	0	3	30	0	49	19
• Independent providers/ traditional sources	59	69	68	51	73	28	64
Means of disposal of household septic waste (percentage of households)							
• In-home connection to piped sewerage	6	3	10	4	1	0	2
• Family labour or independent providers	94	97	90	96	99	100	98
• Near network: connection feasible	(9)	(6)	(17)	(4)	(1)	(0)	(2)

1. Source: Collignon and Vezina (2000).

Invariably it is the less well-off urban dwellers who have to spend time and energy obtaining water from standpipes, independent providers or traditional sources. Small private operators play an important part in the provision of water services in Africa, serving over 75 per cent of the urban poor in Sub-Saharan Africa (Collignon & Vezina, 2000).

It is estimated that an additional 210 million urban dwellers in Africa will need to be served to meet the 2015 goals (WHO/UNICEF 2000). The larger African cities generally have reasonable piped water supplies ranging from 10 to 24 hours a day (from a sample of 17 utilities) (WUP Africa, 2001). However, the proportion of people with in-house connections is low. Many who do not have piped connections are poorer members of the community with limited ability to pay the high charges and costs of new connections. Utilities have limited funds to invest in new infrastructure too, a restriction that suggests innovative alternative approaches need to be explored.

The urban water service levels in India, for example, (as well as other countries in Asia), are characterized by declining hours of piped supply (typically half an hour to six hours each day or every other day), with a proportion of the population having to rely on alternative water sources such as their own borewell. Box 1.1 shows estimated services levels for urban water and sanitation services in India.

Box 1.1. Estimated urban water and sanitation service levels in India[1]

Urban water supply

- Access to safe drinking water - 82 per cent
- Access to tapped water - 65 per cent
- Access to tapped water within premises - 42 per cent
- Unreliable and inadequate services with an unknown quality of water

Sanitation

- Access to toilets - 63 per cent
- Access to toilets within premises - 33 per cent
- Connections to sewerage - 28 per cent
- Only 70 out of 289 Class I cities have sewerage treatment facilities.

---

1. Source: ASCI, CMF background note, 2000.

A similar scenario is reported to be common in other cities in South Asia (see Table 1.2).

Table 1.2. Percentage of households with pipe connections in Asian cities[1]

Asian city	Approximate percentage of households with their own piped connection
1. Delhi, India	53%
2. Ho Chi Min, Vietnam	59%
3. Jakarta, Indonesia	30%
4. Phnom Penn	70%

1. Source: Lyonnaise des Eaux (now Suez), 1998.

Clearly the challenge of meeting both current and future demand for services is huge. Addressing this challenge requires governments to enable water utilities to manage effectively, working with the private sector (both formal and informal) and collaborate with community groups and NGOs, exploiting the comparative advantage of each stakeholder.

The effects of inadequate utility services on poor communities

Most developing country utilities have inadequate funds to invest in the required expansion of water supply infrastructure, usually because they have failed to charge reasonable tariffs over a long period. As there is both insufficient piped water and infrastructure, the rich and powerful tend to be favoured in the allocation of limited resources and the poor often miss out. Politicians may promise cheap water for *all*, but it is mainly the high and middle-income earners, the powerful, who benefit in the end.

The consequence of these poor water services is that many people have to invest time and money in accessing, collecting and storing water from alternative sources, which can be termed 'coping costs'. Added to these coping costs are the indirect costs of both the loss of productive time due to water-related diseases and the costs of medicine to treat them. Higher income consumers may similarly incur additional expenditure when they invest in their own well, borehole, pumps (from water mains or groundwater) and storage tanks.

During water shortages, the rationing of water affects the poor most adversely as their storage facilities are usually very limited. They are also commonly dependent on daily wages through informal sector work (the average percentage of employment in the informal sector in 10 African cities is 56 per cent (UNDP, 1999, cited in Collignon and Vezina, 2000)), which means that any time spent collecting water cuts into their earnings (WSP and PPIAF, 2002).

Why are so many urban water supply organizations slow or reluctant to provide improved water services to unserved areas or informal settlements? One often-cited reason is the political and legal issues associated with land tenure, but there are many instances of these problems being overcome where there is a willingness to communicate and collaborate. There are reports of water supply staff benefiting personally from illegally selling water to vendors, which is as a disincentive to new approaches. In addition there appears to be a mental block amongst many engineers, who traditionally act as managers in the sector, which means they simply do not see the challenge of serving the poor amidst all their other tasks. However, a minority of water suppliers have begun to investigate ways of serving the poor. We describe a selection of these experiences in the next sections.

Pricing and service differentiation to serve the poor

The accepted mode of household water supply in many countries has developed by a variety of routes into metered, full pressure, 24-hour-a-day, buried pipe connections directly into the consumer's house, for distribution internally to a variety of sanitary devices. But the accepted mode is not the only mode.

There are variations on this approach, even within the high-income countries of Europe. For example, only 21 per cent of households in England and Wales (Ofwat, 2002) have meters (up from just 2 per cent in 1989). If metering adds about 25 per cent to the average water bill, and in the English and Welsh setting it only reduces average household water use by 11 per cent, there is an argument as to whether metering is always the appropriate solution to billing for water. Similarly, there has long been the practice in UK to install high-level water storage in the dwelling, though with an off-take on the rising main for drinking water. In other parts of Europe such storage is deemed unacceptable as well as unnecessary.

These variations are described to emphasize the idea that there is no right way to deliver water (notwithstanding the apparent 'inviolability' of national technical standards). It is therefore quite normal to differentiate water and sanitation services, particularly when it achieves the goal of delivering public health benefits. The examples given below illustrates part of the spectrum of possible differentiation of water supply and sanitation.

1.4 Examples of innovative approaches to serve the poor

There are many cases of innovative marketing approaches being used for water and sanitation services in low and middle-income countries where both services and prices have been differentiated. Some examples are summarized below from Durban in South Africa, Manila in the Philippines, Guntur and Rajmundry in India, Buenos Aires in Argentina, El Alto in Bolivia.

Approaches at Durban Metro Water

Durban Metro Water, the public water utility in Durban, South Africa, differentiated its water supply to unplanned peri-urban areas by offering:

- water kiosks where people fetch and pay per 20-litre container;

- water kiosks with storage, where people fetch and pay per 20-litre container;

- individual connections with a 200-litre ground tank in the yard, with trickle feed;

- individual house connections with limited pressure through roof tank; and

- individual house connections with full pressure (conventional 24-hour supply).

Three of these five options promoted by Durban Metro Water are depicted in Figure 1.1.

Durban Metro Water have systematically developed these various options, with the price of water to consumers also adjusted to suit the costs, and then promoted their use amongst poorer communities in newer areas.

The ground tank concept, perhaps the most unusual of the options, was first piloted in 1993. The utility supplies the ground tank (a plastic barrel) once the householder is committed to the approach. The tank is often mounted on an old car tyre, to lift it a little above the ground. The tank is covered to prevent contamination and has a float valve to prevent over-filling and wastage. The tank is connected to the water supply main at a manifold or valve cluster that is situated where it is convenient and cost-effective for the utility to install and access.

In the original concept, the ground tank water system is operated and maintained by a water bailiff, who is selected by the community in the informal settlement and trained by Durban Metro Water. After training by Durban Metro Water the bailiff looked after about 150 ground tank connections and a water kiosk. Where the consumer had paid their water bill in advance, the water bailiff would open the particular valve once a day until the 200-litre ground tank was filled.

Costs, and therefore prices, were significantly reduced (hence made affordable) because householders could pay significantly lower connection charges, there did not need to be a full pressure distribution system locally, and there was no requirement for road-cutting charges or negotiations over access routes. Bill collection costs were also reduced as there

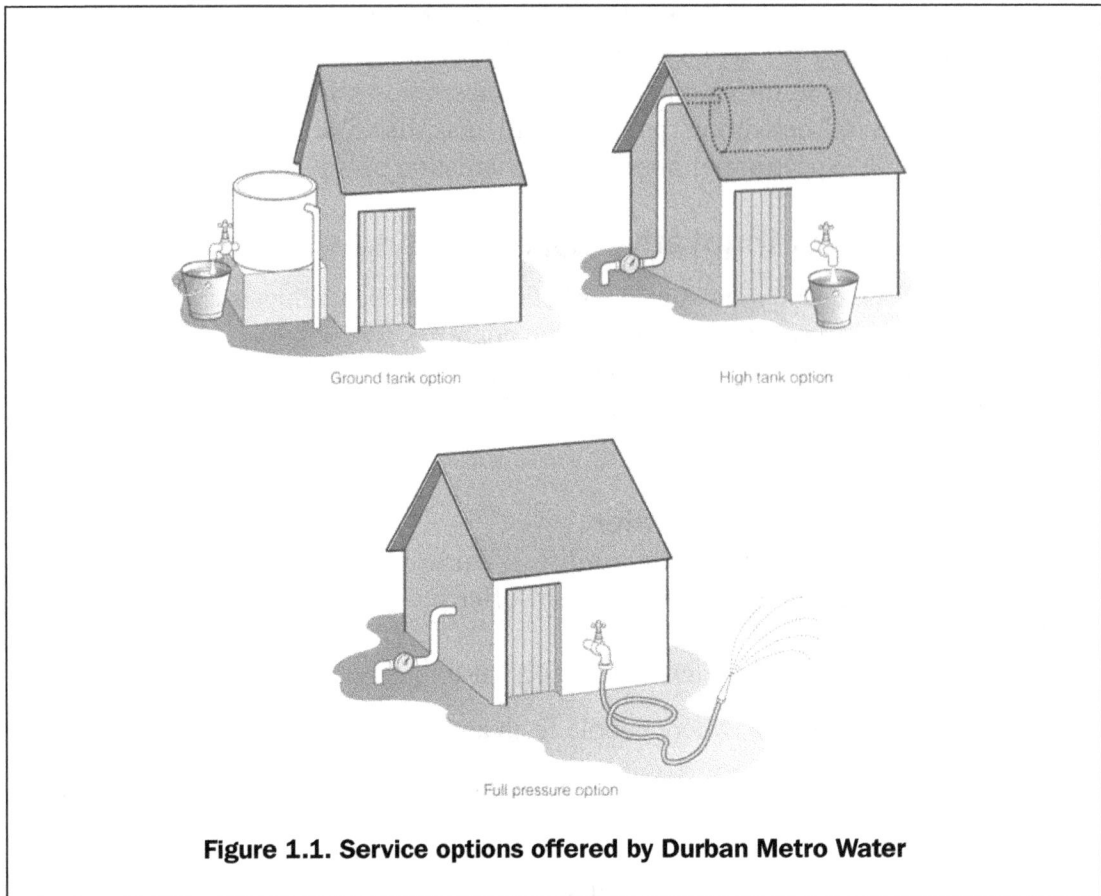

Figure 1.1. Service options offered by Durban Metro Water

was no need for metering, meter reading or bill delivery. Householders did not need to have a formal address, another benefit in an unplanned area. Site inspections reveal extensive use of the various options within specific communities.

More recently the South African policy of free water for the first 6m^3 of a house-hold's monthly water has removed the need for bill collection. But the original concept provides a potential example for adaptation elsewhere.

Approaches in Manila

In Manila, the Philippines, water supply in the city has been made the responsibility of two private operators who manage water services under a concession type of contract, supervised by a government regulator. The demands of the contract for increases in service coverage have encouraged the private operators to differentiate service and price to previously unserved low-income consumers using innovative technologies and approaches - with generally successful results. Examples of these approaches are briefly described below.

Group taps or yard connections for two to five households that follow the concept of the electricity company in providing electricity in low-income areas. In this type of water service, users form groups, register connections and share the cost for usage. Households either form the groupings by themselves or with the assistance of local government officials or area associations. The group is given one mother meter and while it is encouraged to install sub-meters to avoid problems with the sharing of cost, some household groups - usually composed of relatives or close friends - opted not to install sub-meters to avoid incurring further costs. The leader collects payments from each member and pays the official bill to Manila Water.

Bulk water supplies to a community group for on-selling was successfully developed in some settlements where access was difficult. The utility supported the community organization in helping households to fill out and sign the application forms, etc. The majority of the households in one community paid both the connection fees and the additional costs of installing the mother meters. To minimize project cost, the community coordinated and organized their efforts and contributed their labour (men, women, and children alike) by digging, filling, and laying pipes, and concreting the surface to both avoid illegal tappings and protect the pipes. This project initially provided water to about 250 families.

With this approach, installation costs as well as non-revenue water for the utility are minimized. The mother meter is located outside the community area, usually along main roads, where it can easily be seen and monitored for illegal tapping. In this type of service, the non-revenue water is reduced because all water that is lost or consumed legally or illegally after the mother meter is paid for by the community. Billing and collection costs are also minimized, with only one bill for an entire community. Within the community association there maybe some 'community' pressure for the household members to pay bills on time or else the entire community suffers (in the case of a disconnection for nonpayment). So, there is an incentive for the community to urge the late payers to pay, although the community association has to be prepared to continue to manage the cost recovery from people who are connected.

The 'Bayan Tubig' ('water for the community') programme, provides individual household connections in low-income areas. This programme waives the land title requirement and allows households to pay their connection fees by instalment over a period of six to 12 months (in some cases this has been stretched to 24 months). These instalments are combined with the regular monthly water bills so that payment begins only upon receipt of the first bill and not before the installation. To help keep costs as low as possible, in some areas residents who were further away from the entrance of the neighbourhood helped the utility to construct the water pipes for their area.

Technically, this approach involves constructing a conventional underground water main until the narrowness or condition of the access route makes this impractical. From this point in the narrow lanes, the rest of the network is built either above ground or on the ground, partially covered or attached to a wall. This distribution pipe delivers water to a battery or cluster of water meters from where each homeowner makes their own plastic connection. This scheme can be modified depending on the characteristics of the area.

The positive response to the Bayan Tubig shows that, given the opportunity, residents of unplanned areas prefer individual water connections to public standposts. The individual connections resulted in substantially cheaper water than before the connection, when water cost more and quantity was severely limited.

As a result of these initial programmes the researchers observed that the once mostly dilapidated houses have been slowly replaced by structures made of more permanent materials. With more time on their hands and water to use, the women are able to clean their surroundings. This effect of the Bayan Tubig has addressed important health concerns, such as dengue fever, which arises from the storage of water which provided a breeding ground for dengue-carrying mosquitoes. Sanitation in the areas covered has improved as households now have their own toilets and bathrooms within their homes.

(The source of this section is an edited version of Inocencio, 2002.), in Weitz A. and Franceys R., *Beyond Boundaries: extending services to the urban poor, ADB, 2002.*

Approaches in Guntur and Rajhamundry

The poor in Guntur and Rajhamundry in Andhra Pradesh, India depend for their potable water mainly on free public standposts and tankers provided by the respective Municipal Corporations (Narender and Chary, 2002). The water supplied through public standposts is quite inadequate to cover the needs of the majority of the households.

A significant proportion of the poor wanted individual connections and were prepared to pay the required monthly charges. However, they were discouraged by the policy of the Municipal Corporations that charged a one-time connection fee in the range of Rs.5000-7000 (US$100-$130) to provide a household water supply connection. As a result, many poor households were excluded from the system, in effect they were not allowed to enter the 'shop' (water supply system). This has resulted in a proliferation of illegal connections.

However, during sustained discussions with the Corporations, as part of strategic marketing research, their leaders came to appreciate the need to increase the coverage of water services to the poor through innovative approaches. (Studies have highlighted the fact that the poor are willing to pay the user fees for water but not the high connection charges.)

In 2002 the Municipal Corporations leaders made significant efforts to remove the entry barrier. They have not only lowered the connection charges as prescribed in government norms, but also allowed the poor to pay these one_time charges in two or three installments. They have also reduced or waived the associated supervision charges for executing the work. The Mayors and Commissioners have visited several slums, conducted public meetings and issued on the spot connection notices to the willing households. As a result of these sustained efforts, the number of poor households with individual connections has gone up significantly in these cities in the past year. In another variation poor households were encouraged to form groups of six to eight households to access a single connection to reduce the burden of connection and tariff charges.

The Municipal Corporations have also experimented with marketing ideas such as promoting (advertising) new connections in 'Saturday connection camps' and offering the poorest household in a group of ten a special 'bargain' low_cost connection. The experiences of Guntur and Rajhamundry from India demonstrate that city governments are becoming aware of and willing to adopt marketing approaches to increase water services, particularly to the poor.

Approaches in Buenos Aires

A private operator, Aguas Argentinas, was awarded a concession in 1993 to manage water and sanitation in Buenos Aires, the capital of Argentina. The concessionaire had a contractual target of achieving full service coverage by the end of the 30-year contract. They began to develop programmes to serve the poor through differentiating services and in particular connection charges.

The company explained that the key to the pilot projects was to change the approach from a top-down supply-driven pattern to one of partnerships, recognizing that each partner had their own objectives:

- The objectives of the householders in the low-income neighbourhoods were for a normal service with fair costs and social integration.

- The objectives of the government were to create infrastructure and to demonstrate their capacity.

- The objectives of the company were to service all areas whilst controlling investment costs.

In a range of projects the utility found that they had to differentiate their projects to serve the low-income communities - there was no 'one size fits all' approach.

'The Participative Water Service' Projects are described as being based on 'direct links' between the residents of the area (via an association or 'leader' or NGO) and Aguas Argentinas. The company found that this 'barter' operating method, with the community providing the construction labour to reduce costs, is only conceivable for areas where the idea of community work is already accepted.

The utility generally designs the projects and supervises implementation, while the municipality funds materials and the residents construct the system. To promote subsequent payment, a single invoice is given to the community for a year, to see if they are really willing to pay. Meters are installed for the community bill to limit wastage of water. Typically, one person signs on behalf of the neighbourhood, often designated by minuted community committee meetings. Aguas Argentinas has found that there are leaders in poor neighbourhoods who can help resolve people's problems for them. After the trial year is successfully completed, individual billing is introduced, based on an assumption of minimum water usage.

In one Barrio Aguas Argentinas became much more involved with the project design and supervision and altered network standards. Labour for the construction was hired (paid for by government subsidy) and the project was adapted to suit. In another area, reduced cost water supply had been installed, with unmetered (though valved) connections with shallow pipes in each alley and just one meter for the entire area. In this barrio, each family was paying their own bill (unmeasured, using average consumption), and there was no connection fee. To reduce costs and promote participation, all the bills for the neighbourhood were given to one community representative for distribution.

Sanitation in Buenos Aires

A system of shallow sewers was designed because of the high groundwater table, using 'individual or collective septic tanks with liquid effluent transported by small diameter PVC network (75mm instead of 200mm in traditional Aguas Argentinas secondary networks) with shallow gradients'.

'Since the plots were too small ($<<100m^2$) to take both a septic tank and a soakaway, the removal of liquid effluent was essential. The cost of the secondary network (the largest item in the sanitation network) was reduced by more than half by the small diameter network and the low gradients (less excavation is required in areas where the water table is less than one metre below the surface).'

'The effluent collected is at present discharged directly into a nearby river: as a result Aguas Argentinas does not charge for the service. When the company network is extended into this area, the collector will simply need to be connected to the mains: the service will then be charged for.' (Lyonnaise des Eaux, 1998).

This section is based upon Lyonnaise des Eaux (now Ondeo, Suez) (1999) -and site investigations by one author (Franceys) as part of the Business Partners in Development Study Visit in 1999.

Approaches in El Alto

Aguas del Illimani, the private operator in Le Paz, El Alto, Bolivia, has specific performance targets (clearly spelled out in the concession contract) that increase annually until the end of the contract in 2026. To achieve these targets the utility sought to use a marketing approach to target services to the needs of the poor.

Aguas del Illimani has embarked on a series of promotional programmes aimed at raising the company's profile among its users. The 'School Programme' increases awareness about the water and sewerage system by taking children to visit the treatment plants, while the 'Neighbourhoods Programme' advises and explains the procedures necessary to obtain a water and sewerage connection in selected neighbourhoods. The utility also developed the 'IPAS' programme (Peri-urban Initiative for Water and Sanitation). The project objective was to test innovative approaches for sustained provision of water and sanitation services in the low-income areas of La Paz and El Alto. The project promoted the use of appropriate technologies, sound social intervention methodology and access to micro-credit mechanisms for construction costs.

At the project level, IPAS community selection procedures were based on the *Demand Response Approach,* where communities are consulted beforehand about their interest in participating. Aguas del Illimani first approached different communities in their expansion areas and presented the IPAS project, explaining its working characteristic and technology. After internal consultation, the community committed to the project by presenting the signatures of at least 70 per cent of its dwellers. The project was therefore implemented on a first-come, first-served basis.

The next step in the methodology was an area characterization, usually performed by an NGO previously trained by the technical assistance team, to include information about key players in the area, a socioeconomic survey, and a topographical description as an input to the preliminary network design.

The IPAS project introduced an appropriate technology that was used in Brazil, the condominium system. It comprises the introduction of the 'condominium' - or group of users - as the basic unit of service. The condominiums range in size from six to 30 households each. The relaxation of some technical standards allows the participation of the community in maintaining and operating the local network system.

At the social level, the intervention methodology is based on a participatory diagnostic assessment, where the community realizes the need for improved services and acts as an agent - rather than an object - of its own development. The utility also adapted its approach to payment facilities. As a result of savings in installation costs and also as an incentive for participating communities, the utility offered a discounted connection fee of about 60 per cent of the original connection fee, payable in 60 monthly instalments in the water bill with no interest.

The IPAS project also organized with different local micro-credit institutions a credit line specifically designed to improve houses, water delivery, and bathing and sanitary facilities. Guarantees were flexible and interest fixed at market rates. The micro-credit mechanism also allowed families to construct their credit history and later request loans for income-generating activities.

Finally the utility undertook an educational programme to deliver improved hygiene behaviour. The social methodology used by the IPAS project was very effective in educating the newly served about the importance of sanitation practices and the impact on their health. One of the roles of hygiene promotion is to encourage people to use the optimum amount of water necessary for health. Such promotion is best done as part of a broader marketing approach.

This section is based on an edited version of Vargas M. 'Incentives for utilities to serve the urban poor in El Alto, ed Franceys, R. for WSCC, 2002'.

In the above cases the utilities have adopted marketing-type approaches to serve poor communities, whether this has been done consciously or otherwise. They have developed appropriate *products* or service options that they have *promoted* to selected *people* (potential customers) at viable *prices*, using appropriate *processes* in selected *places* where there is demand for service improvements. In doing so the utility has enhanced its *presence* as a consumer-orientated organization. They have therefore been addressing the 7Ps of marketing, which is also known as the 'marketing mix' and is discussed in Chapter 8. It provides a useful framework for developing, promoting and providing different options.

1.5   Conventional 'predict and provide' approaches

The case studies from a variety of countries in the previous section show that it is possible to serve the poor, even in informal housing areas, using innovative marketing-type approaches. But a persistent cause of lack of action is the difficulties of making the case to key stakeholders for more investment to implement improvements, based upon an older, engineering-biased understanding of water supply.

The conventional approach to overcoming the service gap has been to invest large amounts of money in bulk water supply infrastructure to ensure that a sufficient quantity of water is available. The methodology involves predicting the likely population within a reasonable time horizon, taking the standard design criteria of litres of water used per person per day, adding on for commercial, institutional and industrial users, and providing treatment works and transmission mains sufficient to deliver that water to the city.

This approach often fails to take into account the fact that half the water delivered is lost through leakage and theft, whilst the other half is sold to consumers at a price below the operating costs of supplying that water, with thought to recovering capital costs.

Experience also shows that a fair proportion of consumers do not pay their water bills even when they are below cost. This approach also ignores the fact that those operating costs may be unacceptably high due to inefficient equipment and staffing. It also fails to address the point that there has to be investment in distribution networks to get the water to where people live and that the 'illegality' of slums is not a sufficient problem to prohibit water supply to the poor.

Similarly for sanitation, utilities have tended to look at the costs of comprehensive drainage plans and given up in despair before they even consider the concomitant costs of wastewater treatment. 'Knowing' that on-plot and on-site sanitation solutions could pollute the groundwater and also knowing that different government organizations are usually responsible for non-sewerage sanitation, utilities have tended to give up on the unserved population and focus on subsidizing sewerage services to the commercial core of the city.

Moving from the above typical scenario to a demand-responsive, customer-oriented approach therefore requires institutional development as well as a marketing approach. It will still require an element of predict and provide, as the water industry is a capital-intensive, long-term industry. But in particular it will require a new, innovative, creative and partnership-based approach to serving the urban poor. Strategic marketing, the proposed model, can assist in the achievement of these tasks as it provides a framework for organizations to make the case for investment through understanding the perceptions and preferences of different customer groups and their willingness to pay for different types of services. This leads to the development of viable business plans for targeting and promoting appropriate service, payment and management options that can be provided reliably to each of those customer groups or market segments at appropriate prices.

1.6   The marketing approach

A marketing approach is of particular relevance to the water and sanitation sector in developing countries because household consumers, particularly in urban centres, often obtain water from numerous alternative providers and sources. At one level, water utilities 'compete' with alternative water obtained from untreated sources. Across a typical city private vendors, individual household on-selling, family and institutional boreholes, hand dug wells, streams, rainwater and springs complement the conventional utility water, thus illustrating the water market in action.

These 'alternative supplies' that often supplement, replace or substitute direct utility-provided water are accessed through informal human and physical networks. Although often unregulated, unreliable and costly, people use them regularly either through necessity or choice. At some level all these sources of water supply attract reasonably 'loyal' customers and represent degrees of competition to utilities that are required to operate in the same market.

So it is clear that competition exists in the domestic market and that city dwellers do not always automatically look to the utility to provide services. If utilities are to capture neglected or new markets then a customer-focused, effective strategic marketing strategy needs to be developed and implemented.

Successful international companies, including those in the water sector, have found that a key to success is having a clear customer focus and striving to provide good quality services. By seeking to maximize the number of satisfied customers, a water utility can gain many benefits, the most obvious of which is that a utility should receive fewer complaints, resulting in less interference from politicians on operational aspects. Secondly a customer services focus can improve financial sustainability in two ways:

(a) customers who are satisfied with the service they are receiving are more likely to accept and pay reasonable water charges; and

(b) increased numbers of paying customers, where there are cost-reflective tariffs, generate higher revenue and sustainable returns on investment.

The increased revenues from (a) and (b) can then be invested in improving services, which in turn increases customers' satisfaction levels and so a cycle of continuing improvement can develop.

Managing water services (and sanitation) successfully is like any other business where the responsible organization seeks to: keep customers satisfied, increase market share and maximize revenues. In Box 1.2 examples of evidence of how good business performance is linked to market orientation are provided.

Box 1.2. Importance of marketing orientation[1]

The influence of marketing on higher or sustained business performance has been the subject of a number of studies. The conclusions from two of those studies are:

- Hooley and Lynch (1985)] examined 1504 British companies and concluded that the high performing organizations were characterized by a significantly greater market orientation, strategic direction and concern with product quality than the 'also rans'.
- Narver and Slater (1990) focused on the marketing orientation of the senior managers in 140 North American strategic business units (SBUs) and identified a very strong relationship between marketing orientation and profitability. They also found that the *highest degree of market* orientation was manifested by managers of the *most profitable companies.*

---

1. Source: Wilson and Gilligan (1997).

Marketing is about satisfying customers. Jones (1989) has defined marketing as: 'The management process responsible for identifying, anticipating and satisfying customer requirements profitably'.

The implications of this statement are that ongoing communication with existing and potential customers is required to check the effectiveness of efforts to identify, anticipate and satisfy customer requirements. Some government water supply organizations may be uncomfortable with the term 'profitably', but few would argue with the need to generate sufficient funds for future investment.

There are several ways of looking at marketing:

- as a business philosophy;

- as a management process; and

- as a set of tools used to respond to demand.

The more strategic approach to marketing is captured by McDonald (1989, p.8):

'Marketing is a management process whereby the resources of the whole organization are utilized to satisfy the needs of selected consumer groups in order to achieve the objectives of both parties. Marketing, then, is first and foremost an attitude of mind rather than a series of functional activities.'

A water utility with a marketing orientated philosophy would have its entire operations, its personnel and its technical systems, geared to providing improved customer satisfaction and to contributing to meeting its financial objectives.

Marketing can also be viewed as a management process. Typically, it involves the following steps (adapted from Wilson and Gilligan, 1997):

- investigating customer demand for different product options;

- identifying groups of consumers whose requirements could be better satisfied;

- developing reliable products or service options to meet changing demands;

- pricing the product at a level which the market will bear and which will meet its financial objectives;

- making the product or service available through channels accessible to the consumer; and

- promoting the product or service so that a desired unit or revenue volume of demand is achieved.

This process of incorporating marketing approaches throughout an organization can be termed Strategic Marketing where it takes the all-embracing, long-term view. Based upon careful analysis of alternative opportunities, and organizational strengths and weaknesses, Strategic Marketing Plans (SMPs) can be developed for or by a utility incorporating aspects such those described in Section 1.7.

But is marketing really necessary for a monopoly supplier of a basic need? Many water utilities, in principle, now appreciate that the *'Customer is king'* and that they should therefore be treated as 'the fountain of knowledge'. For any business to survive, including enterprises that strive to deliver a 'social good', it is important to build enduring profitable relationships with current and potential customers. Only then can the direct provider be effective and efficient.

A useful concept to achieve this is the *'Customer value chain'*, which can be described as to *know, target, sell and service* knowledge' (SageR. Water Services, , 2000).

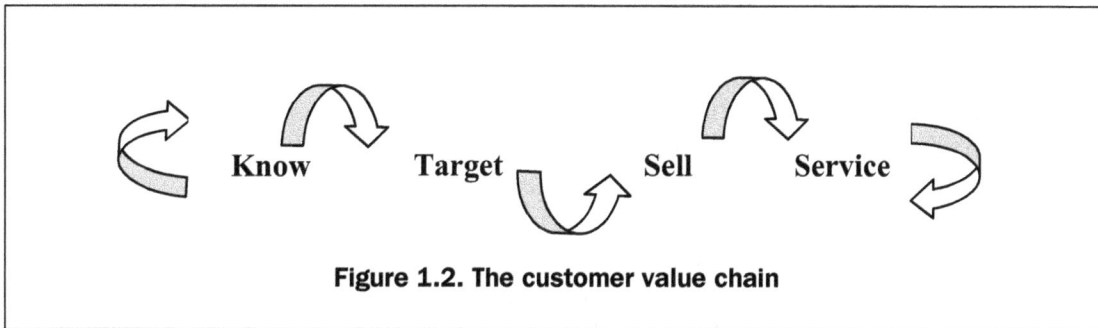

Figure 1.2. The customer value chain

This concept is increasingly used in the commercial sector, and in the context of the water sector it involves the following:

Know and understand the different customer and potential customer groups, including their attitudes, practices, perceptions, preferences and their willingness to sustain payment for improved services. Water and sanitation is often perceived as a 'social good' as well as an 'economic good' and this complicates matters, so more effort is needed to understand people's perceptions. Key methods for getting to know water users include questionnaire surveys, focus group discussions, customer consultative committees and local observation.

Target or prioritize specific areas or consumer groups (e.g. commercial customers, and domestic consumers in low-income as well as high and medium-income areas), with appropriate service options, such as house connections, yard taps and water kiosks or standposts, at appropriate price levels. Targeting should be based on the best available information on the consumer's experiences and preferences, using demand assessment results.

Sell options using suitable promotion techniques and plans, which could include service options and payments options as well as different shared management arrangements together with CBOs or informal small water enterprises. This will often require careful planning and implementation, particularly when dealing with groups who use alternative water supplies or if they have unauthorized pipe connections and do not currently pay. There is a particular role for CBOs and NGOs to act as social intermediaries in the 'selling' process, particularly in informal settlements.

Services should be provided to a high quality standard, delivered through a balance of people, processes and technology by knowledgeable staff. To provide such a standard of service requires utilities to adopt a programme of continual organizational improvement centred around 'the customer'. In addition, effective collaboration between different departments within a utility (such as customer relations, billing, operation and maintenance, financial management, etc.) can enable the resolution of typical customer problems. Servicing the customer will mean that, for example, they are offered payment options to suit their particular needs, such as having a local payment offices rather than expecting them to visit to a distant water office.

The customer value chain approach, adapted to focus on the needs of low-income consumers, is used as a framework for Part II of this document. As it is a fairly simple framework, it is useful for initial pilot projects for services to low-income areas.

1.7   The strategic marketing framework

Strategic marketing for urban water services is a comprehensive approach that builds on the 'customer value chain' described in Section 1.6. It seeks to incorporate good marketing practices in all relevant aspects of a utility's work, so necessarily that is in a utility that has been 're-engineered' to deliver a relatively efficient service.

A 'Strategic Marketing' methodology, as described by Wilson and Gilligan (1997), has been used and adapted for this publication, as part of the research programme in Africa and India. During the research, Strategic Marketing Plans (SMPs) for water services have been developed to test the methodology for a number of cities and towns around the world including: Mombasa, Kampala and Lesotho in Africa and Guntur, Agra and various small towns in Nepal in South Asia. Three of these SMPs (Serving All Urban Consumers - books 4 to 6) are available on the WEDC website at: www.lboro.ac.uk/wedc/projects/psd/

The key elements of the adapted Wilson and Gilligan framework encompass four key questions that logically follow each other and are set out in Figure 1.3.

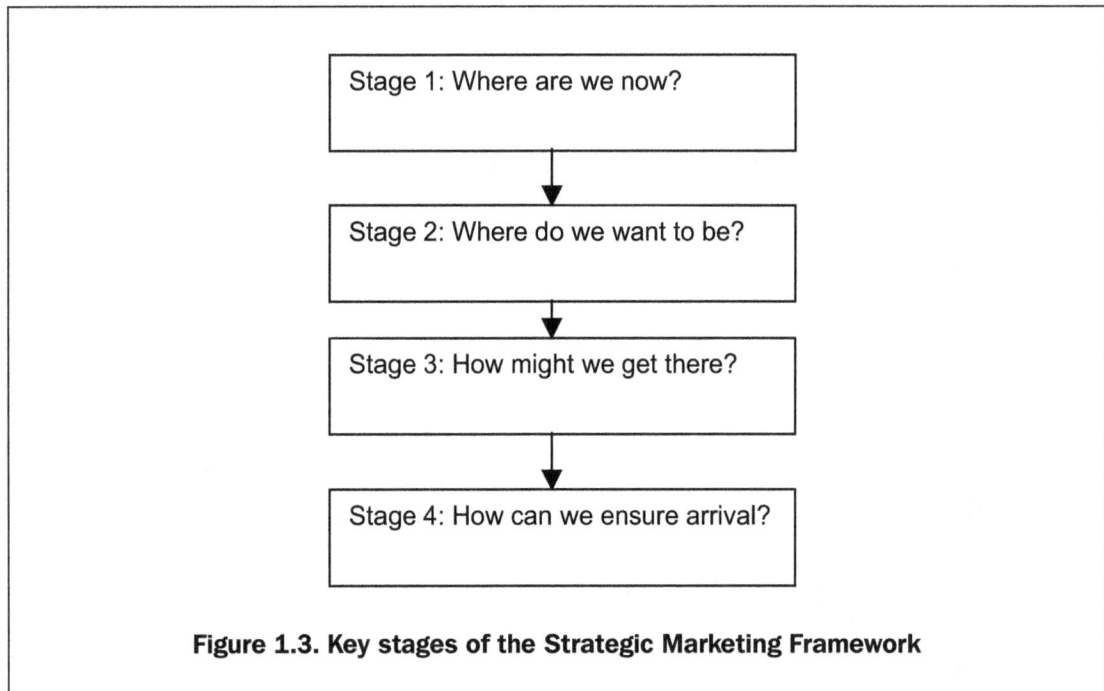

Stage 1: Where are we now?

Stage 2: Where do we want to be?

Stage 3: How might we get there?

Stage 4: How can we ensure arrival?

Figure 1.3. Key stages of the Strategic Marketing Framework

This outline framework has been adapted for the urban water sector in developing countries. The more detailed framework in Figure 1.4 and Figure 1.5 show the typical key aspects that should be considered at each stage in the strategic marketing process, which is described in detail in Part III of this document. This publication, and the urban water sector research that formed the foundation for it, focus more on the first three (planning) stages. For guidance on dealing with stage four (How to ensure success?) we recommend publications on public-private partnerships, institutional development and change management, Total Quality Management (TQM) and other conventional business manuals.

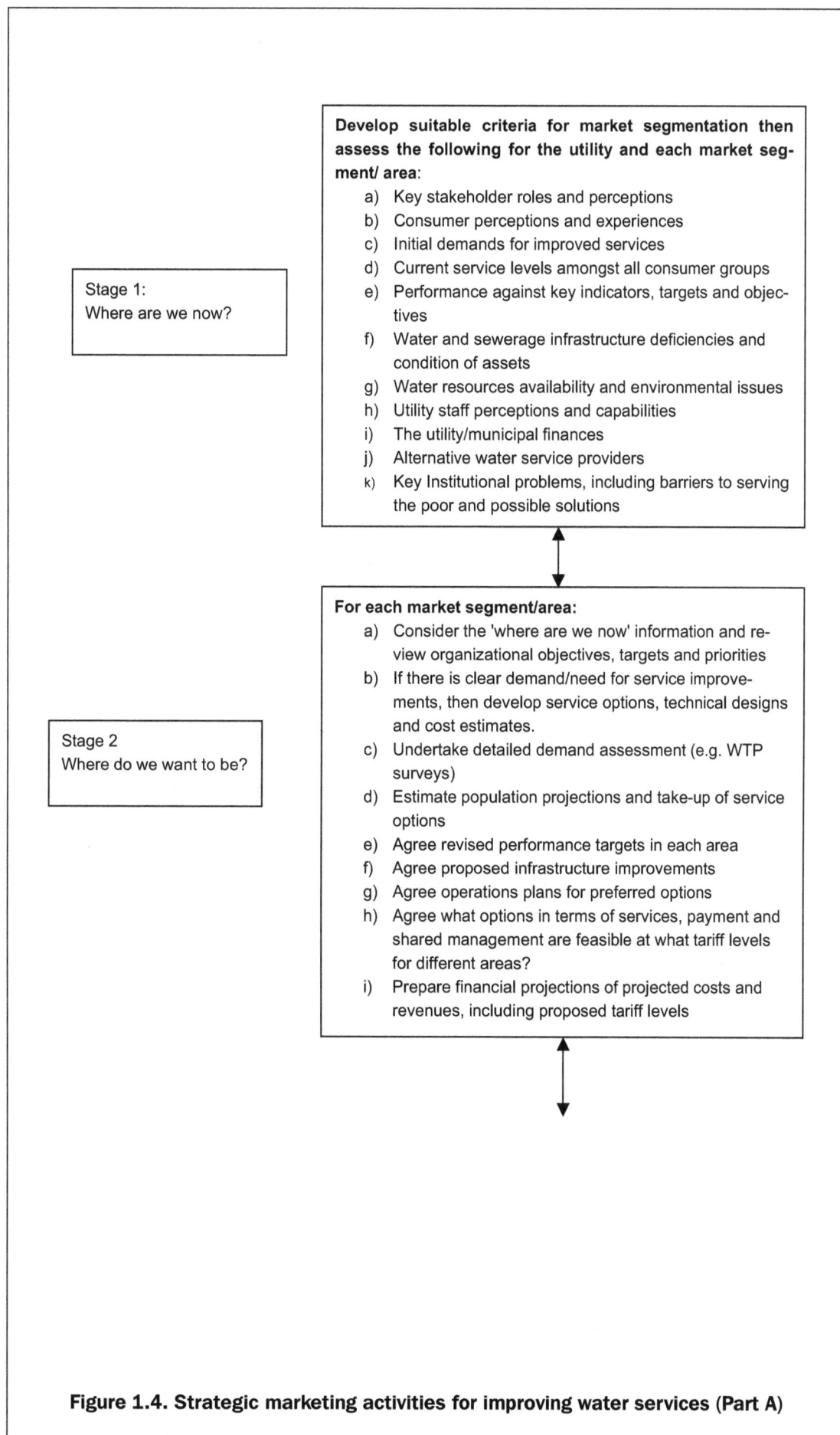

Chapter 6

Stage 1:
Where are we now?

Develop suitable criteria for market segmentation then assess the following for the utility and each market segment/ area:

    a) Key stakeholder roles and perceptions
    b) Consumer perceptions and experiences
    c) Initial demands for improved services
    d) Current service levels amongst all consumer groups
    e) Performance against key indicators, targets and objectives
    f) Water and sewerage infrastructure deficiencies and condition of assets
    g) Water resources availability and environmental issues
    h) Utility staff perceptions and capabilities
    i) The utility/municipal finances
    j) Alternative water service providers
    k) Key Institutional problems, including barriers to serving the poor and possible solutions

Stage 2
Where do we want to be?

For each market segment/area:

    a) Consider the 'where are we now' information and review organizational objectives, targets and priorities
    b) If there is clear demand/need for service improvements, then develop service options, technical designs and cost estimates.
    c) Undertake detailed demand assessment (e.g. WTP surveys)
    d) Estimate population projections and take-up of service options
    e) Agree revised performance targets in each area
    f) Agree proposed infrastructure improvements
    g) Agree operations plans for preferred options
    h) Agree what options in terms of services, payment and shared management are feasible at what tariff levels for different areas?
    i) Prepare financial projections of projected costs and revenues, including proposed tariff levels

Figure 1.4. Strategic marketing activities for improving water services (Part A)

Stage 3
How might we get there?

For each market segment/area:
 (a) Consider utility 'product positioning' (compared to alternative providers such as vendors and private borewells)
 (b) Develop a marketing strategy using the 'marketing mix' (7Ps), including a promotion plan.
 (c) Consider how to support preferred service and payment options
 (d) Consider how to support proposed shared management arrangements either with small-scale providers or community groups
 (e) Develop an institutional improvements plan, considering PPP options
 (f) Develop a 'customer relations management' strategy
 (g) Evaluate benefits and risks
 (h) Summarize Stages 1, 2 and 3 in an Investment or Strategic Marketing Plan (SMP) or business plan and consult key stakeholders
 (i) Seek appropriate sources of funding

Stage 4:
How can we ensure success?

Implement and revise the Strategic Marketing or Investment Plans considering good practice such as:
 (a) Institutional development and sector reform
 (b) Use of appropriate PPP options and regulation
 (c) Well-designed participatory change management approaches
 (d) Total Quality Management (TQM) approaches
 (e) Monitoring and evaluation

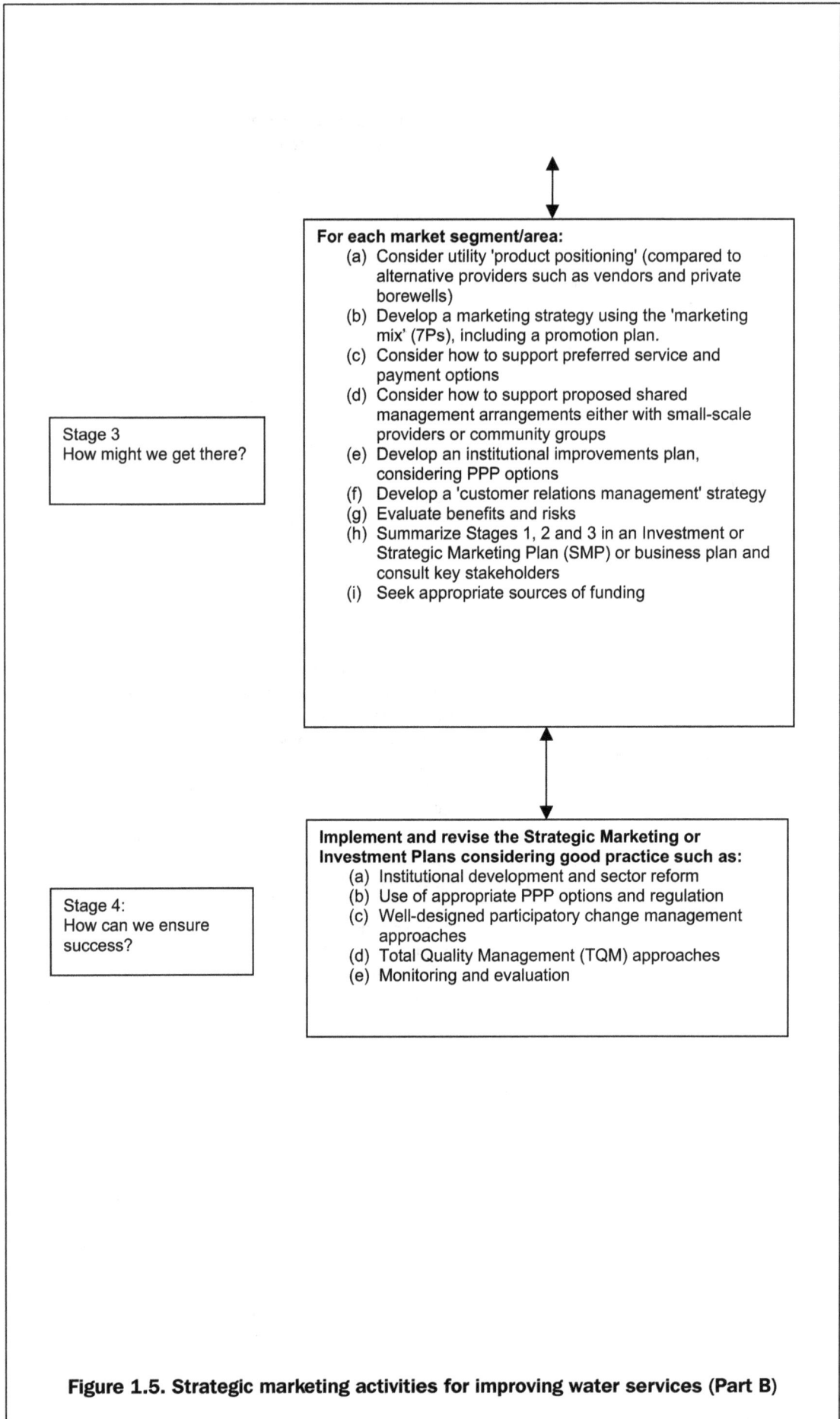

Figure 1.5. Strategic marketing activities for improving water services (Part B)

1.8   Marketing for sanitation

The diversity of the wastewater and sanitation service options that are offered in different low and middle-income cities is illustrated in Table 1.3. The suitability of different sanitation options depends on factors such as: the water supply services that are provided, on-site feasibility of each option, stakeholder pressure for reduction of sewage pollution and the availability of funds for more expensive solutions such as conventional sewerage. A fully operating sewerage system with adequate wastewater treatment is often more expensive than the water supply system. It is for this reason that the use of other less expensive options should be thoroughly explored.

Table 1.3. Wastewater and sanitation technologies[1]

Common service levels	Kampala (Uganda) % Coverage	Dar Es Salaam (Tanzania) % Coverage
Argentina - Comodoro Rivadavia	Conventional sewers, discharge to open water without purification **(85)**	Conventional sewers, secondary treatment, liquid to agriculture **(10)**
India - Bangalore	Household and community latrines, conventional sewers, secondary treatment, liquid discharged to open water courses, sludge dried and retained **(67)**	Household and community latrines, controlled disposal to soils **(23)**
Mexico - Cancun	Conventional sewers, secondary treatment, liquid to deep sea, sludge dried and retained **(69)**	Septic tanks with uncontrolled discharge to soils **(16)**
Philippines - Manila	Septic tank with on-site disposal **(80)**	Latrines with uncontrolled disposal to soils, open water, etc. **(9)**
South Africa - Dolphin Coast	Conventional sewers, secondary treatment, liquid to open water, sludge dried and retained **(59)**	Pit latrines, uncontrolled disposal to soils **(34)**
Zambia - Lusaka	Pit latrines, uncontrolled disposal to soil **(57)**	Conventional sewers, secondary treatment and disposal to open water **(30)**

1.   Source: Blokland et al. (2003).

In this marketing study, with its focus on city-wide sustainability of a utility, we tend to focus more on water supply than sanitation, particularly with regard to serving the poor. The reason for this, alluded to above, is that except in particular situations (such as the Buenos Aires and El Alto examples), sewerage with an adequate level of wastewater treatment tends to be unaffordable for the poor dwelling in low-income areas. The challenge of threading gravity flow sewer pipes at a suitable gradient through illegal, unplanned areas is significantly greater than extending water pipes. This is not to say that such areas do not need sanitation, in fact the reverse is true, as in public health terms the lowest income householders will benefit disproportionately compared to other areas. However a good means of sanitation for the poor does exist, which is on-plot and on-site sanitation.

Because of its individual, discrete characteristics, however, on-plot sanitation does not require the skills of a network utility. Traditionally it has also been co-ordinated by municipal authorities rather than water utilities. Many professionals dealing with on-plot sanitation have realized the benefits of the marketing approaches, whether through 'social marketing' concepts of hygiene promotion, or the conventional marketing of sanitary components such as latrine slabs or pour flush toilet seals. There are good research-based publications available on marketing discrete low-cost sanitation systems for the poor such as:

- *Hands on social marketing - A step by step guide,* by Nedra Kline Weinrich. Sage Publications, London, 1999; and

- *PHAST step by step guide - A participatory approach for the control of diarrhoeal disease,* by Sara Wood, Ron Sawyer and Mayling Simpson-Hebert. WHO, Geneva, 1998.

The PHAST document in particular advises quite intensive interactions with the community. Both publications focus on generating demand for sanitation service improvements. Examples of sanitation options that are normally provided or supported by a utility - i.e. omitting on-plot sanitation and on-site disposal - are shown in Table 1.4.

Table 1.4. Utility-managed or supported sanitation options

Conventional utility/ municipal sewerage network	Low-cost sewerage	Local sewerage network managed by community	Bath housesand public toilets
Conventional sewage treatment	Disposal facilities for suction trucks		

In this marketing study on networked utilities we have focused more on water supply than sanitation. This is because sanitation options in part emerge from the water supply services and their impact on the local environment. However, we would like to emphasize that any strategic marketing plan that does not take into account the needs of sanitation will have failed. In particular, any plan that accepts the continued pricing of sewerage for higher income groups at just 20 per cent of the cost of water supply (when the real cost is likely to be nearer 120 per cent of the cost of water supply) will fail. The result we have seen in some counties is for the courts to become the channel of demand for adequate sanitation through the enforcement of environmental legislation and in one, perhaps extreme, example becoming the de facto manager of the wastewater treatment plant construction programme.

In areas where the use of on-plot sanitation options such as latrines or septic tanks linked to soakaways are causing clear environmental problems, then sewerage system options should be considered. This can arise in areas with high water tables or high population densities. Some of the marketing approaches outlined in this document can be useful in assessing the need for and planning an appropriate sewerage programme. For example, the customer value chain of *know, target, sell and service.* Some key issues under each of these headings are:

Know and understand potential sewer users
If residents in particular areas have invested considerable sums of money in their own septic tanks, they could be reluctant to pay sewerage charges and connect to the sewer

systems. It is important to find out in which areas there is the most demand for sewers and learn the views of potential users before making substantial investments.

Targeting key groups

Which groups will the utility focus on during their initial surveys and promotion work? In Dodoma, Tanzania, where there is a high water table, public and private institutions with more financial resources were encouraged to pay substantial contributions to lay tertiary sewer pipes connecting their properties to the main sewers, so as to remove their sewage pollution. Nearby householders and small businesses then paid for their own connections to these much closer tertiary sewers. This took place between 1988 and 1991 and led to increased connection rates. Where community-managed sewers are feasible, then appropriate strategies for collaborating with such community groups need to be developed.

Selling sewerage connections and reasonable sewerage charges

What combination of incentives and penalties are appropriate to encourage people to connect to sewers and to pay their sewerage charges? Incentives could be in the form of discounts for new connections to the sewer, provided they connect by a certain date. Penalties in the case of non-payment of sewerage charges could be the disconnection of the water service pipe, where water and sewerage bills are combined. Enforcement procedures could be used by local authorities in the case of persistent pollution from overflowing septic tanks. In terms of promotion of sewerage services, the marketing mix 7Ps framework of *product, price, place, promotion, people, processes and presence* (discussed in Chapter 8) can be useful in developing comprehensive plans for implementation.

Sustainable sewerage services

For the provision of reliable and sustainable sewerage services it is necessary to consider the key elements of institutional development such as:

- appropriate environmental and sewerage policies;

- development of sewerage departments than can encourage and respond to the demand for services;

- streamlined systems for O&M and customer services;

- development of staff; and

- provision of sufficient resources.

Using such approaches, strategic marketing or investment plans for sewerage (where there is sufficient demand for services) can be developed following the broad framework outlined in this document for water services.

Part II Marketing water services to low-income consumers

Part II focuses on the marketing of water services to low-income consumers using the customer value chain concept of know, target, sell and service as a framework. The following chapters are included in this section.

- Chapter 2: Knowing and understanding all consumer groups

- Chapter 3: Targeting low-income water consumers

- Chapter 4: Selling and providing services to low-income consumers

For those utilities who wish to use marketing approaches in low-income areas, it is advisable initially to develop pilot programmes in a selected few areas before subsequently scaling-up. Part II focuses on the development of these pilot programmes specifically in low-income areas. Once successful marketing has occurred in these areas it will then be possible for the utility to scale up the overall marketing strategy to develop a comprehensive, city-wide programme.

It is important to gather information about the experiences, perceptions and preferences of all consumer groups. This enables a utility to develop both valuable comparative data to prioritize its investments and resources appropriate and specific marketing strategies for each consumer group. These aspects are dealt with in Chapter 2.

When a utility wishes to move beyond the pilot phase in a few low-income areas and scale up to meet the needs of the entire urban area, the need to balance pricing and service differentiation between the various consumer groups necessitates a Strategic Marketing approach as part of citywide planning. This is the subject of Part III of this document

Chapter 2

Knowing and understanding all consumer groups

2.1 Introduction

The staff of a water utility need to have a good knowledge of the different consumer groups if they are to be able to do their work in a manner that increases customer satisfaction. There has been a tendency for utility/municipal staff to assume that they already know what the consumer wants. Experience in the business sector shows that good quality information about consumer perceptions, experiences and preferences is required if real improvements are to be made. Such quality information can only be gained through well-planned interactions with current and potential customers, using methods such as questionnaire surveys, focus group discussions and semi-structured interviews.

The first stage in the customer value chain, described in the previous section, is getting to know and understand consumers, their wants, their needs, their perceptions, their criticisms. In this category it is necessary to emphasize that we do not only mean existing consumers but also potential consumers, those who are presently unserved by the formal utility.

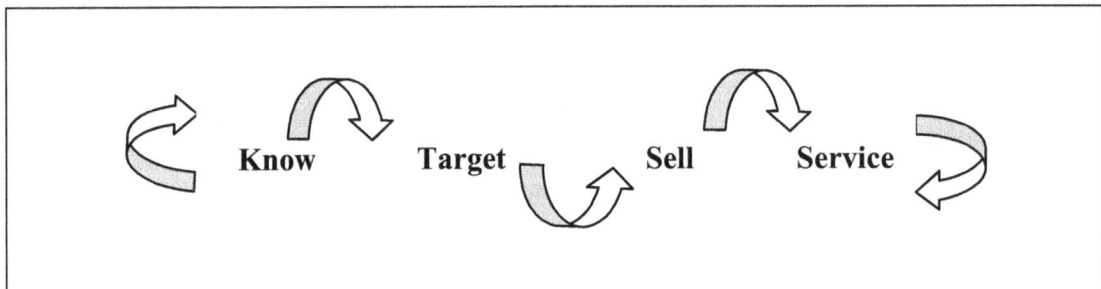

It is important to gather data on all the key consumer groups in a city or town, so that appropriate marketing strategies can be developed that balance the needs and demands of each group. The next section, on market segmentation, considers how best to define these groups or market segments.

2.2 Market segmentation overview

It is clearly impossible to get to know individual water customers, except perhaps for the few largest consumers or perhaps the constant complainers. The marketing approach therefore divides up customers into a manageable number of groups of customers, a process that is known as 'segmentation.' This dividing up for conventional marketing can follow 'social class' lines which incorporate aspects of income or it can follow 'lifestyle' or 'life-cycle stage' patterns which are found to be better predictors of consumer behaviour for particular products. Segmentation has been defined as 'the process of identifying groups of customers with enough characteristics in common to make possible the design and presentation of a product or service each group needs' (Heskett, 1986). The concept of market segmentation is based on the belief that 'people with broadly similar economic, social and lifestyle characteristics tend to congregate in particular neighbourhoods and exhibit similar patterns of purchasing behaviour and outlook (Wilson and Gilligan, 1997).

One of the main reasons for market segmentation is to understand consumer perspectives and develop viable plans to serve the specific needs and demands of *all* consumer groups, and thus avoid some groups missing out, which otherwise often occurs. If we are to 'target specific consumer groups or market segments with suitable service and payment options, at appropriate price levels', as is proposed in the 'customer value chain' section above, then we need to think carefully about how we define our consumer groups or segment the market.

Selection of criteria for market segmentation in the water sector should consider factors such as:

- Is market segmentation feasible and practical using the selected criteria?

- Will the segments be substantial enough for meaningful service differentiation?

- Will the segments be different enough to be distinguished from each other?

- Will the segments be stable enough so that their present and future characteristics can be predicted with a sufficient degree of confidence?

While developing the criteria for market segmentation, it is important to ensure that each market segment has sufficiently similar characteristics to enable appropriate water service options to be provided by the utility.

In many cities in developing countries, needs and conditions differ substantially from one neighbourhood to the next. For example, viable service options in higher income low-density housing areas (such as in-house connections with full internal plumbing) will be quite different from those in informal settlements. It is not realistic, therefore, for the water utility to provide a uniform service to customers whose needs, wants and willingness to pay are so different. It is for this reason that market segmentation has to be used as a means of targeting viable options to appropriate user groups.

One approach to grouping the variables that can be used to segment markets is to define four categories (Wilson and Gilligan, 1997):

- Geographic

- Demographic (e.g. related to age)

- Behavioural (e.g. investment patterns)

- Psychographic or lifestyle

Relying solely on geographical areas such as ward boundaries has been found to be unreliable because even within a small area there can be a wide range of household types and income levels. There can be pockets of slum dwellers in a high-income area, for example, benefiting from their closeness to potential employment.

Segmentation based on demographic or behavioural variables is possible provided good data is available (e.g. from a recent census). But it is difficult to confirm and update the boundaries of the market segment areas on-site using such variables.

For urban water and sewerage services, potential variables for segmentation that have emerged from the strategic marketing research include:

• the type of dwelling and location (e.g. bungalows, flats, informal housing and mixed) which can serve as a proxy for household income levels;

• roofing materials; and

• housing densities (e.g. high, medium and low density).

Based on research in East Africa and India, a suitable and practical criterion for segmentation is the 'type of dwelling or building', described below.

Types of building as a criterion for market segmentation

In many urban areas of developing countries, the type of dwelling that people live in is generally a reflection of their socio-economic status. The people who live in slums and other informal settlements are generally the very poor - although poor people also live in other types of dwellings (tenements and multi-occupancy compounds) and it is not uncommon to find some wealthier householders taking advantage of unplanned areas. Those households in well-planned residential estates tend to be the more affluent in the population or living in housing provided by government for its employees. Housing area is therefore only in part a proxy indicator for income level. The type of dwelling is a better method for a water utility could use to segment the water market. This is more so because a dwelling often defines a household, which is an appropriate unit for the utility to form a beneficial exchange relationship, another definition of marketing.

Market segmentation in Mombasa's residential sector was carried out on the basis of the type of dwellings that households live in. Dwellings were categorized into the following four segments:

• bungalows and maisonettes

• flats

• single, two or three-roomed dwellings (including 'Swahili' type of dwelling)

• dwellings located in informal settlements, constructed using informal building materials such as recycled timber, iron sheets, packaging boards and paper

Using the type of dwelling as a criterion for segmentation, other possible market segments include:

• mixed development, consisting of a variety of different types of dwellings

• commercial, industrial and institutional establishments

Dwellings located in an area with mixed development could be regarded as belonging to one of the four market segments identified above. Commercial, industrial and institutional establishments may be grouped into one segment since they are likely to have similar service requirements.

The use of type of dwellings or type of building as criteria for market segmentation is relatively easy to implement in the field since dwellings are visible and can easily fit into one of the specified market segments. The use of GIS based on up-to-date aerial photographs by utilities can provide good base maps for market segmentation by type of dwelling. Another advantage of this type of segmentation is that viable technical and management options for water provision can be provided to suit different market segments on the basis of type of dwelling. For example, if people are living in small and cramped informal settlements, a variety of service options other than house connections with full internal plumbing are likely to be appropriate.

Socio-economic criteria for water sector market segmentation

Where more detail is required, market segmentation using income as the only criterion may not be practical because it is usually difficult to measure, particularly where many people's earnings are from the informal economy. Utilities can, however, use proxies for income such as household consumer goods, electricity connections, roof types and walling materials - and even, described by one commentator, the presence of television satellite dishes in the informal housing area.

To increase the rigour of the segmentation or zoning process, a basket of proxy indicators could be used to develop a socio-economic index in order to categorize an area of a city into household income segments.

As part of a water quality surveillance zoning exercise in Kampala, Uganda (Howard, 2002) a multi-factored index was used to classify areas into the following broad zones:

- high income
- middle income 1
- middle income 2
- low income 1
- low income 2
- low income 3

For the water quality surveillance zoning exercise in Kampala, the multi-factored index was derived from the variables, weighting, conditions and scores used in Table 2.1. The weightings were assigned because some variables (proxy indicators) were regarded as better proxy measures than others. The information on 'conditions' for each sample household was obtained from a recent census in Kampala.

Such a thorough multi-factored approach to developing a socio-economic index is potentially more accurate for zoning or the development of market segments in a city than using just one indicator. However, it is only likely to be feasible if recent and accurate census data is available. In addition the maps that are produced from the multi-factored index would be difficult to confirm on site and update as changes on the ground occur over

Table 2.1. Socio-economic index variables for water quality zoning in Kampala[1]

Variable	Variable	Conditions	Score
Roof material	4.0	Iron sheets Asbestos sheets Concrete Papyrus Banana leaves/fibre Other	0 1 5 -3 -5
Floor material	4.0	Concrete Brick Stone Cement screed Rammed earth Wood	-1 1 4 0 -5 3.5
Persons per room	2.5	< 1.7 1.8 - 2.1 > 2.1	1.5 1 -1.5
Educational attainment	2.0	None - male None - female P1 - P7 male (Plus other levels of education attainment)	-3 -3 0
Main source of livelihood	2.0	Subsistence farming Commercial farming Petty trading Formal trading Cottage industry Property income Employment income Family support Other	3.5 4 -4 1 -1.5 4.5 0 -5
Average household size	1.0	< 3.4 3.4 - 4.3 4.4 - 4.7 > 4.4	1.5 1 -1.5 -1.5

1. Source: Howard (2002)

time. A multi-factored index based on census data could, however, be effectively used to verify the suitability of a single market segment criterion such as dwelling type or roof material, in a few sample market segment areas.

Using segmentation plans and data

If a utility decides not to base its data collection and marketing activities on detailed market segmentation, then it is recommended that they at least use an area-based approach. This ensures that decision-making and resource allocation are based on the distinct characteristics of each area and the people in it. Effective market segmentation, however, can provide a better approach for dealing with the needs and demands of different consumer groups.

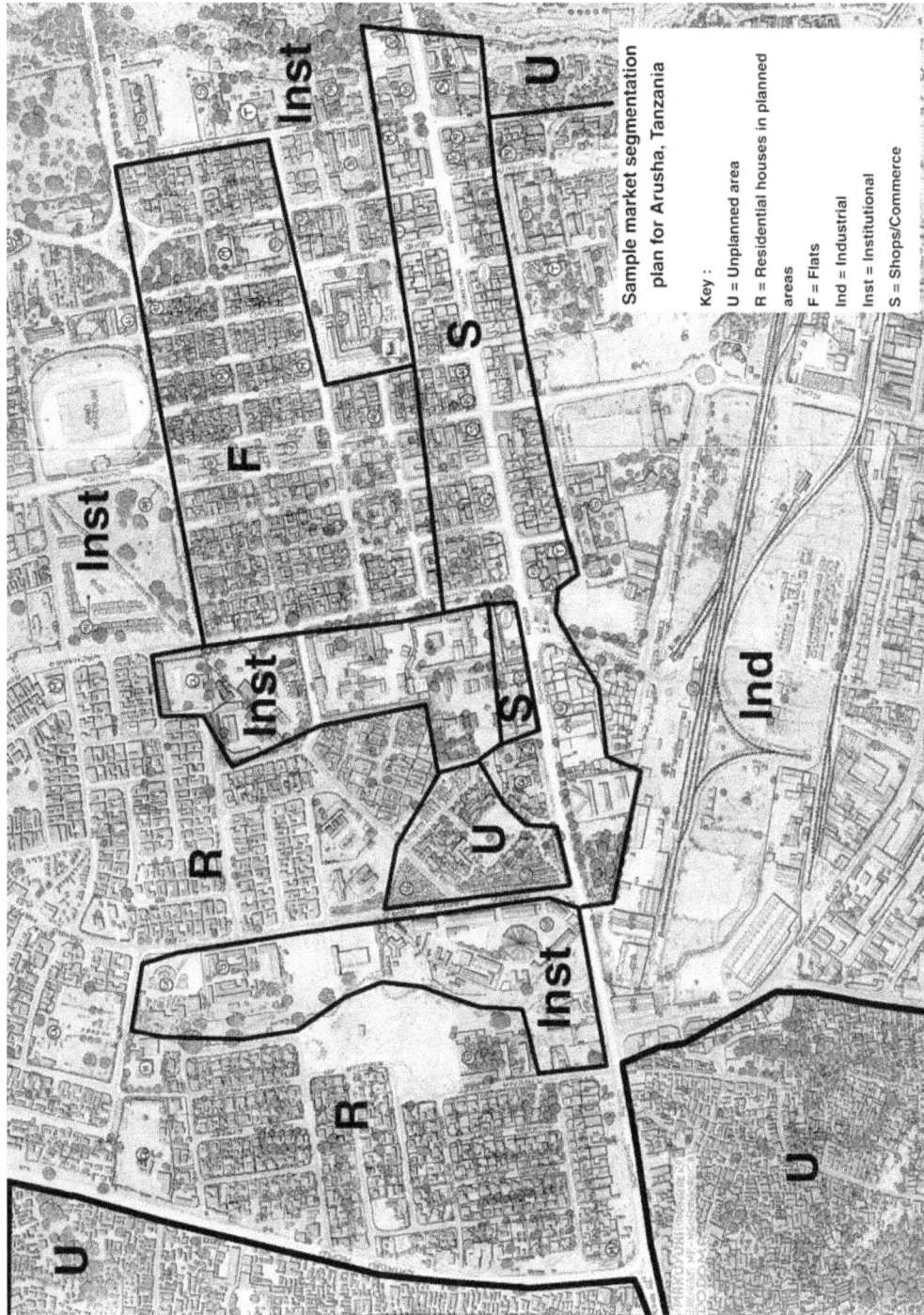

Figure 2.1. Arusha sample market segmentation plan

An example market segmentation plan for an area of Arusha in Tanzania is shown in Figure 2.1. The validity of the segmentation would of course need to be verified on the ground. Such plans are useful in a number of respects including for:

- consumer survey purposes - ensuring that each consumer group and area is adequately represented in the survey;

- developing and implementing marketing strategies for each segment and area;

- linking the location of water infrastructure and service levels with each market segment and area; and

- planning service improvements to poorly served areas or informal settlements.

Note that people living in one unplanned settlement may have quite different service levels, perceptions and demands from another unplanned settlement in the city. So it is important to sample each area.

Table 2.2 illustrates the use of the 'type of dwelling' as a basis for market segmentation as it was used in the Guntur Strategic Marketing Plan (SMP) from India. It is clear that income levels vary substantially between each of these segments.

Table 2.2. Average household income by market segment in Guntur, India[1]

Market segment	Average household monthly income (estimated in Rs*)
Bungalows	1,1765
Independent houses in planned areas	7,833
Independent houses in unplanned areas	4,625
Flats in planned areas	10,078
Flats in unplanned areas	11,180
Slums with some water supply coverage	2,113
Slums with no water supply coverage	605

1. Source: Narender and Chary (2002)
    *Note: the exchange rate is Rs42 to US$1.00 (2002)

Use of type of dwelling or type of building criteria for market segmentation is relatively easy to implement in the field, since dwellings are visible and can easily fit into one of the specified market segments. Another advantage of this type of segmentation is that viable technical and management options for water provision can be provided to suit different market segments on the basis of type of dwelling.

One means of illustrating the resulting segmentation of present and potential consumer groups is through 'social mapping.' An example of a social map from Bolivia is shown in Figure 2.2. Data obtained from a consumer survey was collected and presented on the basis of the identified market segments in order to provide useful decision-support information.

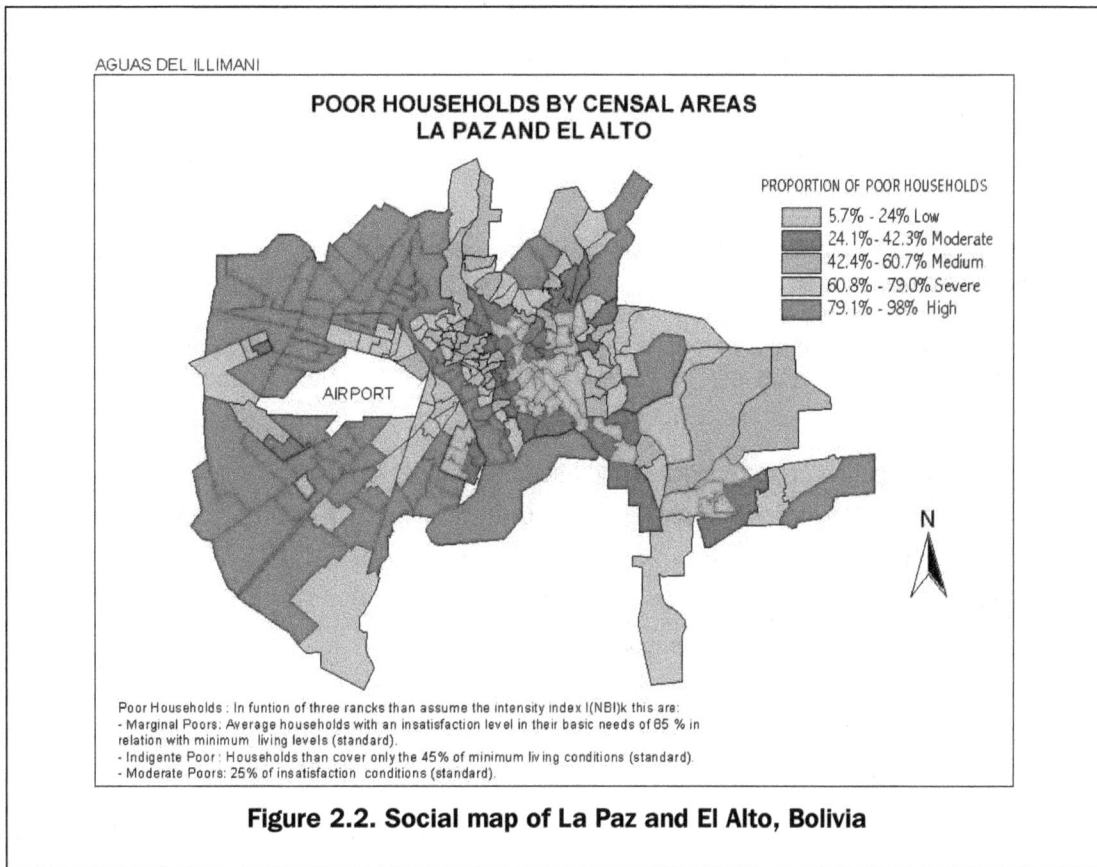

AGUAS DEL ILLIMANI

**POOR HOUSEHOLDS BY CENSAL AREAS
LA PAZ AND EL ALTO**

PROPORTION OF POOR HOUSEHOLDS

5.7% - 24% Low
24.1% - 42.3% Moderate
42.4% - 60.7% Medium
60.8% - 79.0% Severe
79.1% - 98% High

AIRPORT

N

Poor Households : In funtion of three rancks than assume the intensity index I(NBI)k this are:
- Marginal Poors: Average households with an insatisfaction level in their basic needs of 85 % in relation with minimum living levels (standard).
- Indigente Poor : Households than cover only the 45% of minimum living conditions (standard).
- Moderate Poors: 25% of insatisfaction conditions (standard).

Figure 2.2. Social map of La Paz and El Alto, Bolivia

2.3 Use of GIS

A significant challenge for those seeking to improve water services to informal settlements is obtaining comprehensive information on precisely where all the poor and unserved houses are located. Updating existing maps by manually surveying all the new houses and drawing the new buildings on the utility maps is a laborious task and that is rarely undertaken.

A number of utilities, for example in Kampala and Durban, are now using GIS (Geographical Information Systems), which are based on aerial photographs of the utility service area. The photographs are stored digitally on the utility's computers and can be used to produce accurate maps to the required scale for whatever purpose. Some of the key features of the GIS used at Durban Metro Water in South Africa are discussed briefly in Box 2.1.

It is clear from Durban Metro Water's GIS experience that having such valuable and up-to-date information at the 'press of few buttons' has a number advantages:

- Good access to data and management information summaries about different consumer groups (or market segments) including those in poorer areas, which enables well-informed and quick decision-making;

- Where repairs, maintenance work or new connections are required, key technical information about the existing water infrastructure is readily available.

- Enables effective strategic planning to providing services to unserved areas.

- Enables more accurate and speedy responses to customer requests and complaints.

Box 2.1. GIS at Durban Metro Water[1]

Durban Metro Water (now called Ethekwini Water) in South Africa have developed their GIS (Geographical Information Systems) in recent years to enhance the management of water and sanitation services to over 3 million consumers.

The aerial photographic surveys for the GIS are redone each year to produce up to date digitized maps of all properties, at a 'relatively cheap cost'. Such maps are very useful, particularly for locating recently constructed properties in informal settlements that may otherwise be unknown to utility service providers. The Durban GIS system has more than 30 different layers of relevant information that can be shown on its digitized computer maps including the following:

- the precise location of all connected and unconnected properties
- the location of all water and sewer pipes and utility facilities
- the location of all water meters (to enable quick meter reading)
- records of repairs over the years on each water main
- links to each customer's water consumption
- links to each customer's payment records
- links to customer complaint records
- unique numbers for all properties (to enable the speedy location of properties and maintenance problems)
- roads and street furniture
- links to the design or 'as built' drawings of each pipeline

These various layers can be turned on or off to suit the purpose of the member of staff using the GIS, and printouts can be made of the map area under consideration at an appropriate scale.

Durban Metro Water has 700,000 connections and it has connected 98,000 new customers in the last eight years.

---

1. Source: Presentation by Neil McLeod, Head of Ethekwini Water and summarized by Kevin Sansom in December 2003.

Such benefits are best achieved by obtaining and maintaining good quality data on the GIS. Other utilities and government may, therefore, wish to consider this approach.

2.4   Overview of consumer survey techniques

Consumer surveys enable the organization to collect data to:

- understand the different customer and potential customer groups, including their attitudes, practices, perceptions and preferences, as well as water use and buying habits, so that affordable service improvements can be devised;

- develop new service options or modify existing service options and carry out service differentiation;

- estimate future demand;

- estimate affordability to pay for services;

- establish maximum willingness to pay levels for service options; and

- develop a customer care programme and monitor the progress of customer service initiatives.

Many organizations use the traditional method of monitoring complaints and compliments in order to keep track of the views of their customers. By being proactive in finding out about customer concerns and taking prompt action on customers' complaints, the organization saves, rather than spends, money.

Although monitoring complaints enables the organization to actively listen to customers, on average only a small percentage of the organization's customer base actually bothers to complain. Research in America showed that one in 26 people actually take the trouble to complain to the organization (Cook, 1992. The organization should therefore not rely entirely on complaints/compliments monitoring.

In order to make market research a cost-effective task, management should be convinced of the need to carry out the research, and should be committed to the process. Before embarking on a market research programme, management should review data from previous research. Typical questions to ask are (Cook, 1992):

- What do we know about existing and potential customers?

- What do we know about their expectations?

- How well are we meeting their expectations?

- Do we have any information about future trends of customer requirements?

Cook (1992) recommends the following sequence of activities concerned with market surveys in Figure 2.3.

Depending on the objective of the survey, the types of consumer being surveyed, and the intended use of the data, an organization may decide to use one or several of these research methods for data collection:

- **Self-completed questionnaires:** The questionnaires may be delivered to the households or distributed at any point of contact with potential customers. The questionnaires may also be sent through the post. Although they are easy to administer, self-completed questionnaires have relatively low completion rates, may sometimes be biased to a particular category of customers, and may be abused by staff.

- **Enumerator completed questionnaires:** While this approach is more expensive than self-completed questionnaires, it generally produces more reliable data and has a higher completion rate. It is also easier to ensure that a representative sample of the various market segments has been surveyed. Carefully planned training of the enumerators is important for ensuring the validity of the data.

- **Face-to-face interviews:** Interviews may be either structured or semi-structured, depending on the objective. Accurate responses can be collected in a short time. This method also enables the interviewer to probe potential customers for a more detailed explanation of issues. The main disadvantage is the high cost involved.

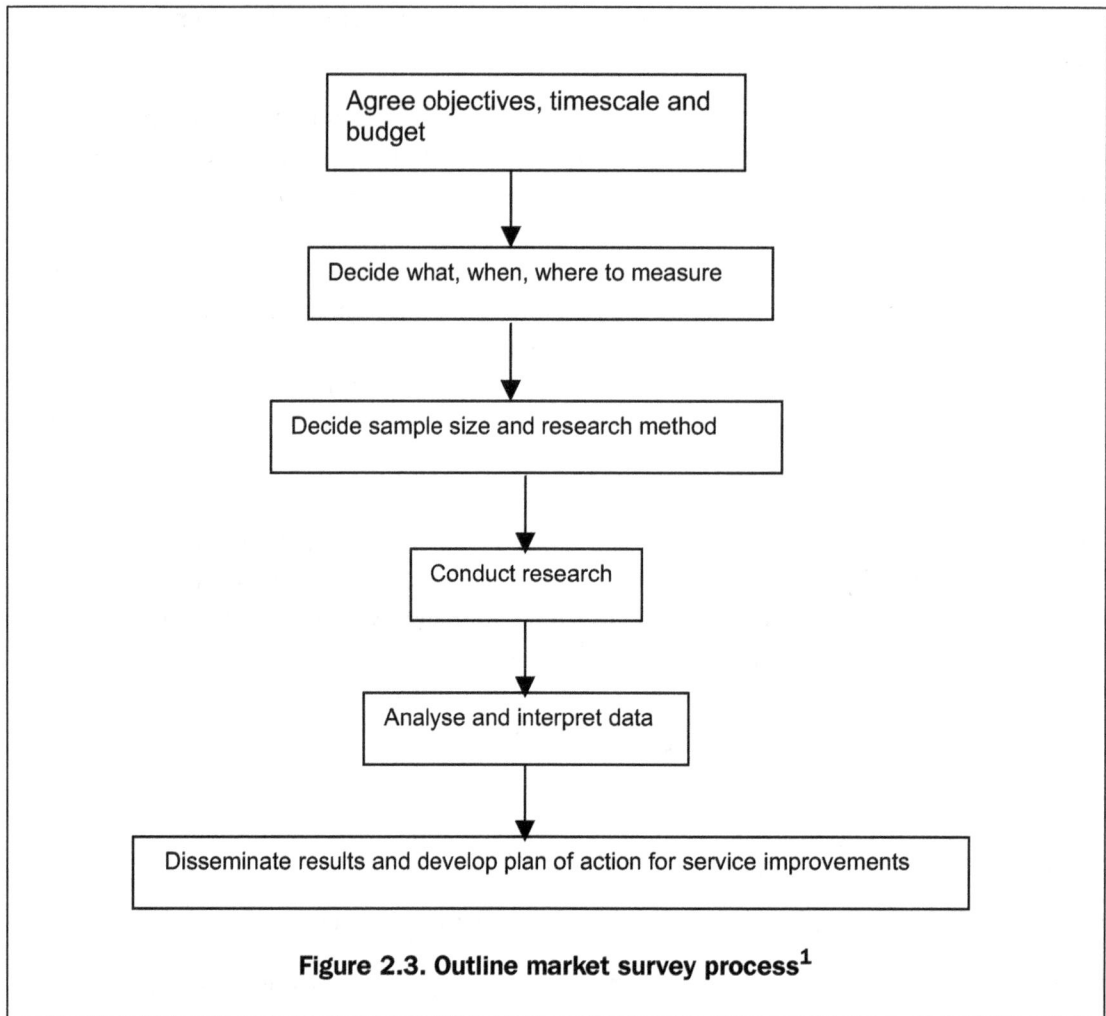

Figure 2.3. Outline market survey process[1]

1. Source: Cook (1992)

- **Focus groups:** These are a powerful means to evaluate services or test new ideas. Basically, focus groups are interviews, but of six to 15 people at the same time in the same group, and therefore act as multiple interviews where interviewees get an immediate response, confirmation or challenge from the group. This leads to immediate validation of the ideas discussed, where the group agrees. However, there is a risk that discussions can be distorted by particular individuals, leading the group in a direction which suits that individual's interests. It is possible to obtain a great deal of qualitative information during a focus group session, but only if it is managed by experienced facilitators.

- **Telephone surveys:** In countries where the telephone network is fairly developed, telephone surveys may be carried out. The advantage of this method is that it gets an immediate response from customers in a short time. It can also be carried out at a relatively low cost. However, this method has several disadvantages: the respondents may consider telephone interviews as an invasion of privacy, and it is difficult to conduct a lengthy interview with customers. Telephone surveys, irrespective of the recent surge in mobile phone use, are extremely unlikely to be representative of the lowest income water users.

For existing customers it is useful to remember to use ongoing means of consulting with them, in addition to the methods described above.

- **Customer service groups or forums and user panels:** These meetings enable the participants to express their opinions on the quality of service an organization provides. The number of participants has to be optimal to keep the discussion focused. Such meetings also enable dialogue and discussion among customers, and between customers and the organization. The main disadvantage is that the participants may not be representative of the organization's customer base.

- **Suggestion schemes:** These are used to solicit for customer opinions on how products and services meet customer requirements, and to identify areas for improvement. However they tend to deliver information only on existing customers.

- **Freephone:** When telecommunication technology allows, customers can provide feedback on the organization through a telephone link fully paid for by the organization.

All social surveys, whether quantitative, qualitative, focus group or questionnaire, require skilled practitioners to undertake them successfully. In general, the lead researcher should be from a reputable research agency such as experienced private consultants, social sciences departments in a university, government-recognized institutes of social research, or capable NGOs.

Enumerators are required to undertake questionnaire surveys, visiting householders individually. Enumerators can be experienced students from university or similar institutions with training in sociology and social methods. Reporters, who could be a research assistant from a reputable research institute, are required to note discussions in focus groups to allow the researcher to focus on facilitating and guiding the discussion.

The lead researcher should be responsible for analysing the text of any discussions and for drawing out the conclusions from any quantitative questionnaires. Focus group discussions are likely to require inputs from an engineer or manager from the water utility to explain technical issues to the researcher and to the group participants.

Communicating with different consumer groups

The technique chosen to obtain information will depend on the type of data required and the characteristics of the particular consumer groups. For example, for larger commercial consumers, interviews may be cost effective, if those consumers then choose to or continue to use utility piped water, rather than their own sources, as they can be a significant source of revenue for the utility.

The use of enumerator-completed questionnaires is a good technique for general customer surveys, where detailed and accurate information is required. It is necessary, however, to design, test and review the questionnaires carefully.

People in informal settlements may have limited trust in or experience in dealing with public utilities. Focus group discussions offer an effective technique for a utility to develop an understanding of the attitudes, practices, perceptions and preferences. It can also be the basis for ongoing dialogue.

A utility needs to consider who will undertake consumer surveys - in-house teams, consultants or a social intermediary such as an NGO. If the required skills and staff are not available within the utility, then it is better to use reputable private companies. Where focus group discussions are the chosen method for informal settlements, capable NGOs or college staff may be the best organizations to facilitate discussions and document the process.

Although it is preferable to survey all consumer groups, there may be times when a utility only wants to survey some market segments or areas. There is no problem with this provided it is clear which areas have been included in the survey and which areas have not and why.

Questionnaire surveys

Key principles of questionnaire development

In order to collect accurate data from customers, an organization should use a good data collection instrument. Carefully designed questionnaire surveys can provide reliable data to inform decisions on future investments plans and improvements in the way staff undertake their work, in order to increase customer satisfaction.

A typical questionnaire development process is outlined in Figure 2.4. Note that the analysis of the completed questionnaires should inform the viability of ideas for service improvements.

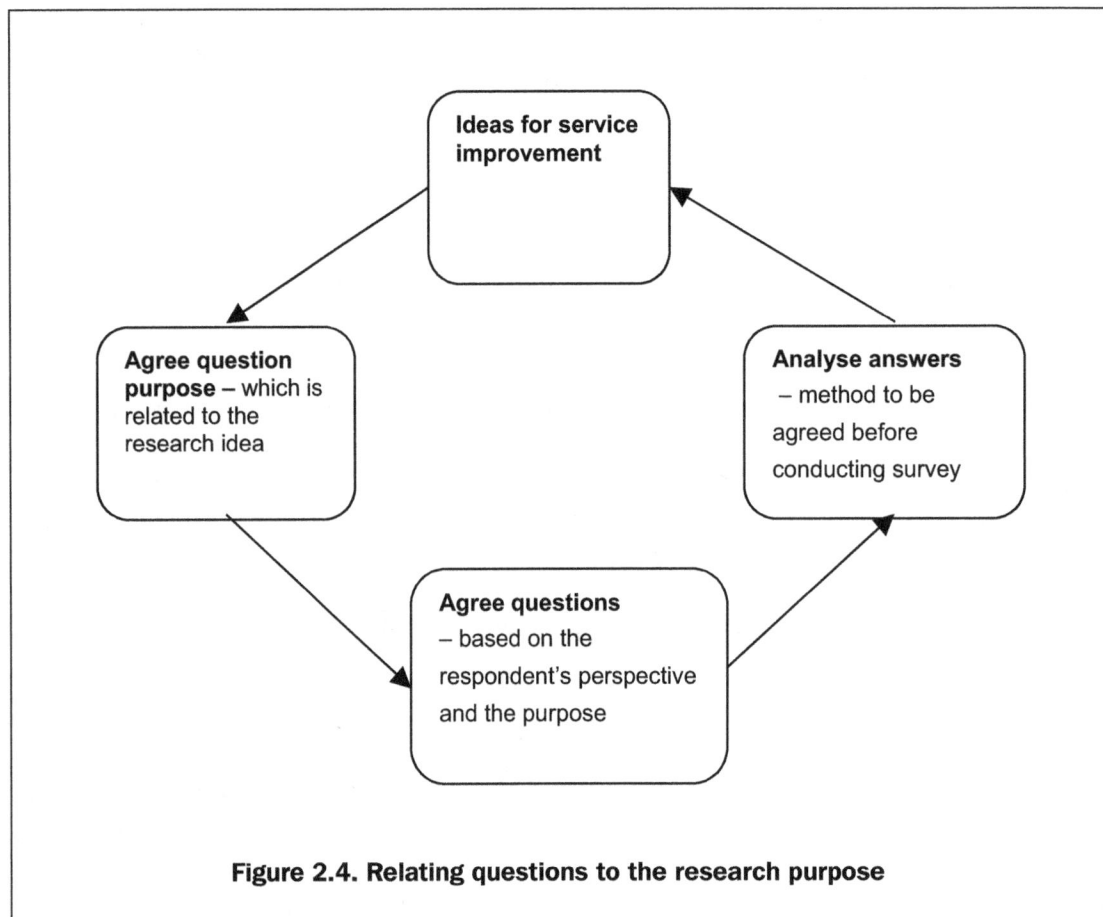

Ideas for service improvement

Agree question purpose – which is related to the research idea

Analyse answers – method to be agreed before conducting survey

Agree questions – based on the respondent's perspective and the purpose

Figure 2.4. Relating questions to the research purpose

Asking the right question is key. So when drafting the form, two issues should be explored:

Is the question necessary? A question should not be included if it is merely interesting, it must relate to the purpose of the research. While it is necessary to keep the length of questionnaires to a minimum, some questions may need to be included to establish rapport and neutrality, particularly when dealing with sensitive subjects.

Are several questions needed instead of one? Once we have ascertained that a question is necessary, we must make sure that it is sufficient to obtain the desired information. Sometimes several questions are necessary to ensure that accurate information is gathered The questionnaire survey format also needs to be easy to read and understand by utility staff, enumerators and other interested parties. For easy analysis, open-ended questions should be minimized and where possible tick boxes for multiple answers should be included. When producing summaries of the analysis, a spreadsheet computer programme can be used to produce summary tables, graphs and bar charts, etc. to communicate the key findings of the survey. Further guidance on questionnaire design is as follows:

- Make the questions as clear and simple as possible, without losing the meaning.

- Decide which questions will be worded negatively, in order to minimize the tendency of some respondents to mechanically choose the points toward one end of the scale.

- Some questions may require respondents to recall experiences from the past that are hazy in their memory. Such recall-dependent questions should be minimized.

- Questions should not be phrased in such a way that they lead the respondents to give answers that the researcher wants.

- Avoid questions that are phrased in an emotionally charged manner ('loaded questions'). Such questions create a lot of bias in the responses.

- The sequence of questions in the questionnaire should be such that the respondent is led from questions of a general nature to those that are more specific.

- Personal information or classification data should be asked for in a carefully worded tone. The respondents should be assured of anonymity.

- The questionnaire should have a good introduction that clearly identifies both the researcher and the purpose of the survey.

Potential aspects to be researched for the water sector

To understand the state of the water supply market in a comprehensive manner, particularly if a utility is to <u>maximize</u> the number of satisfied customers <u>and</u> work towards financial sustainability, the following aspects could potentially be investigated using customer survey questionnaires:

a) **The experiences and perceptions of existing and potential customers with regard to:**

- the water supply services provided by the utility in terms of key service characteristics such as: frequency, reliability, timing, duration, quantity, quality, pressure, or other characteristics that are valued by customers;

- the utility's water charges and billing arrangements;

- the utility's customer services in general, in terms of dealing with requests and responding to complaints;

- the comparative advantages and disadvantages of water services provided by competitors, such as water vendors and private water tankers;

- the coping strategies used by people in the city to deal with poor water services, for example: use of storage and selection of different water sources at different times of the year; and

- opportunities for supply improvements or utility cost reductions, such as new supply options with storage incorporated and tertiary supply systems being managed by community groups.

b) **Information on the socio-economic situation of respondents** for aspects such as housing and income, so that a detailed picture can be developed about the various customer groups in the city, as well as their 'ability to pay'. The specific topic of willingness to pay is discussed in detail below.

A utility may prefer not to get all the data it requires from one survey, in order that the questionnaires can be kept to reasonable length. In addition, analysing the results of a preliminary survey may inform the contents of a further survey. An example of a comprehensive water utility consumer survey form is in Annexe 1; this is based on the Mombasa marketing field research. A shorter survey form based on key indicators for serving the poor is shown in Annexe 5.

Sampling

The sample selected for a survey needs to be both representative and random. Sampling is the process of selecting a sufficient number from the entire group of people, events or things of interest that the researcher wishes to investigate. The entire group is referred to as the population, and a single member of the population is called an element. The population frame is a listing of all the elements of the population from which the sample is to be drawn. The sample is to be drawn such that understanding the properties or characteristics of the sample elements will enable generalization to the population elements.

Sampling is necessary because in a large population it is difficult and expensive to collect data from all elements of the population. A discussion of the different types of sampling is included in a publication called *Willingness to pay surveys - A streamlined approach* by Alison Wedgwood and Kevin Sansom (2003) which is available on the WEDC website.

When considering all consumer groups in the urban water sector, a representative sample should be selected for each of the market segments being surveyed. A good market segmentation plan of sufficiently large scale that is up to date can be a useful aid in selecting which households to visit as part of a representative and random sample.

Pilot testing

Pilot testing is an essential part of any household survey. Pilot testing is a rehearsal for the real thing: it allows the enumerators to practice the questionnaire with members of the public, rather than through stage-managed role playing. It also enables the survey field manager to monitor the ability of the enumerators in the field through observing interviews (Wedgwood and Sansom, 2003).

A key consideration is were any of the questions difficult for the respondents to understand? Were any questions irrelevant? Pilot testing should also be considered an important part of enumerator training. The enumerators can improve their knowledge of the questionnaire in the 'real' environment, away from blackboards and role-playing in the classroom. Persistent problems may emerge after a few interviews have been carried out, which can be addressed during the follow up meeting with the enumerators.

Managing the survey and analysing the results

Developing a questionnaire and then managing a survey requires a considerable amount of specialist work. Hence it is generally better for a utility to contract out the survey design, implementation and analysis of the results. Clearly the utility will have an editorial role over the design of the questionnaire, so it meets their objectives. A typical questionnaire is shown in Annex 1. This form is quite comprehensive, being part of the marketing research that informed the compilation of this publication. Shorter, more simple forms can be developed by utilities provided they provide all the information that is required An example of a short survey form based on selected key indicators is shown in Annex 5.

After the pilot testing, it will be practical for the survey manager to select enumerator team leaders. The team leaders can co-ordinate each day's activities with the survey manager, including where the survey will take place each day. The team leaders can collect the questionnaires at the end of the day and carry out an initial check to ensure that they have been filled in correctly. It is always best to check the questionnaires each day, because if there are any errors or gaps these are more easily rectified immediately. If there are consistent errors in the quality of filled in questionnaires, the only course of action may be to dismiss the enumerator (Wedgwood and Sansom, 2003).

The field manager should act as the general co-ordinator, working with the team leaders. Random checks on the enumerators, observing them during interviews, etc., are vital to maintain the quality of the survey.

Once all the questionnaires have been completed, the next steps are very important. If a consulting firm is carrying out the analysis of data the utility manager can still monitor progress to ensure robust results. Things to look out for include:

- Use of a data entry table to store all key information. This could be a table in Microsoft Excel or a similar spreadsheet programme In the spreadsheet programme each column represents a question from the questionnaire. Each horizontal line represents one completed questionnaire. SPSS is a commonly used statistical programme, this too requires all the data from the questionnaires to be sorted onto one 'page' before analysis can take place.

- At least two members of staff should enter the data, as this provides a constant checking service. Sorting through hundreds of questions, or ensuring that the answer is entered in the correct cell in the Excel or SPSS programme can be tedious and mistakes are easily made. A simple mistake in data entry, inputting a 1 instead of a 0, completely changes the results once analysis takes place.

- Evidence that data has been 'cleaned' to eliminate obvious errors, either on the part of the respondent (answering deliberately untruthfully) or the enumerator (recording the answers inaccurately). The easiest way to look for 'outliers' is to assess the raw data frequency distributions of the answers to each question for obvious discrepancies.

Thorough analysis of the consumer survey and willingness to pay results data is best done using the computer package SPSS, or similar. This allows for cross tabulation of results, which means that graphs and tables of different questions can be joined together. For example, household income or expenditure can be compared with the existing water sources. This will provide the utility with useful information to help them plan new water source options that are more likely to be within the price range of new customers and meet their existing and future water requirements. More information on conducting surveys is contained in publications such as *Designing Household Survey Questionnaires for Developing Countries: Lessons from 15 Years of the Living Standards Measurement Study. Volumes 1, 2, and 3*. M. Grosh. and P. Glewwe, The World Bank, Washington DC, (2000).

Surveys and gender

In order to capture useful information from both male and female consumers it is desirable to ensure that at least 50 per cent of your participants in the survey are women. Where there are concerns that few women will participate, some strategies to consider are:

- At least 50 per cent of the enumerators should be women, to make it easier to interview the senior female members of the households.

- Enumerators could interview both male and female members of the household simultaneously. However, in many cases this might not be possible because either the male or female may be away at the time.

Enumerators should conduct the survey when they think there is a good chance of women being at home.

Presenting the consumer survey results

It is worth thinking about how best to present the survey results in a report, so that important information is clearly presented and the reader can understand the results and consider the implications. Figure 2.5 below shows the ranges of incomes per household for families in a small town in Uganda. The graphical format provides a pictorial summary of family incomes. A quick glance shows the reader that a large percentage of families earn between USh800,000 and USh4 million per year, but also that at least 15 per cent earn only USh300,000 to USh400,000. Caution is required in collecting income data, as people may underestimate their earnings, particularly if they work in the informal economy. In the Bushenyi study by Wedgwood and Sansom (2001), the cash income figures were derived from survey questions on household expenditure.

This form of presentation in Figure 2.5 can also show any potential anomalies in the data, for example if one range has a much higher value than the rest of the data, and such anomalies can be investigated further. An alternative presentation is a table which shows data against a variety of variables, as in Table 2.3. While this presentation requires more detailed reading, it is a useful way of summarizing key information. Other graphical methods of presentation such as pie charts should also be considered as a means of clearly presenting key information.

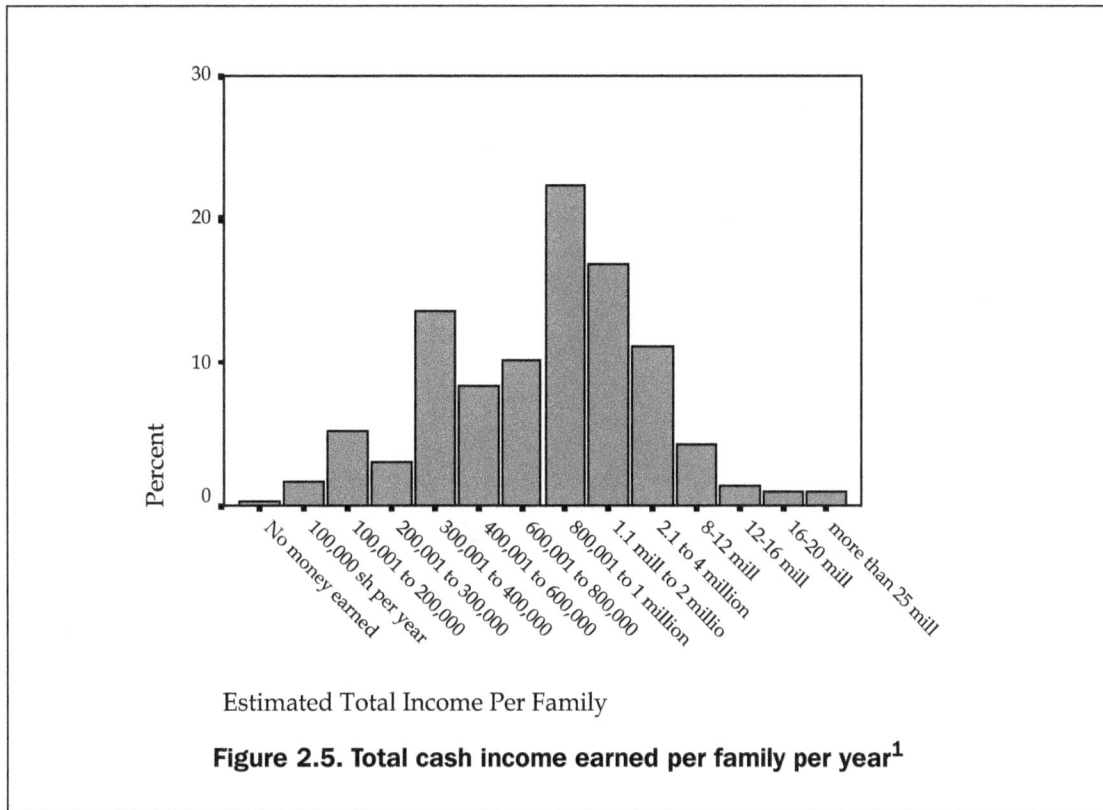

Estimated Total Income Per Family

Figure 2.5. Total cash income earned per family per year[1]

1. Source: Bushenyi CVM Survey 2001 (Wedgwood and Sansom)

2.5 Triangulating and cross-checking results

It is helpful to cross-check the data from specific water and sanitation related studies with broader household survey data. This form of triangulation can lead to greater confidence in the results and the marketing plan that results.

'The Living Standards Measurement Study was established by the World Bank in 1980 to explore ways of improving the type and quality of household data collected by government statistical offices in developing countries. The objectives of the LSMS were to develop new methods for monitoring progress in raising levels of living, to identify the consequences for households of current and proposed government policies, and to improve communications between survey statisticians, analysts, and policymakers.

As of 1997, surveys with several, if not all, of the hallmarks of the Living Standards Measurement Study had been conducted in about two dozen countries. Although the first few LSMS surveys followed a very similar format, as time passed and countries with different circumstances were added, substantial variety arose in the surveys across the different countries' (Grosh and Glewwe, 1996)

An example of the way in which the data from the *Living Standards Measurement Study* can be helpful for planning water and sanitation surveys can be seen in Figure 2.6.

The analysis of LSMS data in Figure 2.6 suggests that the willingness to connect to electricity (upper line in figure [triangles]) at low incomes is far higher than the willingness to connect to water (second line [circles]) and what they term sewer (third line from top). By 'sewer' they appear to mean 'flush toilet', as that is the descriptor most

Table 2.3. Key socio-demographic data for urban population in Uganda[1]

Attribute	Variable	Percentage
Gender	Male Female	48.5 51.5
Age structure	Less than 20 years old 20-50 years old More than 50 years old	60.9 33.9 5.2
Household size	1-2 people 3-5 people 6-10 people More than 10 people	27.9 38.5 29.7 3.9
Access to education	Literate, aged 10 years or older Aged 15 years or more, completed primary school Aged 20 years or more, completed Ordinary Level education	81.4 56.8* 27.1*
Household expenditure (Mean monthly expenditure = USh167,900)	Expenditure on food, drink, tobacco Expenditure on clothing, footware, and household equipment Expenditure on rent, fuel, and power Expenditure on transport, health care and education Expenditure on others	43 11 19 17 10
Type of dwellings	Independent house Tenement (Muzigo) Others	37 51 12
Type of tenure	Owned by household Rented by household Others	36 53 11
Water supply	Households that use piped water as main source Households that use boreholes as main source Households that use protected wells/tube wells as main source Households that use unprotected wells/springs as main source	36* 10.4* 26.9* 19*
Toilet facility	Flush toilet Pit latrine Others	9.2 87.7 3.7

1. Sources: Uganda Statistics Department (1994; 1998) (Only data marked with * extracted from Uganda Statistics Department, 1994)

commonly used in the questionnaires although it does not necessarily imply a sewer connection. The lowest line [+] represents telephone connections, though it should be noted that much of this data predates the very recent growth in mobile telephones.

Various reasons may be cited to explain why low-income families are more willing to pay for electricity connections than water. Does this represent the demand for television by some members of the household? Or is electricity required for cooking or for evening lighting? To answer questions such as these, marketing and investment plans need to be more sophisticated and explore in more detail the characteristics of demand for new services; in particular understanding willingness to pay to acquire different and higher levels of water and sanitation services becomes crucial if a utility is to manage a financially sustainable system.

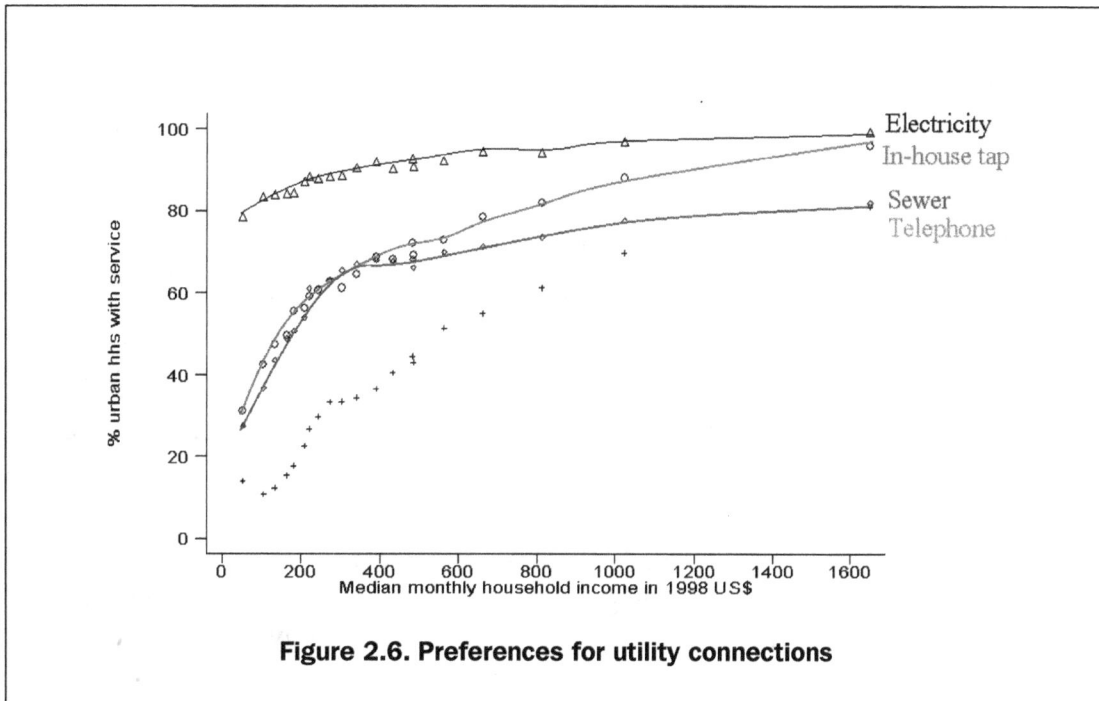

Figure 2.6. Preferences for utility connections

2.6   Understanding water consumer's willingness to pay

When income or expenditure data is collected for each market segment, it can be used to estimate the '[not sure what this open quote belongs to?] ability to pay for service improvements and then be compared to other data. Clearly, just because a particular household earns X amount each month doesn't really prove that they will spend a proportion of X on water services if given the chance to do so by the utility. However, at the very minimum, understanding the levels of earned cash income or expenditure within the poorer districts of cities will provide the utility with an idea of what water services could be provided and which ones are prohibitively expensive and shouldn't be considered. Much more accurate information can be derived from carrying out a Contingent Valuation Survey (CVS) which uses the contingent valuation methodology (CVM) to determine users' willingness to pay for improved water supply services. Willingness to pay data based on the results of a contingent valuation survey is more reliable, but the 'ability to pay' estimates based solely on household income can be a useful check.

CVM is one of a number of techniques to estimate consumers' willingness to pay for improved water supply systems. There are various definitions of willingness to pay (WTP), but the one most used states that:

'WTP is the maximum amount that an individual states that they are willing to pay for a good or service' (DFID Demand Assessment Seminar, December, 1997).

The urban water sector in low and middle-income countries (LMICs) requires good quality data on user willingness to pay in order to:

• justify future investment proposals;

• develop a better understanding of user perceptions and preferences;

- support the selection of preferred service options; and

- set out the scope for future tariff increases and subsidy reduction plans.

There are three ways of estimating WTP:

- observing prices that people pay for goods in various markets (i.e. water vending, buying from neighbours, paying local taxes);

- observing individual expenditures of money, time, labour, etc. to obtain goods - or to avoid their loss. This method might involve an assessment of coping strategies and involve observations, focus group discussions and even household surveys; and

- asking people directly what they are willing to pay for goods or services in the future (contingent valuation methodology).

The first two approaches are based on observations of behaviour and are called Revealed Preference techniques. The third technique is based upon stated preferences and includes the Contingent Valuation Methodology, often shortened to CVM in development literature. In its purest form, the contingent valuation methodology is a tool used by the water sector to elicit the potential service users' maximum willingness to pay (WTP) for carefully selected water supply service options such as house connections, standposts, protected springs, public kiosks, etc.

Observations of the behaviour of people living in low-income communities, plays an important role in understanding how consumers use water, their perceptions on its quality and reliability and how they cope when the water is unreliable, from a variety of sources and a long distance from their homes.

Methods of estimating willingness to pay based on Revealed Preference techniques can develop a better understanding of user perceptions and support the selection of preferred service options without the need for large-scale rigorous surveys. Therefore, Revealed Preference techniques are a useful tool to tackle the first stage of the customer value chain, of getting to know consumers. The contingent valuation methodology draws on more sophisticated uses of surveys and analysis to understand consumers' potential use of new water supply and sanitation options, how much they are prepared to pay for these services and which services they prefer. Therefore, CVM is a more useful tool in targeting consumers and suitable areas for investment and is discussed in Chapter 3.

2.7   Revealed preferences: Coping strategies and costs

It is often assumed that utilities cannot provide water services to poorer communities because the poor are unwilling and unable to pay water tariffs and so any efforts by the utility to recover costs and maintain a quality water supply will fail. Yet a number of studies reveal that poorer households often pay a high price for their existing water supplies; this might be cash paid to vendors or the economic opportunity cost associated with spending many hours per day collecting water instead of carrying out other essential tasks.

Low-income consumers adopt a series of coping strategies, often drawing on many different water sources depending on the end uses of the water and the season. Even the very poorest households spend cash purchasing water in most urban slums. Revenue that could be captured by the utility to provide a more reliable and cheaper service to consumers is lost through a network of independent water suppliers that source water either from the utility or from poor quality groundwater supplies.

Table 2.4 summarizes the findings from a study in Dehra Dun in India which demonstrates the real cost to consumers of using different water supplies.

Table 2.4. Coping costs for water users in Dehra Dun, India[1]

	Public tap	Individual connection	Weighted average
Average income (Rs/month)	1969	5908	4862
Average coping costs (Rs/m3)*	33.2	2.32	10.5
Average water bill paid (Rs/m3)	0.6	3.8	3
Average total price paid (Rs/m3)	33.8	6.12	13.5
Estimated quantity of water consumed (m3/month/hh)	3.9	15.9	8.4
Average monthly costs for water(Rs/month/hh)	132	97	113
Average percentage of income spent on water	6.7%	1.6%	2.33%

1. Source: Choe et al (1996) cited in World Bank,India (1998)
   *Note: 'Coping costs' include the value of time spent collecting water, as well as costs incurred for pumps and filtered water and occasional purchases from a private tanker.

Although tariffs for households with individual connections are higher, the economic cost to the household using public taps is much higher because of the time spent queuing and collecting water. Furthermore, standpost users not only have higher average monthly costs for water than people with individual connections, they also spend 6.7 per cent of their income on water compared to 1.6 per cent for households with individual connections.

To illustrate the high coping costs paid by all consumers for inadequate water supplies, a summary of the calculated coping costs in Guntur, India are presented below, based on a marketing study (Chary and Narender, 2002) [missing from regs]. Most high and middle-income earners in Guntur have to rely on their own or shared boreholes and municipal piped water, while people in slum areas rely on public standposts and water tankers.

The Guntur coping cost estimates are based on:

• annualized capital expenditures by the household

• annualized operating and maintenance costs by the household

• opportunity cost of time spent in collecting water

• expenses incurred on waterborne diseases

• expenses on boiled/bottled water

• any other relevant costs

The actual costs for each of the above items were estimated based on the data collected through household interviews and surveys and the coping cost was estimated as a percentage of household income.

Because of the inadequate and intermittent access to piped water supply, households have adopted various coping strategies that result in additional coping costs. The household survey found that those on low incomes and people living in slums invest a significant amount of time collecting water from standposts and other sources. The monetary value of this coping cost can be quite large, as shown in Table 2.5

Table 2.5. Opportunity cost of time spent collecting water

Income group (Rs.per month)	Opportunity cost as percentage of income
<2000	15.10
2000-5000	2.9
5000-10000	1.01
>10000	0.55
Average	4.81

As a preventive measure against waterborne diseases, households have spent money buying water purifiers or mineral water, or boiling water, as shown in Table 2.6.

Table 2.6. Expenses on boiled/mineral water (as a percentage of income)

Income group (Rs.)	Percentage of income
<2000	0.2
2000-5000	0.3
5000-10000	0.23
>10000	0.38
Average	0.27

Households have also invested in pumping equipment to cope with the inadequate pressure of the water supply in Guntur. In total households spent 15 per cent of their annual income coping with their poor water supply (see Table 2.7).

The Guntor study has also calculated the total coping costs as a percentage income (see Table 2.8), which is high for low-income households and also quite high for middle and higher income groups. These results demonstrate the great potential benefits to the city residents of a much-improved piped water supply.

Table 2.7. Total annual capital expenditure (TACE) as a percentage of income

Income group	Municipal	Non-municipal	TACH
<2000	9.7	10.0	19.27
2000-5000	4.4	16.0	20.4
5000-10000	2.3	10.0	11.7
>10000	1.4	9.2	10.6
Average	4.45	11.3	15.4

Table 2.8. Coping costs as percentage of income[1]

Income group	Percentage of income
<2000	18.0
2000-5000	16.0
5000-10000	9.4
>10000	9.2
Average	13.15

1. Source: Narender, Chary and Samson, 2004

2.8 Revealed preferences: Small scale providers and informal market

Over 75 per cent of the urban poor in Africa get their water from small-scale providers (vendors, water tankers, etc) (Collignon and Vezina, 2000) and about half of the African urban population have no piped water supply. The gap created by the low service coverage is often filled by small-scale independent water service providers. Table 2.9 shows the contribution of small-scale independent water service providers in ten selected African cities.

As these figures show, in many cities a large portion of households rely on independent providers and point sources as their principle water source. Good opportunities exist for water utilities and municipalities to capture a higher percentage of the water market, not for the sake of competition or to put private entrepreneurs out of business, but to provide improved services in a sustainable manner.

The amount of money that low-income households are prepared to pay to water vendors, usually through lack of alternatives, represents their existing willingness to pay for a good utility supply. Some householders have to pay water prices to vendors that are often higher than European water prices (see Box 2.2). However, this approach has led to problems, such as in Buenos Aires for example, where the apparent high payments to vendors did not mean that households were willing to connect to the new distribution system because of the extraordinarily high connection fee of about US$1,500.

Table 2.9. Small-scale providers' market share in 10 African cities[1]

City	In-home connection	Standpipe water fetched by household	Independent providers or traditional sources
Abidjan, Cote d'Ivoire	76%	2%	22%
Nairobi, Kenya	71%	1%	27%
Dakar, Senegal	71%	14%	15%
Kampala, Uganda	36%	5%	59%
Dar Es Salaam, Tanzania	31%	0%	69%
Conakry, Guinea	29%	3%	68%
Nouakchatt, Mauritania	19%	30%	51%
Cotonou, Benin	27%	0%	73%
Ougadougou, Burkina Faso	23%	49%	28%
Bamako, Mali	17%	19%	64%

1. Source: Collignon & Vezina (2000)

Box 2.2. High vendor prices in East Africa[1]

In Nairobi, Mombassa and Kampala, the usually price for water from a kiosk vendor in an informal settlement ranges from US$1 to US$5 per cubic metre. This level is common in other Africa cities. Only about 30 per cent of the people living in these cities hase direct access to piped water. The rest depend on point sources (shallow wells, etc.) and on small service providers such as water kiosks, handcarts, tankers and borewell operators.

1. Source: UNDP-World Bank WSP (2000)

During water shortages, vendor prices can increase dramatically. In an informal settlement in Nairobi called Kibera, for example, water kiosk prices can range from KSh5 to KSh20 per jerrican, compared to the typical level of KSh2 per jerricanUS$1 = approx KSh73). Figure 2.10 shows the range of water of prices quoted in focus group discussions in Kampala (Kayaga and Sansom, 2004).

Table 2.10. Water Price Range in Kampala poor communities

Water source	During normal period (Ush per kilolitre)		During periods of piped water scarcity (Ush per kilolitre)	
	Range of costs	Most common	Range of costs	Most common
Non-utility? • Protected springs? • Vended water	Nil 2,500-5,000	Nil 2,500	Not readily available 10,000-20,000	10,000
Utility - indirect? • Vended water	5,000-10,000	5,000	10,000-20,000	10,000
Utility direct? • Landlord supplied? • CBO/NGO tap? • Public standpost? • Direct customer	2,500-5,000l 5,000-70,000 (*per month) 1,650-2,500 2,500-5,000 500-750	2,500 6,000 (*per month) 2,500 2,500 750	Not applicable	

The data displayed in Table 2.10 shows that normally consumers in low-income settlements who are not direct customers of national water and sewerage corporations (NWSC) pay between three and seven times more than direct customers. However, during periods when there is a scarcity of piped water in the area, the main source of water for peopleliving in low-income settlements is vended water, and the price surges up to 13 times the price charged by NWSC for domestic customers.

In many cases, vendors do not pay the utility for the water that they sell on to their customers, which is therefore lost income to the utility. Indeed unauthorized water connections for which the utility receives no revenue are common in many countries. A more proactive marketing style could enable a utility to substantially increase both its customer base and revenues.

It should be noted that all the small-scale providers are also water users, as they often buy or collect water before selling it on to their customers. Chapter 4 considers the subject of partnerships for improving services to informal settlements, including partnerships with small-scale providers to enhance services. A utility may be considering supporting and regulating water vendors to improve services in areas where the utility will not be able to provide a service for some time. In that case it would be worthwhile assessing the perceptions, experiences and preferences of the small-scale providers in those areas. This is probably best done through methods such as meetings and focus group discussions, as part of an ongoing dialogue that can encourage the development of trust and mutual understanding.

The high direct costs and indirect coping costs that people pay for inadequate water services, particularly the poor, makes a compelling case for utilities to seek to capture more of their local water market with good quality piped water services. This entails developing different services and payment and management options that will meet the needs of different consumer groups.

2.9   Focus group discussions and the 'PREPP' approach

People living in informal settlements may have limited trust in, or experience in, dealing with public utilities. Focus group discussions (FGD) offer an effective technique for a utility to develop an understanding of their customers' (or potential customers') attitudes, practices, perceptions and preferences. It can also be the basis for ongoing dialogue.

A refinement of focus groups, PREPP - 'Participation, Ranking, Experience, Perception and Partnership', has undergone development and testing in East Africa and India (Coates et al., 2004. This approach provides a practical method of directly addressing some of the issues that arise from the miscommunication between the utility and the poor. Too often that relationship is one where low-income consumers do not see themselves as valued customers at present or in the future.

PREPP is a practical way for utilities to consult low-income consumers about their experiences, perceptions and preferences. Developed with the assistance of utility engineers, social scientists and economists and piloted in low-income communities in Kenya, Uganda, Zambia and India, PREPP is grounded in the belief that a utility and a low-income consumer can have a mutually profitable relationship.

PREPP methodology outline

This methodology has a number of benefits and possible uses but one of its strengths is that it is a reasonably rapid means of gaining quality information about a community's experiences and perceptions about water services, together with their preferences for alternative service options (Coates et al., 2004).

The process involves water engineers, facilitators (usually drawn from local councils, NGOs, university departments or consultants) and low-income consumers in a mutually beneficial exercise based around a comparison of proposed service options with existing sources and supply. It serves a number of purposes, not least demonstrating the decision-making process used to select 'best for purpose' water supply options by the utility and the consumer.

In focus groups, usually segregated by gender, the PREPP facilitator and engineer take the participants through a set of carefully prepared steps providing a framework for informed dialogue between the water engineer and his/her potential customers. Another person needs to document the responses of the focus group to questions raised by the facilitator. The whole process takes on average less than a couple of hours to facilitate and is proving to be an eye-opener for the engineer and water users alike. The key Steps 1 to 5 are shown in Table 2.11 below.

The researchers have found that just as engineers and utility managers often have entrenched perceptions about the viability of service provision in informal settlements, the residents may have ill-conceived views of utility motives and interests. The PREPP dialogue is valuable because among other things it clears up misunderstandings.

54

Table 2.11. PREPP - The basic steps

Topic/research area	Tool used to facilitate
1. Existing experiences (sources, supply and coping strategies)	Water ladder, group probing and discussion
2. Existing preferences (exploration by type)	Household voting, group probing and discussion
3. Consumer perceptions (of the utility)	Questions and probing
4. Service option preferences (existing options compared to new)	Costed option ranking Pocket chart voting
5. Household expenditure	Household expenditure charts

The key step for determining future services is costed option ranking. Here the purpose is to determine which service options should be considered by the utility for future marketing in the same or similar market segments. The consumers are informed that the utility wishes to find out what local consumer preferences are for potential future service options, compared with the existing water services and sources. The group is presented with pictures showing a mix of two types or categories of service option - potential options with estimated costs for the following year and the most popular existing sources determined during Step 2 of the PREPP process. This enables the utility to find out information regarding the consumer's first, second and third preferences for a range of service options as part of a negotiated demand process.

Potential PREPP benefits and outputs

PREPP is primarily a tool for water utilities. The information gained through approach can be used directly by the utility to make decisions about service options to be offered and marketing strategies that could be used to target low-income consumers. The approach's primary purpose is to benefit the poor and low-income consumer. Benefits include:

- Greater utility understanding of the nature of consumer preferences for the different potential service options that it is both willing and able to offer.

- Improved utility understanding of both consumer preferences for existing sources and consumer coping strategies.

- Improved mutual understanding and trust between the utility and its potential customers, built upon open dialogue that can continue after the PREPP process.

- Improved knowledge of the utility's comparative advantage - or disadvantage - against other providers.

- The information generated by PREPP can contribute effectively to a utility's normal investment planning.

PREPP is consistent with a partnership approach and draws on techniques that are familiar to social scientists, economists and engineers. It can assist utilities to think strategically about how to both engage with the urban poor and maintain the customer-utility relationship thereafter. Potential PREPP outputs in relation to the 7Ps of marketing are summarized in Table 2.12.

Table 2.12. Potential outputs from PREPP surveys

	Potential outputs of PREPP
Product	Knowledge of existing provision - by all suppliers including traditional sources and small-scale providers Knowledge of type of service and payment options preferred by the communities and comparative advantages to existing sources
Price	Knowledge of existing informal and formal tariff structures and seasonal fluctuations Cost of provision for storage, queuing, treatment and scarcity (coping costs) The relative preferences of community groups for costed service options Knowledge of attitudes toward connection schemes and payment options
Promotion	Knowledge of existing communication patterns between utility and consumers, and potential marketing opportunities Potential for active on-going customer-utility dialogue Enables the development of future targeted promotion strategies for each area
Place	Knowledge of where alternative providers operate, where new potential markets exist Better sense of specific local problems and living conditions, to enable the development of realistic solutions Improved estimates for service option take-up in each area
People	Knowledge of present and potential customers, income distribution, behaviours and practices, resistance to change Knowledge of community groups who are interested in collaborating in shared management arrangements
Process	Establishes the beginning of a consultative planning process between the utility and the communities, as part of realistic negotiated demand
Presence	Establishes a means for future mutually beneficial exchanges Improved utility corporate identity and image

Armed with this information the utility can now begin to make informed decisions about which service, payment and management options are most feasible. Planning for services that involve the primary stakeholders enables mutually beneficial solutions to be found. The information gained during PREPP surveys can also be triangulated against household semi-structured interviews and observation at existing water points, in order to verify information.

One thing is very clear, once engineers and utility managers step out and enter such dialogue with their existing and potential customers, there should be no going back to the 'supply-driven' ways.

The demand assessment aspects of the PREPP approach, such as the results from the costed option ranking, can also be used to 'target' investments, which is discussed in the next chapter.

Chapter 3

Targeting low-income water consumers

3.1 Introduction and summary

Funds for improving services in poorly served areas are often limited, so careful thought is required on where to target resources. Effective targeting or prioritizing of future investments and efforts for low-income areas is best done considering:

- The development of feasible service, payment and management options based on lessons learnt elsewhere and locally. Innovations should be considered, such as the use of local water storage tanks where water supplies are intermittent. The development of options should be guided by the principles of maximizing revenues but also providing the best feasible supply to poorly served areas until the utility can provide better services (such as house connections) in those areas.

- Assessing consumer demands for existing and new service options using appropriate techniques such as WTP surveys or PREPP. Such studies will inform the likely future take-up of different options and the scope for increasing tariffs, which is invaluable for utility financial planning.

- Exploring opportunities for working with other stakeholders such as CBOs, NGOs and small water enterprises is important when working in informal settlements, because utilities often do not have all the resources and skills to work in such areas. It is worthwhile finding out which NGOs have experience of working in those low-income areas that the utility is considering.

- The selection of priority areas on the basis of agreed objectives, using the best available information about the needs and demands of consumers for different service and payment options, together with utility performance data against key indicators.

These issues are discussed in more detail in the following sections. When initial pilot programmes for working in low-income areas are being developed, the targeting of which areas to work in is likely to be less rigorous. Larger programmes should include more systematic targeting so that issues of need, equity and consumer demand are adequately addressed.

3.2 The need for innovation

The approaches to understanding consumers that were described in the last chapter will inform the marketing strategy about the water and sanitation services that are being used at present by various different groups, the price they are paying and what they think of these services relative to the other demands on their limited resources.

For those people who receive good full pressure 24-hour water services, the service options which the utility might want to promote may seem somewhat limited. Good water utilities, however, seek to introduce viable options wherever they can, such as payment and service options, in order to improve customer satisfaction. The potential to introduce more service and shared management options increases substantially in situations where services are currently intermittent and/or inadequate, particularly in developing countries as described above.

To meet the challenges of improving current service levels and providing for future needs, innovative approaches are necessary that match consumers' preferences and paying capacity. For example, if utilities support the on-selling of water by vendors, or by households selling to their neighbours, then incremental service improvements can be made, without incurring the full cost of providing everybody with household connections.

Some of the potential improved service options that can be offered to consumers are compared to typical existing water sources in Table 3.1. Existing water sources are listed in the left-hand column and potential options as part of incremental improvements are in the right-hand column.

Table 3.1. Examples of existing and improved water options in informal settlements

Typical existing water sources	Potential improved service options
· Unregulated water kiosks · Handcart vendors (expensive) · Unauthorized connections · Public standposts from which little or no revenue is collected · Contaminated pools or rivers · Distant springs or boreholes · Seasonal dug wells	· Utility-supported private water kiosks · Regulated small-scale providers or vendors · Community-managed kiosks · Community-managed local water distribution pipes · Shared water connections with on-selling to neighbours · Individual connections · Prepaid metered kiosks · Water kiosks with storage tanks

Such incremental improvements are often a more realistic process, particularly where a utility is trying to improve services to as many people as possible. Whatever options are developed, a key objective is for the utility to recoup its investments or at least to cross-subsidize to the agreed level.

The following sections on service options, payment options and management options show examples of innovative approaches to improving services that have been successfully tried in various parts of the world, building on the examples described in Chapter 1. If utilities are to offer more of such options to existing and potential customers, then they will invariably need to be more flexible in terms of their design standards and procedures, as part of an effective strategic marketing strategy, so that customer satisfaction can be improved.

3.3 Service options

Many water utilities provide some limited options such as house connections and standpipes or water kiosks, but the scope for introducing more options to improve customer satisfaction is considerable. A key aspect of improving customer services is developing different service options that can be used to address the demands of consumers in different market segments. These options should be technically feasible and financially viable. The service option should also be priced taking into account peoples' willingness to pay and it should be environmentally feasible.

In technical terms, water service options may generally be grouped into seven basic categories, in the context of utility provision, as follows:

- **Individual house connections** with various pressure regimes and frequency of water supply. There may be a variety of means of connecting to the water mains, for example by conventional buried pipe, possibly metered, or through informal connections to an individual manifold or meter some distance from the dwelling. Water is obtained from a tap in the house which is usually the desired level of service.

- **Individual yard connections** at various pressure regimes and frequency of supply, where water is obtained from a tap outside the house. The house is unlikely to have internal plumbing.

- **Shared group connections** with a few households or a 'street' sharing one connection at various pressure regimes and frequency of supply in order to minimize connection charges and any fixed standing charges. Alternatively one household with a yard connection may sell on water to neighbours.

- **Bulk supply connections** where the utility sells water through a bulk meter at special rates to a community or private contractor, possibly with on-site storage capacity, for selling on through a private distribution net-work to household connections or even to water kiosks.

- **Water kiosks**, essentially communal/public water points, technically similar to standposts where people buy water. A water kiosk may be sheltered (with a structure) or open and may include storage and/or bathing facilities. A utility, a private operator or a community group may manage the water kiosk and sell water at a predetermined price per container, although different payment methods may be adopted.

- **Standposts**, communal/public points where water is collected by many people. Standposts, as opposed to kiosks, are usually unmanned and there is no direct charge for the water provided (particularly in South Asia).

- **Supply by vendors**. Vendors may transport water in various ways such as using bicycles, handcarts, animal-pulled carts and motorized delivery vehicles (trucks) to deliver water to consumers.

- **Supply by water tankers**. The utility or a private provider may deliver water to an area using a water tanker, especially in cases of water short-ages.

For each of the above basic service options, different payment mechanisms and management systems could be adopted. Apart from these basic service options, others can be developed depending on the particular circumstances faced by respective water utilities and on consumer demand. In general terms, where intermittent water supplies are common, more options tend to be worth considering including local water storage tanks either at water kiosks/standposts or as part of a yard connection. Many of the variables such as water point delivery, supply hours, water pressure, etc. that can be used to develop different service options are shown in Table 3.2.

Table 3.2. Water service options for selected variables in urban areas

Location of water delivery point	Max 100m	Max 25m	Yard	House
Pressure	As in conventional network	Roof (1st storey)	Ground	Trickle feed
Hours of supply	24, 12, 9, 6, 2 hours (do those hours only apply to column 1?)			
Type of dwellings	Bungalows and maisonettes (with internal plumbing)	Flats (with internal plumbing)	1, 2 or 3-roomed (without internal plumbing)	Dwellings in informal settlements
	Commercial premises	Single or two-storey	Multiple storey	Tenement rooms/flats
Water point Delivery	Multiple taps	Single tap	Water kiosks	Valve clusters with hosepipe offtakes
	Standposts	Standpost vendors	Locked shared standposts	Machine dispensers
	Standposts or kiosks with storage tanks	Smart card or pre-payment meters	Neighbourhood on-selling	Handcart vendors
	Flow restrictors / trickle flow	Storage containers	Shared connections	Water flow regulator
	Site storage	Area storage		Tanker vendors

In developing service options that are suitable for their market segments or selected consumer groups, it is worthwhile for utilities to learn from elsewhere. The next section considers some typical service options that have been used in various parts of the world.

Examples of service options that utilities can provide or support

Different service options are applicable to different situations depending on the existing water supply infrastructure and the perceptions of consumers. The most important consideration is that the proposed service options should be at-tractive to customers and viable for the utility. Fourteen options are illustrated below and their potential advantages and disadvantages, from the perspective of both the consumers and the utility, are briefly discussed. Several of these options might have been seen as 'second best' or even 'illegal' according to conventional approaches. To achieve universal service to the poor however, we cannot afford to be conventional and the recommendation therefore is to absorb the ideas that people have, out of necessity, developed for themselves. Then adapt them slightly to ensure that they are 'good enough' and incorporate them into the revenue base of the utility, all without destroying the essence of what made them attractive in the first place.

Individual house connections

This is generally the preferred option for both utilities and consumers, where there are sufficient financial resources to fund the development of the infrastructure and where it can be sustainably managed with adequate and reliable services.

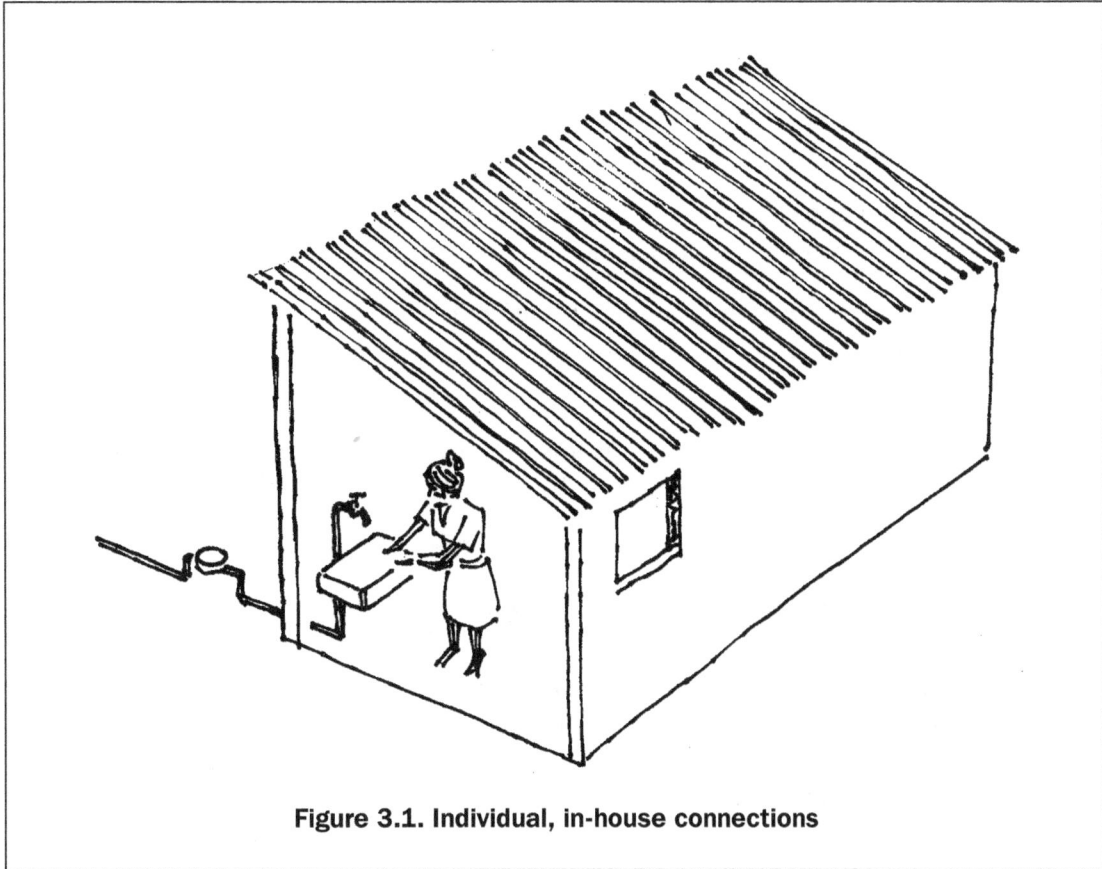

Figure 3.1. Individual, in-house connections

Potential advantages (for customers)

- This is a convenient method of water delivery, as water is available from a tap inside the dwelling, offering a high level of service if the pressure is sufficient.

- Residents are potentially able to use more water from in-house connections and therefore reduce the risk of water-related diseases.

- In the case of intermittent supply it is relatively easy to fill storage containers within the house.

- Water is received directly from the distribution system, with less chance of contamination in the process of water collection

- The household has full control of their water service, and little chance of disagreements with other customers

Potential advantages (for utilities)

- Providing house connections within a given area enables a utility to sell more water (compared with other service options), thereby increasing revenues and thus recouping the investment in water supply infrastructure more quickly.

- It is easier to hold customers accountable for payment of bills, compared with other options such as water kiosks.

Potential disadvantages (for the utility)

- An expensive method of water supply in terms of both the capital and operational investment.

- Limited control of water use, for example customers may have leaks or sell on water to other people. This is more of a problem where there are no individual meters.

- If there are serious water shortages, it can be difficult to limit wastage of water on activities such as watering gardens.

- There is more potential for waste and leakage, as the size of the network is increased considerably compared with other options.

- More wastewater is generated, and this often requires some form of wastewater collection and disposal system. A proper sewerage and wastewater treatment system is usually very expensive.

For consumers the main disadvantage of this option is cost, in terms of both water and sewerage charges plus connection costs, so the customer has to be willing and able to meet these costs.

Individual house connections - flexible pipes by household to meter/valve clusters

This option entails the utility laying a limited pipe system in an informal settlement at a shallow depth or above ground, then installing clusters of valves and meters (as is shown in the figure below), from which residents can connect plastic pipes from their own meter to their dwelling. This option has been successfully used in Manila in the Philippines.

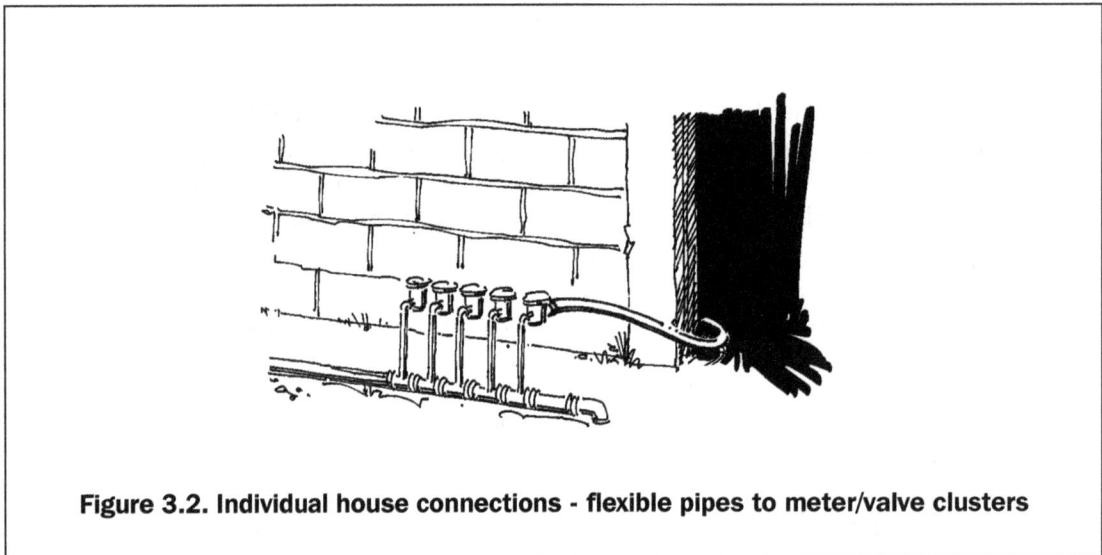

Figure 3.2. Individual house connections - flexible pipes to meter/valve clusters

Potential advantages (for customers) - similar to the first option (house connections)
- This is a convenient method of water delivery, as water is available from a tap inside the dwelling, offering a high level of service if the pressure is sufficient.

- Residents are potentially able to use more water from in-house connections and therefore reduce the risk of water-related diseases.

- In the case of intermittent supply it is relatively easy to fill storage containers within the house.

- Water is received directly from the distribution system, with less chance of contamination in the process of water collection.

- The household has full control of their water service, and limited chances of disagreements with other customers.

Potential advantages (for utilities)
- Providing house connections within a given area enables a utility to sell more water (compared with other service options), thereby increasing revenues and thus recouping the investment in water supply infrastructure more quickly.

- The valve cluster option is cheaper than a water distribution system built to standard designs and can easily be adapted as the settlement develops.

- It is easier to hold customers accountable for payment of bills, compared with other options such as water kiosks.

- Provided the meters continue to work it should be relatively easy to locate possible sources of non-revenue water (such as illegal connections and physical leaks).

- This option shows key stakeholders that the utility is doing its best to serve poorer communities.

Potential disadvantages (for the utility)
- Adequate disposal of wastewater can present problems.

- More expensive in terms of both the capital and operational investment, compared to alternative options such as water kiosks.

- There is more potential for leakage, as the pipes are laid at a shallow depth or are above ground.

Potential disadvantages (for consumers)
- The cost in terms of water charges plus connection costs can be higher than other options, so the customer has to be willing and able to meet these costs.

- Adequate disposal of wastewater can present problems.

Individual house connections - daily filled overhead tank

This option entails the utility providing a pipe system and overhead tanks for those communities or households that want them. Figure 3.3 below shows the type of arrangement that has successfully been used in Durban, South Africa.

Figure 3.3. Individual house connections - daily filled overhead tank

Potential advantages (for customers)
Similar to the house connection option, but because the utility provides the overhead tank greater storage is provided, so that a more reliable service is likely, particularly where intermittent water supplies are common.

Potential advantages (for utilities)
- Similar to the house connection option, but this option also shows key stakeholders that the utility is doing its best to serve poorer communities.

Potential disadvantages (for the utility)
- Adequate disposal of wastewater can present problems, compared to options that typically provide a smaller volume of water.

- More expensive in terms of both the capital and operational investment, compared to alternative options such as water kiosks.

- Expensive in terms of the capital cost of providing the storage tank on the roof.

- Where the ball valve or stop cock that shuts off the flow into the tank is not working, the water will continue to flow into the tank, causing it to overflow and water will be wasted.

Potential disadvantages (for consumers)
- The cost in terms of water charges plus connection costs can be higher than other options, so the customer has to be willing and able to meet these costs.

- Adequate disposal of wastewater can present problems.

Individual house connections - daily filled ground tanks

There are examples of utilities providing ground tanks, but more often householders invest significant sums of money to buy their own ground tank that is filled from the water distribution network. These tanks can fill during the night or at other times when water is not used, and can substantially increase both the available quantity and reliability of supply compared to customers without such tanks. In some situations householders ensure that their tank is filled by installing a suction pump on the mains. In other settings it is more common to find a pump used to fill an overhead tank to ensure adequate pressure in the household taps. This is common in regions where people are concerned about the adequacy and reliability of their supplies.

From the perspective of the utility and other customers, such tanks can cause problems, particularly where the ball valve that shuts off the flow into the tank is not working. In this case water will continue to flow into the tank, causing it to overflow leading to the wastage of water. is therefore in the utility's interest to check occasionally that the ball valves in private tanks are in working order, though less critical if there is a meter before the tank inlet.

Individual yard connections/taps

This approach is similar to individual house connections except that the only tap on the service pipe connection is outside the house in the yard or compound.

Potential advantages (for consumers)
- This option costs less than in-house connections and is therefore more affordable to households, as the house need not have internal plumbing.

Figure 3.4. Individual yard connections/taps

- It is generally easier to collect water from a yard tap than, say, a water kiosk.

- The household has a fair amount of control as the connection, though outside, is not shared with other households.

- If the householder wants to they can let their neighbours to use their yard tap, perhaps charging those neighbours for this service, which can make the pipe connection more affordable.

- Selling on water from yard taps can provide competition for water kiosks and therefore help to keep down the price of water.

Potential advantages (for the utility)
- Yard connections can be an intermediary service level between a water kiosk/standpost and an in-house connection, where the utility can potentially sell more water and generate more revenue than they would if there were only kiosks available and people did not have internal plumbing.

Potential disadvantages (for consumers)
- Some inconvenience from carrying water into the house.

- Reduced control over the use of the water tap, which is outside the house, and possibility of others using the water (especially at night).

- Waste may be a problem, leading to problems of drainage, breeding of mosquitoes, etc.

- Increased risk of water becoming contaminated after leaving the tap as it is carried to the house and stored.

- In some cultures women complain that it gives them a similar burden in having to carry water into the house while at the same time reducing their opportunities to meet other women at the standpost.

Individual yard connection with ground tank

This option has been used in Durban, South Africa, where the utility provided the tanks. In other countries customers have provided their own tanks.

Figure 3.5. Individual yard connection with ground tank

Potential advantages (for consumers)

The benefits are similar to those of the yard connection, but with additional security with regard to reliability of supply. The water stored in the ground will be available to households at the tap even when water is not flowing in the network.

- This option has the potential to improve the reliability of water supply in capacity constrained cities where water rationing is the norm.

- Consumers are less likely to have to queue at inconvenient times to collect water where local storage is provided.

- When the ground tank is full there is the option of extending the pipe supply into the house, to a kitchen sink, for example, to receive piped water for the first period of consumption.

Potential advantages (for the utility)

- Yard connections can be an intermediary service level between a water kiosk/standpost and an in-house connection, where the utility can potentially sell more water and generate more revenue, than they would if there only kiosks were available and people did not have internal plumbing.

- Often less water is consumed, postponing the need for high capital investment in bulk supply, treatment and distribution.

- If the householder wants to, they can let their neighbours use their yard tap, perhaps charging those neighbours for this service, which can make the pipe connection more affordable.

- Selling on water from yard taps can provide competition for water kiosks and therefore help to keep down the price of water.

- Where the utility supplies the ground tank, complete with sealable cover, it can be more sure of maintaining the potable quality of the water.

Potential disadvantages (for consumers)
- Same as for yard connections, but in addition this option is more costly as a tank has to be provided for each connection (if the customer purchases the tank).

Potential disadvantages (for the utility)
- Where the ball valve or stop cock that shuts off the flow into the tank is not working, the water could continue to flow into the tank causing it to overflow and water will be wasted.

Communal or shared yard connections/taps

As an alternative to standposts or kiosks a utility may offer a number of shared or group connections to particular areas, typically to be shared by between two and ten households. This option is becoming more common in some countries.

Figure 3.6. Communal or shared yard connections/taps

Potential advantages (for consumers)
- This service option is relatively low cost and more affordable since several households can share the cost of one connection. Sharing the connection reduces the unit cost of services per household.

- It is easier to collect water from a shared tap than a water kiosk and it is likely to be cheaper than an in-house connection.

- This service option may not require a wastewater collection system, and can be provided to poor areas that do not have a sewerage system.

- Water from shared yard taps can provide competition for water kiosks and therefore assist in keeping down the price of water.

Potential advantages (for the utility)
- Shared connections can be an intermediate service level between a water kiosk/ standpost and an in-house connection, where the utility can potentially sell more water and generate more revenue than they would if only kiosks were available and people did not have internal plumbing.

- Often less water is consumed, postponing the need for high capital investment in bulk supply, treatment and distribution.

- The water utility ends up having fewer customer accounts, hence it is potentially easier and less expensive to deal with in terms of customer service, billing and revenue collection.

Potential disadvantages (for consumers)
- There is some inconvenience from carrying water into the house.

- No control over the use of the water tap, which is outside the house and is shared by several households, and there is the possibility of others using the water (especially at night).

- Unless one household takes responsibility for managing the shared tap, there is potential for disputes among those families who are sharing the tap.

- Increased risk of water being contaminated after leaving the tap, as it is carried to the house.

- Waste may be a problem, leading to problems of drainage, breeding of mosquitoes, etc.

Potential disadvantages (for the utility)
- The households sharing the tap may disagree on payments, and the utility could therefore lose revenues.

Communal yard connections with a high level or ground tank
A variation on the idea of shared or group connection but with the addition of a water storage tank (to ensure availability).

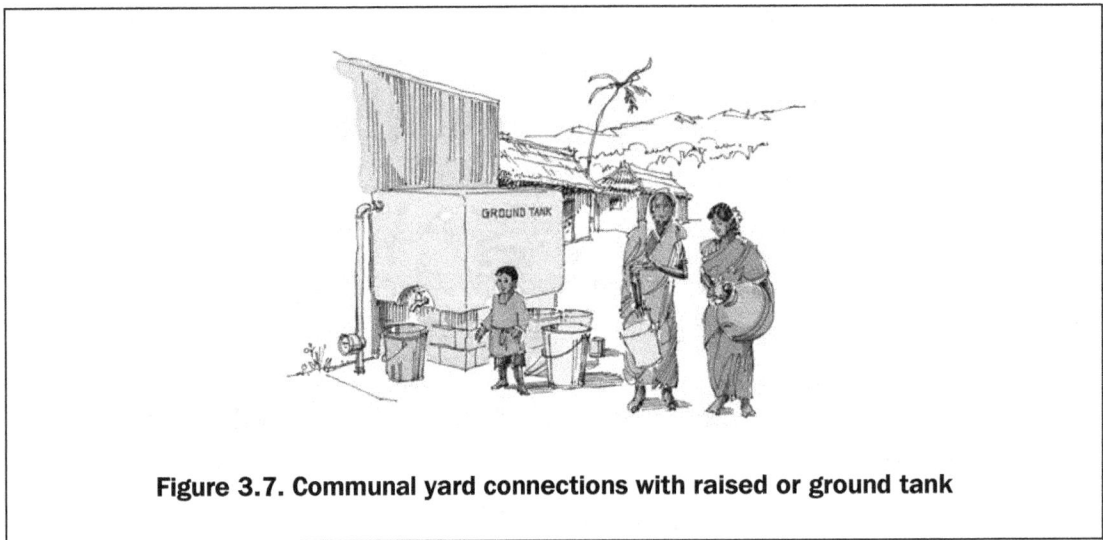

Figure 3.7. Communal yard connections with raised or ground tank

Potential advantages (for consumers)
- The same advantages as for group connections, with the additional security with regard to reliability of supply.

- The ground tank stores water that may be available to households at the tap even when water is not flowing in the network.

- This option has the potential to improve reliability of water supply in capacity-constrained cities where water rationing is the norm.

- Consumers are less likely to have to queue at inconvenient times to collect water where local storage is provided.

Potential advantages (for the utility)
- Where water supplies are intermittent and where people in poorer areas have more local storage in the local pipe system, it gives the utility more flexibility in terms of what time of the day it can supply water to these areas. This can lead to improved services and increased consumer satisfaction.

- The capacity of the water distribution system can be lower where customers have local storage tanks, because the tanks can fill at off-peak times.

Potential disadvantages (for consumers)
As for communal yard connections with, in addition:

- There is some risk of water contamination directly into the tank, especially if the tank is at ground level or is not properly sealed.

- This option is more costly, since a tank has to be provided for each connection.

Potential disadvantages (for the utility)
- If the utility decides to subsidize the costs of the storage tanks, it will incur significant additional costs.

- Where the ball valve or stop cock that shuts off the flow into the tank is not working, the water will continue to flow into the tank causing it to overflow and waste water.

Public standpost - staffed (kiosk)

Water kiosks may be managed by a private operator, a community group or the utility itself and are common in Africa. A person (a vendor) is usually required to stand by the kiosk to sell water to customers at an agreed price per plastic jerrican or other container. Some kiosks have shelters for the vendors to protect themselves from the hot sun.

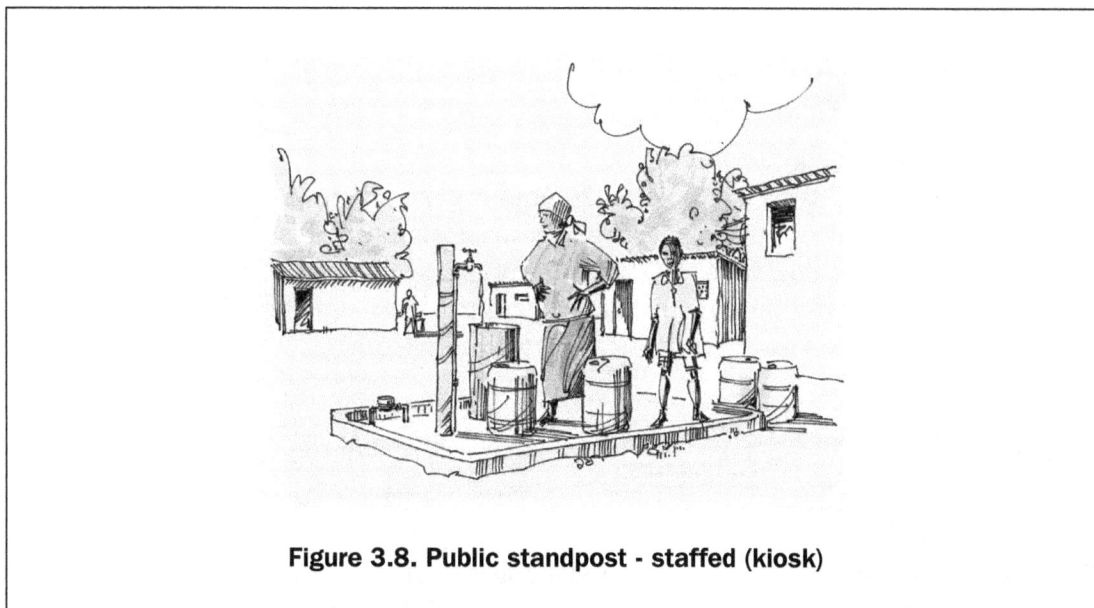

Figure 3.8. Public standpost - staffed (kiosk)

Potential advantages (for consumers)
- Water is sold in small quantities, and this is often more affordable for low-income customers than house connections.

- This is a popular option in Africa in urban areas where people do not have any other suitable service option.

- There is little or no wastage or stagnant water because water is metered and sold by volume.

- Effective cost recovery for the group or person managing the kiosk, because customers pay up front as they collect the water.

Potential advantages (for the utility)
- This is a low-cost service option for the utility, because many people can be served by one kiosk. Also, kiosks often do not require an extensive distribution system, making this method suitable for areas where it is difficult to lay pipes.

- Billing is convenient for the utility, if there is a working meter for the kiosk, as only the kiosk operator is billed.

Potential disadvantages (for consumers)
- The price per unit volume of water is often very high compared with household connections.

- In periods of water shortages the price of water from unregulated vendors with limited competition can go up dramatically.

- Availability of water is limited to kiosk opening times.

- Time may be wasted because of queues at water kiosks, especially if kiosks are far apart or if the water pressure in the distribution system is low.

- It is tiring carrying the water, since the kiosks can be 200m from the household or further.

- Water can become contaminated at the supply point and/or while carrying or storing the water.

- If the kiosk does not have a storage tank it will only have water when there is water available in the local pipe network. This is a common problem in systems with intermittent supplies.

Potential disadvantages (for the utility)
- Only limited amounts of water per household is generally sold from kiosks, particularly when people are also using informal (unprotected) sources because of the high cost of kiosk water. So relatively low levels of revenues are generated from kiosks for the utility (most of the amount charged goes to the vendor), so it is difficult for the utility to recoup its investment in infrastructure unless other service options are used as well.

- In some cases informal water kiosks are supplied by illegal connections, so the utility receives no revenues from such kiosks.

Public standpost with water storage - staffed (kiosk)

This option is a variation on the staffed standpost (water kiosk), with the storage tank provided to increase the service reliability. In some examples the tanks are below ground, where pressure is particularly low, and are accessed using handpumps, which studies in Dhaka, Bangladesh, have shown limits water use. Other variations have the tanks above ground, built from brick or with circular concrete rings as in Kathmandu, Nepal or Bangalore, India.

Figure 3.9. Public standpost with water storage - staffed (kiosk)

Potential advantages (for the consumers)
- The same advantages as for the staffed standpost (kiosk) above, but with additional security with regard to reliability of supply.

- The ground tank stores water that may be available to households at the tap even when there is no water in the network.

- This option has the potential to improve the reliability of the water supply in capacity-constrained cities where water rationing is the norm.

- Consumers are less likely to have to queue at inconvenient times to collect water where local storage is provided.

Potential advantages (for the utility)
- Where water supplies are intermittent and where people in poorer areas have more local storage in the local pipe system, it gives the utility more flexibility in terms of what time of the day it can supply water to these areas. This can lead to improved services and increased consumer satisfaction.

- The required capacity of the water distribution system can be smaller where customers have local storage tanks, because the tanks can fill at off-peak times.

Potential disadvantages (for consumers)
Similar disadvantages as with the kiosk without a storage tank, in addition:

- There is some risk of water contamination directly into the tank, especially if the tank is at ground level or is not properly sealed.

- This option is more costly, since a ground or raised tank needs to be provided.

Potential disadvantages (for the utility)
- Similar to the communal yard connections with ground tank.

Public standpost - pre-paid
This option has been used in South Africa and Uganda and offers an innovative alternative to more labour-intensive water kiosks. Nowadays pre-paid public standposts are likely to use electronic measuring systems such as 'smart cards' rather than the tokens that have been more commonly used in the past.

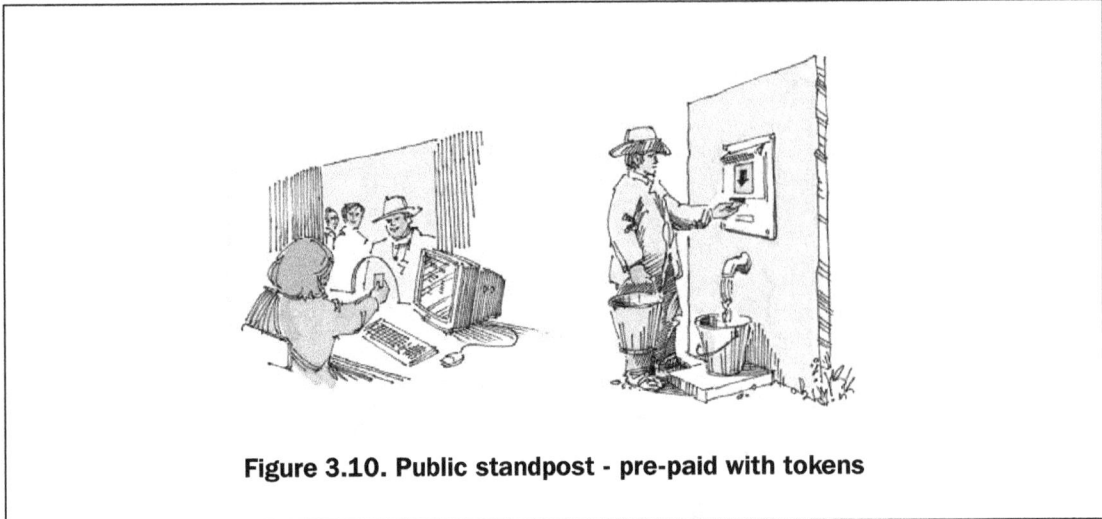

Figure 3.10. Public standpost - pre-paid with tokens

Potential advantages (for consumers)
- There is no need for a vendor to stand by the kiosk and sell water by the container, so it has potentially cheaper running costs, which should be reflected in the cost of water.

- The smart cards avoid the problems associated with dealing with cash and accounting for that cash.

- The smart card option can be programmed to give credits to individual customers, and this can be used to apply limited subsidies for some specified minimum consumption.

Potential advantages (for the utility)
- Cost recovery is reliable because customers pay before collecting water.

- As the system is computerized, the financial accounting can be automatic.

- It is relatively easy to change tariffs, as the system is computerized.

- It is relatively easy to establish how tariff change affects water consumption.

Potential disadvantages (for consumers)
- Some customers may be reluctant to buy and use the tokens or cards because the system is unfamiliar.

- If the system fails due to technical problems the water dispenser will not work and consumers will need to find alternative water sources.

Potential disadvantages (for the utility)
- Relatively high installation costs.

- This option is relatively high tech and requires specialized maintenance, which might not be readily available in some cities of developing countries.

- Requires a reliable power supply for proper operation, with a 24-hour supply for the main computer. This may not be available in some areas.

- Significant training is required for operators in order to provide back-up support for this option.[not really clear who the 'operators' are]

- Requires high pressure in the distribution network, and only operates at a pressure of at least 10 bars.

- This option is not completely foolproof, and may be tempered with.

This option carries the substantial risk of becoming a technical solution to a social problem. If that is the case it will fail. Where it is introduced with community agreement as a means of enabling people to pay small amounts as they find convenient, to budget their scarce resources whilst ensuring a continuing, conveniently located, quality water supply, then it has potential, provided there are enough of these pre-paid meters in a particular area to make the specialised maintenance and repair viable.

Public standpost

The public standpost system, where people can come and take water without paying an agreed sum per container, is common in South Asia. User payment may be in the form of small monthly or quarterly payments.

Figure 3.11. Public standpost

Potential advantages (for consumers)
- A relatively low or zero financial cost option which makes it more affordable, particularly for poor consumers.

- This option may not require a wastewater collection system, just adequate standpost drainage, and it can be provided to poor areas that do not have a sewerage system.

Potential advantages (for the utility)
- A relatively low-cost option in terms of construction cost. People tend to collect less water from standposts compared to other options, so infrastructure investment requirements are lower, however the utility is likely to receive very little revenue, if any, from this option.

Potential disadvantages (for the utility)
- Invariably the revenues from standpost users are low compared to other options, because it is not always clear who uses the standposts regularly in cities and so is difficult to obtain payments from users.

- Where no water charges are levied, this option sends the wrong message of 'water is free' to the people, who may be reluctant to pay for water again.

- People can waste a lot of water when they do not pay on a volumetric basis. Standposts with broken taps are a common sight in some areas.

- Maintenance of the standpost is likely to be a problem, as no-one is responsible for its proper use. With the utility not getting any revenue from this option, there is little motivation to maintain it adequately.

Potential disadvantages (for consumers)
- Poor maintenance of standposts is common, as something that is everybody's property ends up not being looked after by anyone, so poor performance can result.

- In areas where there are not enough satisfactory alternative water supply options, long queues are common.

Private vendors, price regulated
The handcart option is common where small water enterprises carry water from distant water points to sell it to people in areas with water shortages. A variation of this option is to use bicycles, although the number of containers that can be carried is very much limited with this option.

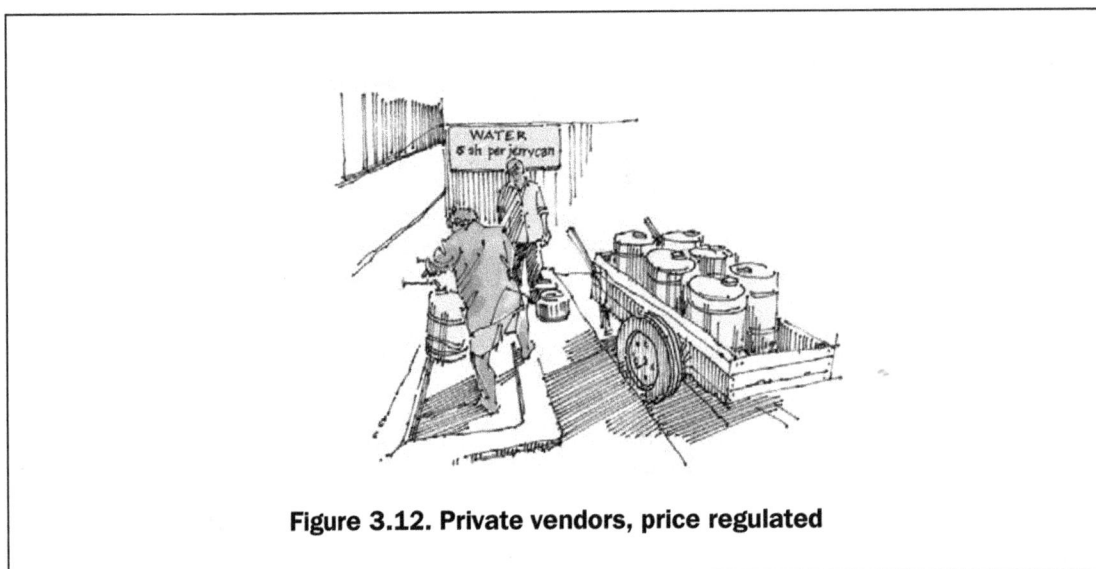

Figure 3.12. Private vendors, price regulated

The service provided by handcart vendors can be improved where the utility regulates and supports their activities. For example, the utility can provide a convenient water collection point for the vendors and can potentially regulate the price that is charged to consumers by publicizing the price that is charged to the vendors. This can be done to some extent by the utility, who can put up a sign up showing the cost of the water at the collection point, as is shown in the figure below. Alternatively, community groups or even local government can be empowered to take on this monitoring role.

Potential advantages (for consumers)
- It can be convenient for consumers to have water delivered to their houses. In marketing terms, the customers are receiving an added value which, if it is cost reflective, is a good service.

- Consumers spend less time collecting water than they would if they used alternatives such as water kiosks or standposts.

- If the utility is supporting and regulating the cart vendors, then consumers can receive a better service, hopefully at a reasonable price.

Potential advantages (for the utility)
- The cart vendors can serve areas that the utility is unable to serve adequately in the short to medium term.

- By working in partnership with the handcart vendors, the utility is more likely to be perceived by consumers and politicians as an organization that is doing its best under the circumstances.

Potential disadvantages (for consumers)
- Water from handcart vendors is usually very expensive because the vendors charge for all the time and effort it takes to collect, transport and sell the water.

- In some cases water may not be from a protected water source and could therefore be contaminated. Regulation can minimize this problem.

- This option may not be reliable if the vendor is not working or if water is sold to others instead.

- The price can be set by criminal gangs claiming monopoly rights over supply in certain areas.

Potential disadvantages (for the utility)
- Consumers who are served by the handcart vendors represent a missed opportunity for the utility to sell water in their city.

- If a sizeable proportion of consumers are served by vendors at expensive prices, the utility is likely to be perceived by key stakeholders (politicians and consumers) as an organization that is not doing its required job.

- The vendors may not be paying for the water they are selling, or in some cases they may be buying the water illegally from utility employees rather than from the utility itself.

It should be noted that the service options that should be adopted will depend on local circumstances, especially regarding feasibility of options and perceptions of customers.

Public or private street tank/water tankers
Tankers may be provided by the utility or a private company who regularly deliver water to areas experiencing serious shortages. The tanker can fill a local street tank or fill people's containers directly. Public supply to street tanks is common in drought-prone areas.

Potential advantages (for consumers)
- This method is effective in emergency situations, as water tankers can be mobilised relatively quickly. However it is also used in some prolonged water shortage situations.

- Water tankers are suitable for transient communities, where people are only settled temporarily, such as in emergency situation.

Potential advantages (for the utility)
- This method requires minimal infrastructure investment, apart from procurement of a tanker and perhaps a pump. Water can be pumped directly into a tank feeding a single tap-stand. There is no requirement for a pipe distribution network.

Figure 3.13. Public or private street tank/water tankers

- It is easy to train people to use this method of delivering water compared to other methods.

Potential disadvantages (for consumers)
- This method of distributing water is very expensive in terms of the cost of water per container. In some cases utilities or municipalities subsidize this lifeline option.

- Not suitable for areas with limited access, such as informal settlements.

- Water tankers can damage poorly constructed roads.

- Consumers are likely to experience inconvenience in terms of queuing for the tanker water and not being sure when it may come to their area.

- This method can create dependency, when no alternative supply has been planned.

- This is not a sustainable method in the long run unless users can afford to pay high prices for water.

Potential disadvantages (for the utility)
- Can be expensive for the utility where it is providing a subsidized service.

- Where consumers are relying on tankers, the utility is liable to receive pressure from politicians and other stakeholders to provide a better level of service.

- If tankered water is common, it can have an adverse effect on the utility's corporate image, which can reduce customer's willingness to sustain payments.

Water transported using this method may need to be chlorinated to a higher dosage when it has to be transported long distances, because the water will be sitting for longer before being used, hence the need to use more chlorine.

Public handpump in urban or peri-urban areas

Handpumps are usually associated with rural areas but are also common in peri-urban areas, particularly where there are good groundwater yields and where adequate pipe systems have yet to be provided. In some cases the water is provided free to people who use the handpump, in other locations charges for are levied as people collect water from the handpump or as part of a general tax. Handpumps are not usually provided by a utility but they may be provided by a government department.

Figure 3.14. Public handpump in urban or peri-urban areas

Potential advantages (for consumers)
- Water is either free or sold in small quantities, and this is often more affordable for low-income customers compared to other options.

- This option can provide a clean source of water, provided the groundwater is not contaminated.

- A good temporary option where the nearest pipe distribution network is far away.

- It can provide a back-up option where piped water services are unreliable.

Potential advantages (for the utility)
- Many utilities do not provide this option. A handpump can provide a temporary option for a new area until piped water is provided.

- It can provide a back-up option where piped water services are unreliable, otherwise the utility may have to provide more tanker supplies.

- It is a low-cost service option, because many people can be served by one hanndpump.

Potential disadvantages (for consumers)
- Time may be wasted due to queues at handpumps and the time taken to pump and carry the water.

- It is tiring using a handpump and carrying water, and the nearest pumps could be a long distance from the household.

- Handpumps often fall into disrepair and it is not always clear who is responsible for maintenance.

- Possible contamination of the groundwater from septic tanks and leaking sewers can lead to contaminated handpump water.

- Often only limited volumes of water are available from handpumps due to the problems outlined above.

Potential disadvantages (for the utility)
- Consumers who are served by handpumps represent a missed opportunity for the utility to sell water in their city.

- If a sizeable proportion of consumers are served by handpumps, the utility is likely to be perceived by key stakeholders (politicians and consumers) as an organization that is not doing its required job.

The selection of service options to be promoted for a particular town or city will depend on local circumstances, especially regarding the feasibility of the various options and perceptions of customers. Where utilities are contemplating offering more service options to different consumer groups, it is preferable to undertake consumer surveys and dialogue. Section 4 on 'Understanding water users' discusses approaches that can be used to reliably investigate consumer perceptions and demands for different options.

Consumer-organized service options

Where services in a particular area are inadequate, consumers will often seek to develop their own water sources. In some cases such sources can in effect be competition to utility-managed services, and should be taken into account in any investment programme. In areas where the utility cannot provide piped water in the medium term, it would be good public relations for the utility to provide information on the most viable alternative water sources.

Examples of consumer-organized service options are set out below. It is important for a utility to find out the extent of the use of such consumer-organized service options, in order that they can understand the local water market in their city, prior to investment in new infrastructure.

A sensible marketing strategy is to develop trust in the utility amongst existing and potential customers. One way of developing such trust in areas that are likely to remain poorly served with pipe water for some time, is to be helpful to potential customers about alternative water sources.

a) Private individual or community boreholes

In situations where groundwater is available, consumers may install their own borewell with electric pumps, so that they have an adequate and reliable supply. Individual boreholes are very widespread in South Asia. In Guntur, India, for example, the extent of the use of such alternative water sources is clearly demonstrated in Table 3.3, with 70 to 100 per cent of households in a number of consumer groups having their own borehole or sharing one.

Such extensive use of alternative water sources is significant 'competition' for the utility or municipality and needs to be borne in mind when the utility develops its investment plans. If customers have already invested a lot of money in alternative water sources such as boreholes, they may be reluctant to pay large water tariff increases. This has been borne out in a willingness to pay survey conducted in Guntur (Narender, Chary and Sansom, 2004).

b) Private individual ground-level storage tanks

Some customers invest significant sums of money by buying their own ground tank, which is filled from the water distribution network, often with a pump connected to their overhead tank. This is common in some regions where people are concerned about the adequacy and reliability of their supplies. These tanks can fill during the night or other

Table 3.3. Alternative water sources in Guntur

Consumer group	Alternative water source	Percentage use
Bungalows	Individual borehole	80%
Independent houses in planned areas	Individual borehole	70%
Flats in planned areas	Shared borehole	100%
Independent houses in unplanned areas	Own borehole	33%
	Own open well	33%
Flats in unplanned areas	Shared borehole	100%
Slums with some water supply coverage	Public borehole	32%
	Own borehole	54%
Slums with no water supply coverage	Municipal tanker	96%
	Open well	0%

times when water is not being drawn from the network for immediate use and can substantially increase both the available quantity and reliability of supply compared to customers without such tanks.

From the perspective of the utility and other customers, such tanks can cause problems, particularly where the ball valve that shuts off the flow into the tank is not working. In this case water will continue to flow into the full tank, causing it to overflow and wasting water It is therefore in the utility's interest to occasionally check that the ball valves in these private tanks are in working order.

c) Roof catchments

The collection of water from roofs into tanks is used in both rural and urban settings as a means of supplementing other water sources. It is particularly useful in urban areas that the water distribution system does not reach. An example of the successful use of roof catchments in Tegucigalpa, Honduras is briefly described in Box 3.1

Box 3.1. Roof catchments in low-income shanties in Tegucigalpa, Hondurash[1]

In a survey of two low-income areas in Tegucigalpa with inadequate piped systems it was found that more than half the households used rainwater as their principal source of water, while 90 per cent of inhabitants collected at least some water from their roofs. The mean area of the iron sheet roofs varied from 23 to 45m^2.

Most households stored water in 200-litre oil drums, while about a quarter had somewhat larger cement tanks known as *pila*. Research findings revealed that provision of loans for fully equipping roofs with guttering and for building pila with up to 2000-litre capacity could be repaid over a relatively short time, using money saved from not having to purchase water from vendors.

---

1. Source: Brand and Bradford (1991), cited in Gould and Nissen-Peterson (1999).

The Tegucigalpa case demonstrates the viability of this service option in poorly served urban areas. This technique is also successful in many other areas around the world, in both wet and semi-arid regions. Problems have been experienced, however, where there are high levels of air pollution, such as heavy industry and coal-fired power stations, which make rainwater unsuitable for drinking or cooking (Thomas and Greene, 1993).

Water utilities are not generally in the business of providing materials for roof catchments. However, a utility wishing to demonstrate that it is concerned about existing and potential customers may wish to provide information about roof catchments and potential suppliers in areas that it cannot serve for some time.

The range of alternative water sources that people have to resort to in newly constructed areas in Kampala are evident from Table 3.4.

Table 3.4. Coping strategies of new middle-income residents in Kampala

Water source	Frequency	Percentage
Roof catchment with portable storage	99	66%
Roof catchment with underground tank	4	3%
Protected spring	104	70%
Water vendors	20	13%
Open well	16	11%
Privately operated powered borehole, pre-paid	14	9%

d) Individual or community open wells

Open wells are common in some urban areas where there is a high water table. If it is known that water from these wells is contaminated, the utility or municipality may wish to promote piped water as a safer alternative, provided they are confident that the piped water is clearly better than the well water. It is preferable if there is third party verification of this claim from a health department, regulator or NGO.

One approach for promoting piped water for drinking as an alternative to well water would be to undertake participatory water tests with community groups. This will enable increased awareness of a contamination problem and possible health impacts.

Unprotected or unauthorized water options
In areas where service provision is poor, many people may resort to alternative service options that are either unprotected sources or unauthorized such as:

• untreated water taken directly from rivers or ponds;

• water from a leaking pipe (often made easier to access by digging a hole under the leak);

- leaking pipes above ground; and

- illegal connections to piped supplies.

The first two options are likely to entail clear contamination risks. The best means of discouraging these practices is to provide alternative service options that are more convenient and are affordable. Well-designed hygiene promotion programmes can be useful in discouraging people from using the above options, provided there are viable alternative protected sources. To reduce the occurrence of the third and fourth possibilities the utility needs to be proactive in undertaking surveys and implementing strategies for reducing these sources of non-revenue water.

3.4   Payment options

Successful international water utility companies generally have a wide variety of payment options for their customers. This is essentially because they know that if they make it easy for customers to pay, they are more likely to pay their water bills promptly. They know that people living in a city have a variety of different lifestyles and preferred payment methods. Severn Trent Water in the UK, for example, offers a number of payment options, enabling customers to payby the method they choose:

- by post

- by direct debit

- at a bank

- at a building society

- at a post office

- at a payment point ('Paypoint') in a shop

- by home or telephone banking

- through the internet, via the utility website

Severn Trent have also found that not all customers are able to pay in the normal pattern of two payments per year. They have had to accept small payments on a monthly and even weekly basis to help those on low incomes or social welfare benefits.

While a utility in a developing country may not offer quite the same list of options to its customers, they still need to think about suitable payment options for their high, medium and low-income customers. The method of payment is most important in the urban areas of low-income countries where many households have a low disposable income. In a World Bank study of ten cities in Africa, for example, more than 80 per cent of these countries' residents live on less than a dollar a day (Collignon and Vezina, 2000).

In Kampala, Uganda, the preferred means of payment amongst customers is through vendors rather than the utility, as can be seen from Box 3.2.

Utilities serving low-income communities may wish to consider more flexible payment options, rather than monthly payments for individual connections. Utilities could negotiate with community groups or private individuals to manage water kiosks or shared connections, so that consumers pay the owners of the kiosk or shared connections small

---

Box 3.2. Payment option preferences in Kampala[1]

In September 1999, a questionnaire was sent out to a random sample of registered customers of the National Water & Sewerage Corporation, Uganda, to solicit their perceptions on the quality of service. Respondents were asked whether they agreed or disagreed with the following statement:

'Water vendors are able to receive payment for their services easier than NWSC because the terms for sale are simple and more convenient to customers.'

Of the 510 valid responses, only 137 customers (27 per cent) disagreed; 232 respondents (46 per cent) agreed with the statement. The rest of the respondents (26 per cent) were undecided about the validity of the statement.

---

1. Source: Sam Kayaga (2001)[missing from refs, need details of title and where.]

sums of money when they take water and the kiosk or shared connection owners pay the utility each month. Or the utility could set up local payment offices in poorer areas and allow weekly payments of water bills.

There are several dimensions of payment options. The options could outline different ways to pay in terms of:

*   where to pay;

*   how to pay;

*   when to pay;

*   whom to pay; and/or

*   a combination of all these dimensions.

Table 3.5 shows a choice of options for payment, arranged according to different dimensions such as those listed above. A utility can develop its own payment options based on the choices shown for each dimension in the table. Whatever options are preferred, it is worthwhile being systematic about the option development process, which is discussed below.

3.5   Shared management options

It can be beneficial for a utility to share the management of water services together with other partners such as community groups or vendor groups, particularly in low-income communities or areas that are poorly served. This is true for both publicly and privately managed water utilities. Such arrangements can reduce the utility's operational management costs and enable the vendors or community groups to be more effective in service provision. Examples of the latter are discussed below.

Shared management between a utility and community groups
Shared management of water services between a utility and local community groups can be cost efficient and both empower communities to manage their services and enable improved service provision in areas where a utility may be unable or reluctant to operate. For example, in Arusha (Tanzania) and Dhaka (Bangladesh), community groups manage water kiosks that are supplied with water by the utility and payment is based on meter

Table 3.5. Payment option summary

Dimension	Payment choices
Method of payment	Cash Cheque Bank debits Prepayment cards or tokens Water stamps A combination of methods
Where to pay	Pay at a cash point at utility head office Pay at a cash point at utility zonal office Pay at a cash point at utility zonal and head offices Deposit cash or cheque onto a bank account Through direct debit of your account Pay to a water vendor Pay to a private operator of a standpipe or kiosk Buy a pre-payment card/token from a water cash office, chainstore, or bank Pay to a community water user committee Pay to a landlord Pay as part of a local tax rate A combination of places
When to pay	Per month, per quarter, half-yearly, annually, etc. in arrears Per day Every time one draws water Per month, per quarter, half-yearly, annually, etc. in advance Whenever convenient but with a time limit A combination of these
Basis of payment	Fixed charge Volumetric charge, basing on metered rates Per house value Per plot value Estimated consumption A combination
Who to bill?	Utility Collective community billing using a bulk meter Street billing Landlord billing Household billing

readings. In Kibera (Nairobi), Haiti and Dakar (Senegal), community groups manage small tertiary water distribution systems and pay the utility or municipal council for the bulk water supply.

Such arrangements for managing water services are best explained by example. Box 3.3 and Box 3.4 summarize a successful case in Port-Au-Prince, Haiti.

Box 3.3. Shared management of water services in Haiti (Part 1)[1]

Programme context

Port-Au-Prince is a rapidly expanding capital city of 2 million inhabitants, where the population has increased 10-fold during the last 30 years. The water distribution network has not kept pace with this growth. Approximately 55 litres per capita of water are available each day, but only about 12 per cent of families have water connections in their homes. For the remainder of consumers the standpipes have not been functioning regularly. CAMEP, who are the public water company, are reported to be heavily in debt. Consequently Port-au Prince has seen a rapid increase in water distribution by the private sector. Water is sold to private individuals who do not have their own pipe connection by the water carriers at a price of $3 to $5 per cubic metre.

Programme to serve 14 shanty towns

A programme of improvement was developed that was led by GRET (a French NGO), with technical assistance from HYDROCONSEIL. The project aims were to supply water to the shanty towns through new pipe distribution networks that would be managed by local community associations. The construction works were undertaken by local private companies from 1995 to 1998. Particular attention has been paid to technical surveys and the design of the new pipelines, in order to avoid conflicts over land rights and to reduce the risk of breakdowns. As the CAMEP network only has water pressure for a few hours a day, additional water storage was provided in the system to allow for more reliable distribution of water.

On completion of the construction work, water was provided to poor neighbourhoods via the main urban network, which is managed by the public operator (CAMEP). This avoids the need to use private transportation for water. Water is distributed to users via standpipes in the shanty towns, where water is sold at an average cost of $1 per cubic metre, which is considerably cheaper than the water provided by the independent service provider chain.

A key to the success of the programme is the active and capable participation of the neighbourhood water committees. An intensive mobilization and training process was, therefore, carried out by GRET and SOLAM, who are a local NGO who specialize in social mobilization work in the shanty towns. The committees are made up of representatives from all the community organizations in the neighbourhood. They decide what work is to be done (e.g. choosing the number and location of standposts) and collect the revenue from water sold at the standposts.

The division of responsibilities between the water company and the water committees is shown in Figure 3.15 below. CAMEP maintains the pipe network and bulk supply of water up to the flowmeter just outside the shanty town, while the local water committee maintain the pipelines and stand posts inside their community area.

Water is purchased from CAMEP at $0.3 per cubic metre by the local committee and the monthly bill is based on the flowmeter readings. The users pay about $1 a cubic metre at the standposts. This difference in price enables the committees to pay the water sellers at the standposts, provide a small payment to committee members and finance the O&M of their local pipe network. The remaining profits (15-20 per cent) are invested in other public facilities such as drains and walkways.

1. Source: A summary case study based on Collignon (1998)

Box 3.4. Shared management of water services in Haiti (Part 2)[1]

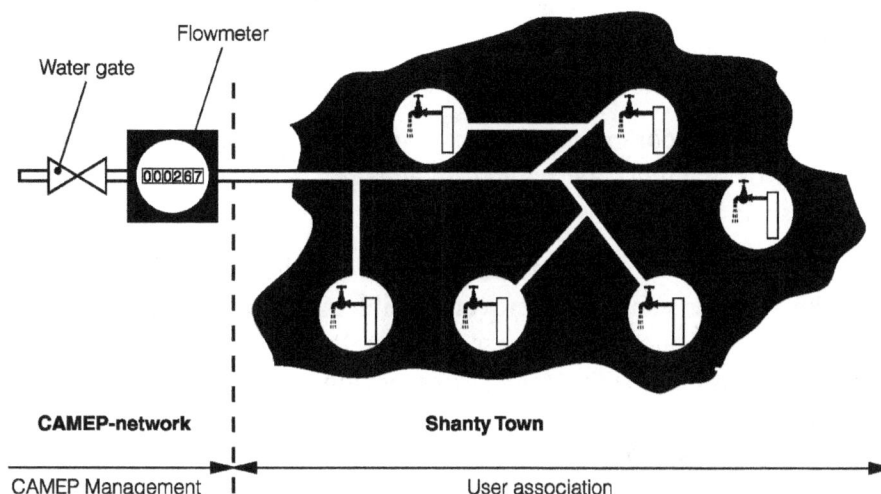

Figure 3.15. Water services in Port-Au-Prince shanty towns

Results

By 1998 20 kilometres of pipeline had been constructed, providing water to approximately 60 new standposts. No water bill presented by CAMEP has yet gone unpaid, which is a good indicator of the success of the programme and encourages the water company to serve more informal settlements using this management arrangement. The introduction of this new competition to these areas has had the effect of reducing the price previously charged by water vendors, who have come to accept the new system, and there have been no cases of sabotage.

The volume of water sold by CAMEP to the first eight water committees increased from zero in October 1995 to 15,000m3 per quarter in July 1998. This shows that the new system is meeting the demands of the users.

However, it is interesting to note that during the rainy season consumption declines as people opt for cheaper sources such as rainwater collected from rooftops.

The water committees have shown great maturity in dealing with conflicts within the communities and managing funds effectively. The successes that have been achieved in Haiti would suggest that it would be worth adapting the management arrangements described above to provide improved water services to informal settlements elsewhere in the world.

1. Source: A summary case study based on Collignon (1998)

Some of the key factors for a utility to consider when contemplating collaborating with community groups for the shared management of water or sanitation services are as follows:

• Are there community or user groups who are able and willing to take on the management of distinct service provision tasks?

• Do the groups have the necessary skills to undertake the identified tasks, or are there clear opportunities for them to develop their capacities to the required level?

- Consideration should be given to where the community groups have 'comparative advantage' over other management arrangements. For example, if a community group wants to manage O&M and/or cost recovery for water services in their own informal settlement, they have the advantage of understanding what is and is not acceptable in that community. In addition they are likely to be competitive in terms of labour costs in their own area, because they may want to improve services for themselves and neighbours and they do not have to incur travel costs.

- When negotiating with community groups it may be easier and more effective to use an intermediary or facilitator, perhaps from an NGO, who has good experience of working with such communities and has suitable communication skills.

- To minimize the cost of monitoring and evaluation of the work of community groups, it is best to keep matters simple wherever possible. This can be achieved by having easily measurable indicators for success and simple payment terms. For example, indicators of success may be the number of working water kiosks and connections, as well as the prices they charge compared to vendor prices. The payment terms for, say, a community group managing the water distribution system in their area, could be based on readings of the bulk flow meter on the water main that supplies their pipe network.

3.6   Processes for option development

Having considered the range of possible options, the outline process of developing new products or options is set out below in Figure 3.16. This process could particularly apply to new service or payment options, where there are novel aspects not tried in the region before. Even where there is a reasonable level of confidence that a new option or product is viable, it is worth testing or piloting it in a particular area to confirm its viability before scaling up to a broader use of the option/product.

The key factor which has not been discussed in relation to these various service options is price. Ultimately, customers, present or potential, make their choice according to the value they perceive they can obtain from the product or service, relative to its price. Figure 3.16 requires the planner to check whether the proposed service 'will have an attractive price and value.' To achieve the 'mutually beneficial exchange relationship', the goal of marketing, it is therefore necessary to sell the service at a price the customer is willing to pay but also at a price which covers the costs of the supplier. For all the options listed above it is possible to determine the specific direct costs of the variations relative to alternatives. However, the actual price of the water (or wastewater) service can only be determined having undertaken the strategic marketing or investment planning exercise described in Part III.

The iterative process therefore requires pilot programmes for low-income consumers that are priced as close as possible to the final price, but that final price cannot be known until the concepts are proven and some estimate can be made of the take-up of the idea throughout the city or service area. Marketing is relatively simple in concept, but in practice it is remarkably hard to balance all the necessary factors.

```
┌─────────────────┐                    ┌─────────────────┐
│ Consumer        │                    │ Ideas from      │
│ preferences in  │                    │ options tried   │
│ different market│                    │ elsewhere       │
│ segments        │                    │                 │
└─────────────────┘                    └─────────────────┘
            ╲                          ╱
             ╲                        ╱
              ┌─────────────────┐
              │ Ideas           │
              │ generation      │
              └─────────────────┘
                       │
                       ▼
              ┌─────────────────┐
              │ Idea screening to│
              │ eliminate weak  │
              │ ideas           │
              │ (Consider       │
              │ potential       │
              │ advantages and  │
              │ disadvantages)  │
              └─────────────────┘
                       │
                       ▼
              ┌─────────────────┐        ┌──────────────────────┐
              │ Concept         │        │ Check whether:       │
              │ development     │◄──────►│ • The product's      │
              │ and testing     │        │   benefits are clear │
              └─────────────────┘        │ • It will have an    │
                       │                 │   attractive price   │
                       ▼                 │   and value          │
              ┌─────────────────┐        │ • There is enough    │
              │ Outline         │        │   demand for the idea│
              │ marketing       │        │   amongst the target │
              │ and business    │        │   group              │
              │ assessment      │        │ • The probable       │
              └─────────────────┘        │   market is big      │
                       │                 │   enough             │
                       ▼                 └──────────────────────┘
              ┌─────────────────┐        ┌──────────────────────┐
              │ Product         │        │ Agree:               │
              │ development     │◄──────►│ • What should be     │
              │ or refinement   │        │   tested?            │
              │ and testing     │        │ • How long should   │
              └─────────────────┘        │   the test be?       │
                       │                 │ • How should the     │
                       ▼                 │   results be used?   │
              ┌─────────────────┐        └──────────────────────┘
              │ Adopt,          │        ┌──────────────────────┐
              │ modify or       │        │ Full launch,         │
              │ drop the        │───────►│ monitor and          │
              │ product or      │        │ review               │
              │ option          │        │                      │
              └─────────────────┘        └──────────────────────┘
```

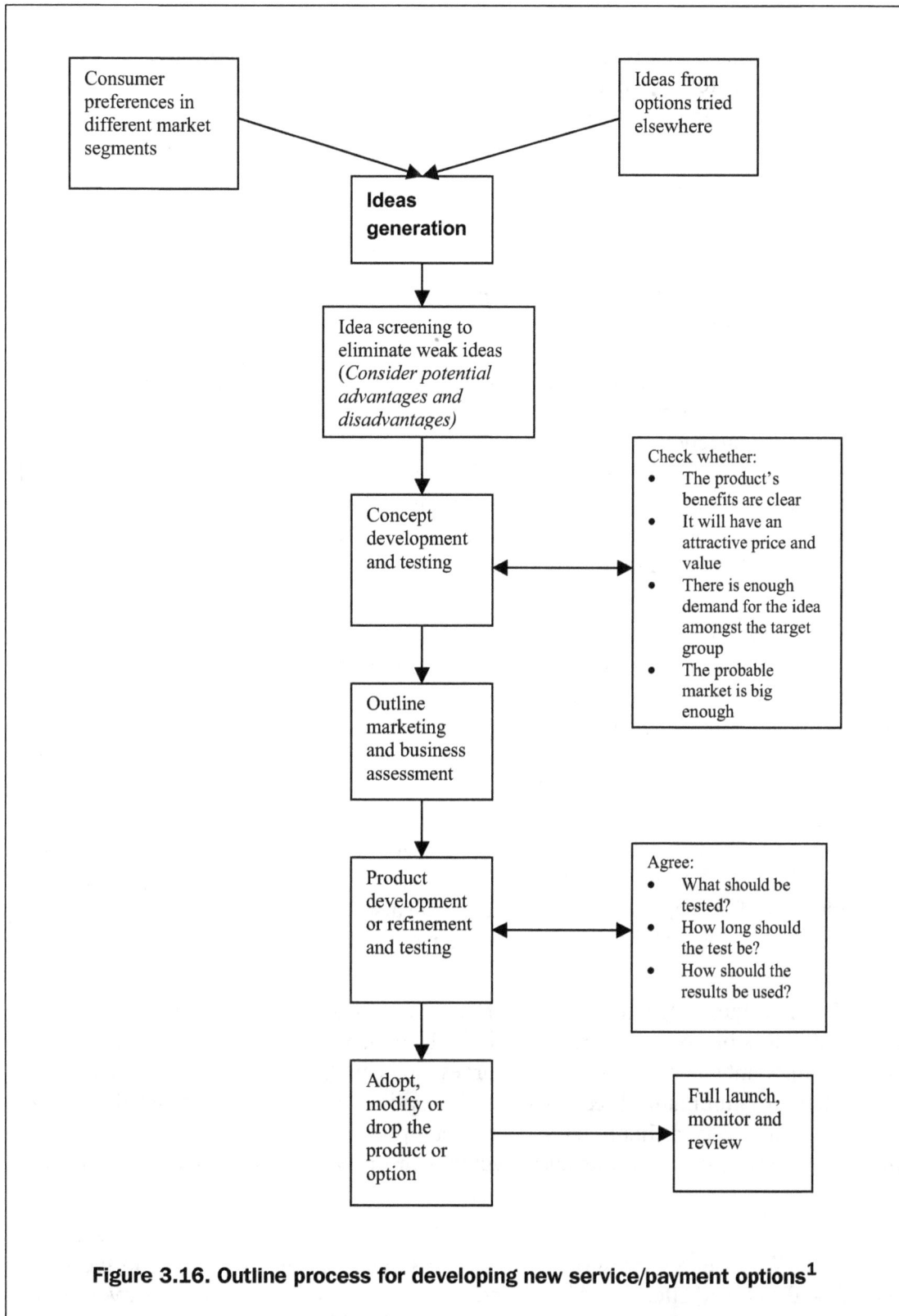

Figure 3.16. Outline process for developing new service/payment options[1]

1. Source: Adapted from Wilson and Gilligan (1997)

3.7 Demand assessment - the Contingent Valuation Method

A number of demand assessment methods were outlined in Chapter 2. The method that provides the most reliable data for the maximum WTP of consumers for particular service options is CVM.

Outline of CVM

Contingent valuation surveys principally entail carrying out house-to-house surveys using carefully designed forms and asking respondents a range of questions. Typically, the main topics on a CVM survey form are:

a) the consumers perceptions of their existing water supply system;

b) key socio-economic factors such as household expenditure; and

c) a hypothetical scenario for potential service options that are offered to the respondent at various prices to determine their WTP.

When undertaking (c) the potential service options are presented to respondents to determine what kind of water and sanitation services users want and are willing to pay for. The economic concept that CV surveys are trying to capture is the maximum amount that a respondent would be willing to pay for the proposed improvement in water services in the context of the existing institutional regime within which households are free to allocate their financial resources (Whittington, 1997). An example CVM questionnaire based on market research in Mombasa can be found in Annexe 1.

The most important part of the contingent valuation methodology is creating a realistic contingent valuation scenario, which has accurately priced water supply 'options' reflecting the levels of prices that the water service provider would be willing to charge in order to provide the service. The respondent is asked about their preferences and is effectively asked at what price they would be willing to 'buy' the water, based on the level, quantity and quality of service (Wedgwood and Sansom, 2003). A bidding game approach is usually used. This could entail the enumerator asking the respondent if they are prepared to pay the highest value of a range of prices for a particular service option, then going to the next lowest bid, until the respondent says they are willing to pay that particular price for that service level. Bidding can also start low and move higher until the respondent confirms that they are prepared to pay a stated price.

The CVM manager needs to ensure that the service options included in the CV survey are technically feasible without been prohibitively expensive to build and maintain. It is equally important when conducting CV surveys to keep the range of options offered to the respondent to a minimum (three to five service options are recommended). Otherwise the survey becomes very difficult to conduct, is complicated for the enumerator when in the field, and analysis of the results and development of realistic tariff models becomes too unwieldy.

Ideally the WTP survey questionnaire and the service options to be used in the survey should be developed after the analysis and dissemination of the consumer survey results. This should enable the development of more feasible options based on consumer preferences and perceptions in the different market segments.

A typical CVM process is shown in Figure 3.17 and Figure 3.18. The last two steps (10 and 11), which use CVM to develop tariffs and ensure that the results inform policy, are often neglected - but they are very important to maximize the benefits of the survey.

Phase 1 – Preparation

Step 1 – Select interview technique

For example should it be a personal interview, mail survey or phone interview ?

Step 2 – Develop a sampling strategy

Include agreeing a sample size and how to achieve a random and representative sample.

Step 3 – Develop the CVM scenario

Including defining the service options and deciding how the options will be offered to the respondents.

Step 4 – Decide which elicitation method to use

For example, you could use the bidding game, referendum voting or contingent ranking.

Step 5 – Cost the options

Options should be based on the range of costs that could realistically be charged for each option.

Step 6 – Write household survey and CVM questionnaire

The survey and questionnaire could include, for example, Section 1 – Socio-economic data, Section 2 – Existing water supply, Section 3 – Elicit WTP.

Phase 2 – Implementation

Step 7 – Enumerator training and pilot testing

Including enumerator selection, role playing, sampling in the field and pilot testing.

Step 8 – Implement survey

Consider translation and gender issues, as well as the field manager's role.

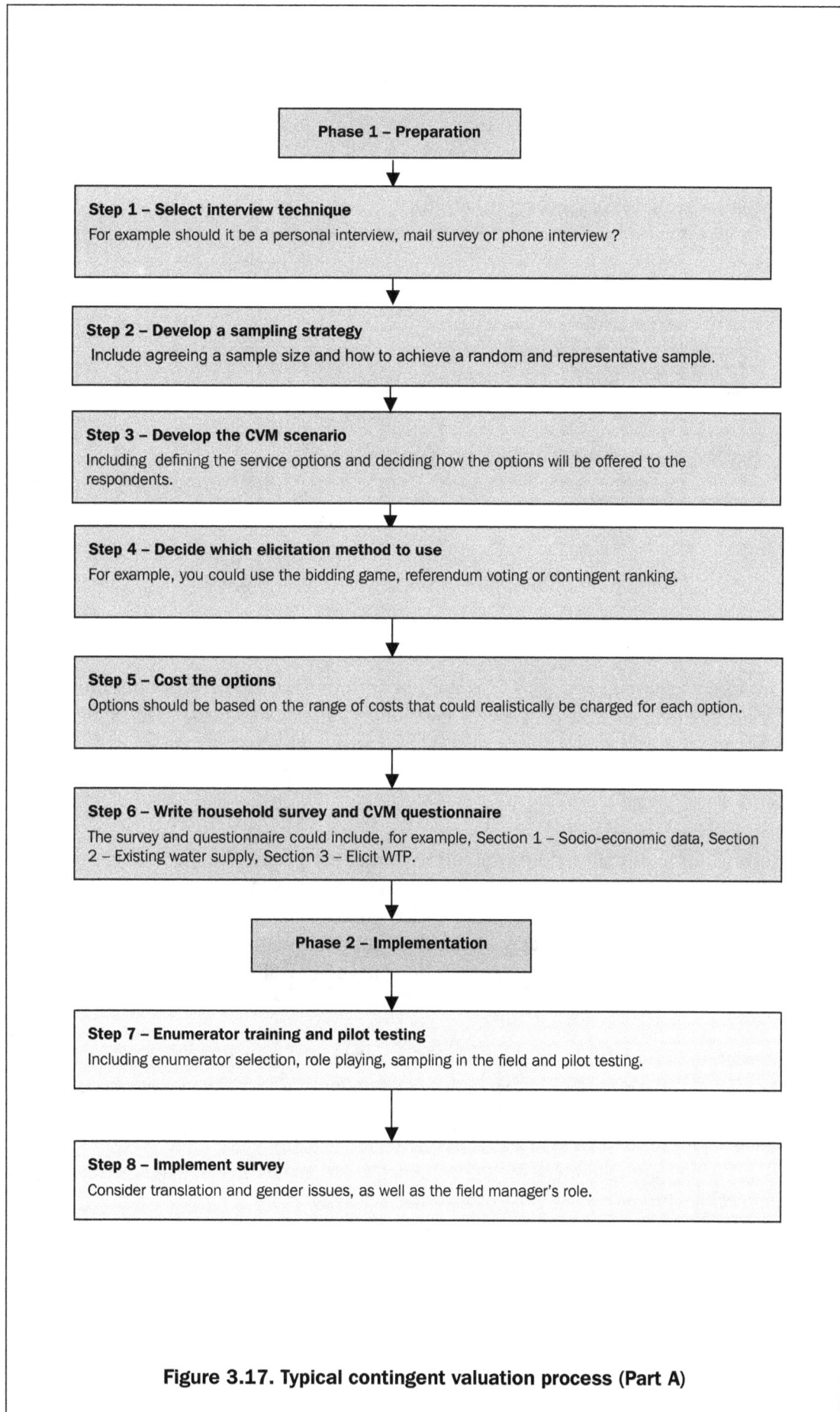

Figure 3.17. Typical contingent valuation process (Part A)

```
┌─────────────────────────────────────────────────────────────────┐
│                                                                   │
│              ┌──────────────────────────────────────┐            │
│              │  Phase 3 - Data analysis and policy    │            │
│              │           implications                 │            │
│              └──────────────────────────────────────┘            │
│                                 │                                 │
│                                 ▼                                 │
│   ┌──────────────────────────────────────────────────────────┐  │
│   │ Step 9 – Data entry and analysis                          │  │
│   │ Including checking the validity of the data and           │  │
│   │ considering how to present the results.                   │  │
│   └──────────────────────────────────────────────────────────┘  │
│                                 │                                 │
│                                 ▼                                 │
│   ┌──────────────────────────────────────────────────────────┐  │
│   │ Step 10 – Using CVM results to develop tariffs            │  │
│   │ Includinge developing financial sustainability analyses   │  │
│   │ by using spreadsheets and consider options for subsidy    │  │
│   │ reduction.                                                │  │
│   └──────────────────────────────────────────────────────────┘  │
│                                 │                                 │
│                                 ▼                                 │
│   ┌──────────────────────────────────────────────────────────┐  │
│   │ Step 11 – Ensuring that WTP studies inform policy         │  │
│   │ Including how to use the results to both support new      │  │
│   │ projects and advocate changes such as an improved         │  │
│   │ 'willingness to charge' amongst key stakeholders.         │  │
│   └──────────────────────────────────────────────────────────┘  │
│                                                                   │
│        Figure 3.18. Typical contingent valuation process (Part B) │
└─────────────────────────────────────────────────────────────────┘
```

Figure 3.18. Typical contingent valuation process (Part B)

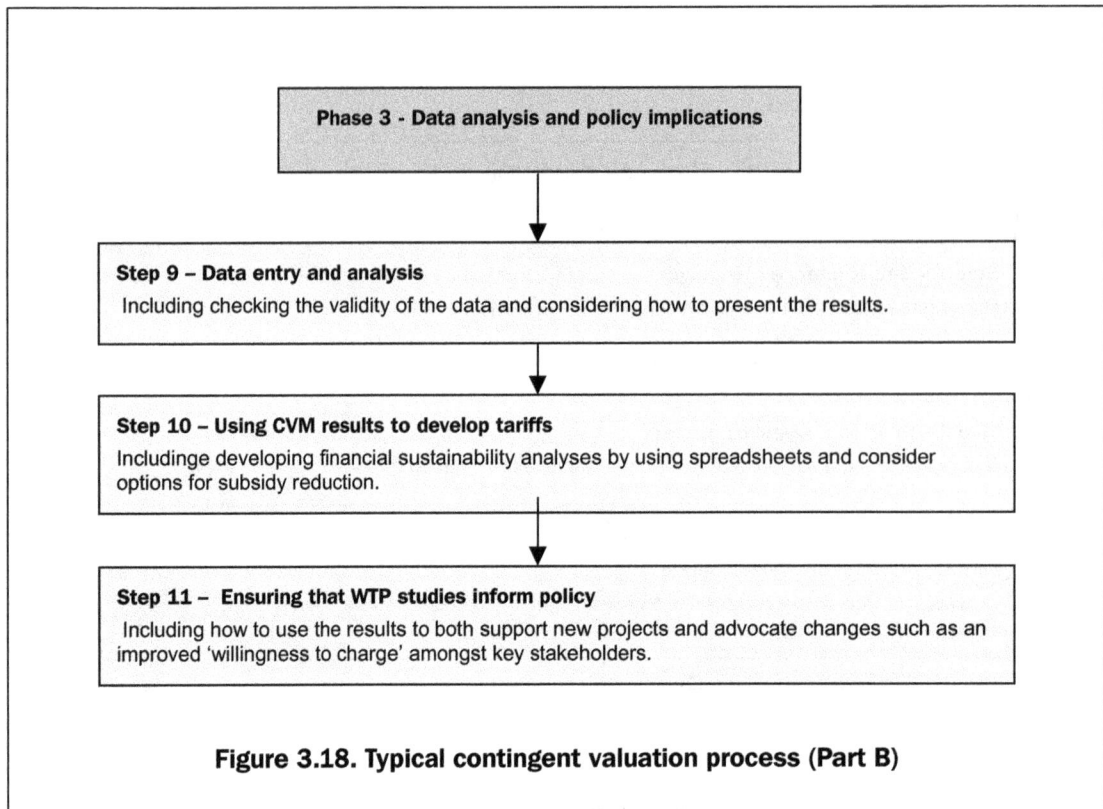

An example WTP survey questionnaire is included in Annexe 2, based on research in Mombasa that was conducted in 2001. The research in Mombassa split households into four market segments based on type of dwelling (bungalows, flats, 1, 2 or 3-roomed swahili houses and informal settlements). This was done so that disaggregated data can be presented for these four consumer groups to aid decision-making in how to improve services for each group.

The results of the willingness to pay studies are analysed to reveal the average amounts that users are willing to pay for improved water services. A simple frequency distribution curve of households' willingness to pay bids for improved water services, obtained from a contingent valuation survey, can be used to support management decision-making. Figure 3.19 shows such a frequency distribution curve of WTP results from the Mombasa survey.

It can be seen in Figure 3.19 that 6 per cent of respondents are willing to pay the first bid amount of KSh2500 per month. 74 per cent of respondents are willing to pay over KSh700 per month for this service. The weighted mean willingness to pay for this service level is KSh1124 per month. 54 per cent of respondents are willing to pay the weighted mean. These WTP values are considerably higher than the utility tariff levels that were charged at the time of the survey.

Mombasa WTP survey - Service Level 4: Continuous water supply to a shared yard connection in a planned area with 1, 2 or 3-roomed dwellings or Swahili houses

WTP (KSh) Service Level 4

WTP (KSh) Service Level 4

Figure 3.19. Mombasa example WTP survey results

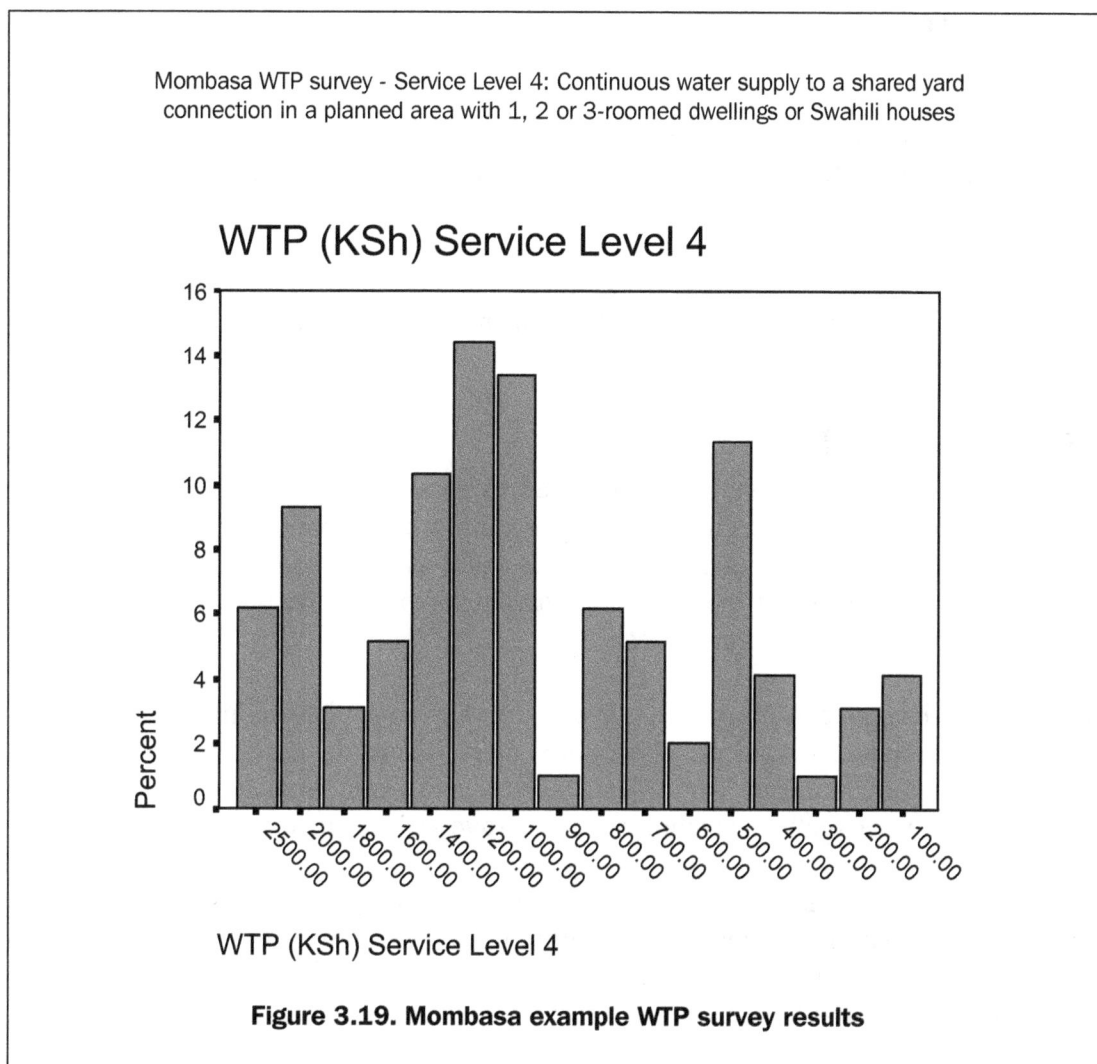

Benefits and potential drawbacks of CVM

Other demand assessment techniques such as revealed preference techniques and PREPP provide useful information on understanding user experiences, perceptions and preferences for different options. Well-designed CVMs are also able to provide such information but, in addition, CVMs provide reliable data on people's maximum willingness to pay for different service options. This is invaluable for developing investment projections and guiding future water tariff policies.

Some critics may claim that respondents will not answer truthfully, and what they say they will pay does not reflect what they would actually pay. It is true that some respondents might bias their answers: selecting expensive options in the hope that the government would eventually pay for them if the customers cannot or will not. Various techniques have been developed to minimize biased responses. In particular, the way that the CV scenario is presented to the respondent, and how the willingness to pay question is asked, can be very specifically designed to reduce bias.

Assuming that the utility contracts specialist consultancies to write, manage, and analyse the CVM survey results then the utility manager's awareness of the limitation and advantages of CVM will assist in writing more focused terms of references to ensure that the end report can be used to provide financially sustainable water services to low-income communities.

For more detailed information on conducting and managing a contingent valuation survey for the water sector refer to Wedgwood and Sansom (2003) WTP Surveys - A streamlined approach: Guidance notes for small town water services.

The question of how willingness to pay results can be used in a utility's investment planning process is discussed in Chapter 7 - 'Stage 2 - where we want to be', as part of strategic marketing, and is shown in Figure 7.1.

3.8   Selecting priority areas

As funds are invariably limited, utilities need to agree which areas are a priority for improved services. Market segmentation plans, utility performance data, as well as the results of consumer surveys and demand assessment surveys, provide an effective and impartial basis for selecting the priority areas, thus avoiding the potential criticism of favouritism during the selection process.

As many low-income consumers often live in informal or unplanned areas that typically experience inadequate services, these are often likely to be priority areas for improvement. Governments with clear poverty reduction strategies are likely to encourage utilities and other stakeholders to improve services in such areas.

Initially, when comprehensive city-wide data may not be available, a utility is likely to want to target certain low-income areas to pilot work based on limited information. This is a sensible strategy initially, because there is a need to 'learn by doing', but ultimately when planning for city-wide services this needs to be done based on more comprehensive survey information.

Chapter 4

Selling to and providing services for low-income customers

4.1 Introduction

The outline approach to marketing described in the previous three chapters of Part II is based around the customer value chain framework of: 'know, target, sell and service'. Having determined how potential customers receive water and sanitation services at present and what options they might want if their needs are to be properly addressed; it is necessary to consider how improved services might be promoted and sold and then serviced over the long term.

Informal housing settlements, slums, compounds or peri-urban areas provide viable though often unexplored revenue bases for utilities. The fact is that many of the consumers who are not served directly by the utility live in such areas and continue to have inadequate access to basic water and sanitation services. This means that they need to obtain water from elsewhere, and it is often expensive and of poor quality. For the community and household this means that related social and economic factors, including chronic health problems, are made worse. For the utility a sizeable percentage of its potential revenue base remains untapped. This need not be the case.

In determining how best to sell and provide services in informal settlements, we firstly consider the potential barriers and solutions to serving these areas, such as: high connection costs, government and utility staff attitudes, land tenure issues and the 'spaghetti' problem. We then move on to consider how best to improve services in informal settlements using carefully designed participatory projects and partnerships with other key stakeholders.

If we are to maximize the support to service providers and other stakeholders in serving the poor, then appropriate incentive mechanisms and policies need to be in place. Example initiatives are proposed. Finally, as new approaches are piloted, lessons need to be learnt for scaling up across a city or town. This requires strategic planning and marketing approaches, which are examined in Part III.

4.2 Overcoming barriers to serving informal settlements

A number of common barriers to improving services in unplanned or informal settlements and strategies for overcoming such problems are briefly discussed in the following sections.

Land tenure issues

Often, urban water utilities are faced with difficulties when extending water and sanitation services to parts of some cities or towns, particularly informal settlement areas, due to complexities in the land tenure system. These complexities usually make it difficult for the authorities to enforce regulations. This in turn contributes to a proliferation of unauthorized dwellings being erected.

In addition, both companies and individuals in cities in developing countries employ people on low wages, and those employees and informal sector workers tend to reside in unplanned settlements because that is the only accommodation that they can afford. A summary of how the Cato Crest informal settlement developed in Durban, South Africa is included in Box 4.1.

Box 4.1. The history of informal settlements in Durban, South[1]

In 1990 Durban City, the second largest city in South Africa, experienced rapid urbanization, mainly caused by political violence, severe drought and unemployment in the rural areas, and sparked off by the socio-political changes in the country. The first informal settlement in Durban City was Cato Crest, which is located about four kilometres north-west of the city centre, off the Western Free Way. The first inhabitants of Cato Crest forced their way onto empty land belonging to the central government in the mid-1970s, fleeing political violence in the surrounding areas of Kwazulu-Natal. The migrants constructed simple temporary structures, known as shacks, or *umjondolo* in the local Zulu language.

With changes taking place in the political arena at the time, and as the number of squatters increased tremendously, officials of the City Council could hardly evict the migrants. By 1991, there were about 370 shacks in Cato Crest, with a population of about 1,600 people. It was estimated that about 600,000 people lived in informal settlements in Durban Metropolitan Council areas by 1995.

---

1. Source: Adapted from a presentation to the 5th Global Forum, WSSCC on "Incentives for Utilities to Serve the Urban Poor: The case of Durban, South Africa" by Sam Kayaga.

Land tenure systems can have adverse affects on the provision of water services in several ways:

- acquisition of land for lay water installations, transmission and distribution mains.

- Difficulties in establishing clear and specific addresses for the end-user customers.

- Approvals for laying pipes for house connections and standpoosts or water kiosks.

Different forms of land tenure systems exist in different countries. Similarly, a wide range of legislation to enforce the land tenure system is in place in various countries, where the strictness of enforcement also varies considerably. For the purpose of providing water services in an urban area, land tenure systems may be categorized as follows (Lyonnaise des Eaux, 1998):

Public land, which is more easily accessed by squatters, and may be sub-divided into:

- inalienable public land, which authorities cannot give up under any circumstances;

- inalienable public land, which the authorities are willing to sell, rent, or grant as a concession. This type of land is attractive to potential squatters; and

- 'available' public land, such as forests, national parks, etc, which is not allocated to anyone but is governed under the public land system. This is the type of land most easily accessible to spontaneous urbanization.

Private land, which is more difficult for the squatters to access, and may be subdivided in the following categories:

- Properly and legally registered private land that clearly has an owner poses no specific problems, as the utility can negotiate with the registered owner.

- Illegally registered private land, which may have been illegally allocated by local authorities with no reference to the central government land registry office. The best option is to follow up formalization of the registration procedures.

- Unregistered private land, which loosely comes under the sovereignty of a community or some other customary group, and is governed under a law which is not necessarily laid down in writing. The boundaries of such land is not always clearly established.

General guidelines have been suggested by Lyonnaise des Eaux (1998) (now Ondeo, Suez, on the general course of action to be taken by a water utility in acquiring land to extend water services, particularly for the benefit of low-income communities. This is based on their experiences as an international water operator. These adapted guidelines, which are shown in Table 4.1, are characterized according to the attitude of the responsible authorities.

It is relatively easy for water utilities to acquire land to extend water and sanitation services into the public land categories. It is more difficult for utilities to acquire land from private owners for the purpose of developing water and sanitation systems. In some instances, the costs of land compensation are so prohibitive that projects are abandoned altogether.

It is recognized that land tenure laws and systems are difficult to amend overnight. It is therefore suggested that governments should reassess and amend their legal frameworks to circumvent such land tenure constraints. Examples of potential initiatives for improved water services in illegal or unauthorized settlements include:

- regularizing appropriate unauthorized settlements;

- de-linking the rights to services from tenure status;

- seeking to resettle some people without legal title (WSP and PPIAF, 2002);

- compulsory acquisition of land by utilities from landlords for extension of water services to low-income settlements, at a fee agreed by independent arbitration, according to the regulations;

- granting of 'easement' areas for the utility to construct and maintain water and sewerage facilities, with appropriate levels of compensation for disruption paid to landowners, according to the regulations. The utility requires ongoing free access to the facilities constructed for maintenance and rehabilitation purposes, with planning restrictions enforced on building over pipelines;

Table 4.1. Implications of status of land for extension of water services[1]

	Public land			Private land	
	Inalienable	Alienable	'Available'	Registered	Unregistered
A. Status of land registration procedures					
1. Land with recognized title deeds	Extreme caution	Caution	Possible intervention	Avoid	Clarify or steer clear
2. Land with doubtful title deeds	Avoid	Clarify or steer clear	Clarify or steer clear	Avoid	Avoid
3. Land occupied with no title deeds	Only intervene if the communities are large and have a political advantage. In that case use the land for a project that is specifically beneficial to the communities.				
B. Status of attitude of the authorities toward an area					
1. Officially accepted occupation	*This is a rare case* Handle carefully	*This is a possible case* Intervention is possible	*Highly feasible* Intervention is okay	*This is a rare case* Clarify or steer clear	*This is a possible case* Handle carefully
2. Implicitly accepted or rejected occupation	Analyse, evaluate with care; do not make any commitments, even verbally, without an official decision being made by authorities.				
3. Officially rejected occupation	Steer clear. If the communities concerned are large, analyse and evaluate so as to be in a position to react in the event of a change of status. In the meantime use the land for a project that is specifically beneficial to the community.				

1. Source: Adapted from Lyonnaise des Eaux (1998) (now Ondeo,Suez)

- acquisition of land for extension of water services to low-income settlements by the central or local government, i.e. the government pays the landowners and owns the land over the pubic water facilities.

Flexibility should be encouraged to explore which potential solution is the most appropriate in each case. The legal framework should support the preferred options for action. Such initiatives make it easier for utilities to work in unauthorized settlements and hence are likely to increase their willingness to work in those areas.

In most cases laying of water pipes through plots in informal settlements is likely to increase the value of the land, and therefore landowners should not require compensation payments. Disputes about the routes of new pipes can be addressed through negotiation and there should be a presumption against compensation payments. There are, however, likely to be some exceptional cases where some compensation payment would be reasonable. In such cases a streamlined arbitration system could facilitate speedy dispute resolution, so the progress of projects are not unduly delayed. Appropriate government policies and procedures are required to allow such a process to be introduced, together with adequate promotion of the new streamlined process amongst interested stakeholders.

Land tenure issues can be overcome, provided sufficient time is allowed for negotiations. Positive examples of this have occurred in cities around the world, including the brief case studies in Chapter 1. In some places, laying temporary mains has overcome objections.

Connection fees, procedures and costs

In many cases water mains are a considerable distance from houses in informal settlements, so new house or standpost connections are very difficult. In such cases there is a clear need for the utility to provide water mains closer to such areas, provided they think that there is sufficient demand for their services.

Even where public water mains are close to or within low-income areas there are many constraints to households obtaining a legal pipe connection. These relate to:

- the utility/municipal connection fee;

- costs of constructing the new household pipe connection; and

- the utility connection procedure (both formal and informal).

A high utility connection fee can act as an effective barrier to households entering the market for utility water, which will result in lost revenues for the utility. Many enlightened utilities have reduced their connection fee in recent years to encourage more connections. Utility costs associated with new connections can be recouped later through slightly higher water charges.

The high cost of constructing the pipe connection from the water main to the house or yard can also be an effective barrier to more connections. In Buenos Aires and Durban the utilities have explored ways of reducing these connection costs in poor areas, using such measures as encouraging residents to participate in the construction of the pipe connection, with successful results. Where government's and utilities have poverty reduction strategies, reducing connection costs for low-income areas through targeted subsidies can be an effective poverty reduction strategy as people will use more water and they can sell on to neighbours. This can lead to both economic and health benefits.

The formal utility connection procedures may seem logical on paper and may include aspects such as: taking the land title deeds to the utility office, arranging for the utility surveyor to visit the site, commissioning approved construction drawings, followed by site inspections. But poor households can find such a process particularly onerous when it involves many visits to utility offices. There may also be 'informal' aspects to such a procedure, for example payments to utility staff for transport to visit the site. Utilities can therefore seek to streamline procedures to make it easier to connect. In low-income areas the utility can also go to potential customers to encourage them to connect, reducing the need for people to visit their offices, through specific projects for informal settlements.

Staff attitudes to serving informal settlements

Some typical statements that are made in relation to why informal settlements are left without utility-provided services include:

'the poor can't pay'

'they (the poor) are looked after by donors and NGOs'

'we (the utility) are only just managing to serve the rest of the city without supplying people who are living on land illegally'

At worse some utilities simply do not recognize informal settlements as a customer base. But the expected percentage of people living in unplanned or informal settlements is likely to increase over the coming years to 40 to 60 per cent of the population in many cities, so this issue should not be ignored. Such government/utility staff attitudes can be influenced by disseminating and discussing the implications of government poverty reduction strategies and exposing such staff to best practice in serving the poor from elsewhere.

The challenge for utilities and governments is to change the assumptions that exist about informal settlements and their potential for revenue. This means recognizing the scope for growth in these areas and devising simple and achievable methods for capturing people's willingness to pay for services.

The 'spaghetti' problem

Where water mains are a long way away from housing areas, often a few households are able to afford to lay a long private water connection pipe to the mains, which may be more than 100 metres in length. Their neighbours may then wish to connect to this private pipe. Owners of these private connections are often not enthusiastic about allowing their neighbour's connections, because it will mean a reduction in the water pressure in their own taps. The pipe owners often exploit the neighbour by charging a high 'permission to connect' fee. Over a period of time more connections are made to these private pipes and a 'spaghetti' of small diameter and often leaking pipes emerges, may of which may be unauthorized. Supplies from such pipes are often inadequate or unreliable because they have not been properly designed and constructed.

This is common in many low-income areas in cities in Africa. The best solution to this problem is for the utility to lay new water mains of adequate capacity closer to and into these areas, replacing the 'spaghetti' pipes if necessary.

Culture of free or cheap water

In countries in Africa and South Asia where previous government regimes have promoted either free or cheap water to help the poor, there is often substantial resistance to raising tariffs to sustainable levels. Where tariffs are low there is generally insufficient resources and water to serve all consumer groups and the rich and powerful are generally allocated much of the scarce resources and water. This leads to the poor missing out in the allocation of investments and piped water, so the very people who are supposed to benefit from the low tariff policy (i.e. the poor), suffer the most. In most countries charging adequate tariff levels is the only way to generate sufficient revenues to invest in expanding services to unserved areas.

Chapter 7 describes a process of determining sustainable tariff levels and cross subsidies that is rational and equitable.

Differing priorities for men and women

In poor areas it is usually the responsibility of women to collect water, so they have a clear vested interest in the provision of improved water services closer to their homes, whereas men may not be willing to spend some of their limited income on new piped water sources. It is therefore important to engage both men and women's groups on projects when discussing the benefits of new water service options and seeking their participation.

Having considering common barriers to serving informal settlements and related potential solutions, we move on to consider positive strategies for selling improved water services and serving such areas.

4.3   Utility projects for serving low-income areas

Utilities often have limited water services in informal settlements. Typical services that they do provide include a few water kiosks/standposts and in some cases temporary solutions such as water tankers may be provided. If a substantial improvement in service levels is to be achieved through actions such as increasing the number of active house or yard connections with on-selling to neighbours, then specific initiatives need to be developed and implemented. Potentially worthwhile investments and targeted subsidies for serving the poor are likely to include:

- extending water mains closer to and in to informal settlements;

- paying for and supporting special participatory projects, with both substantial hardware and software components, for providing more piped water connections in informal settlements;

- subsidizing both the connection fee and connection costs in defined low-income areas;

- allowing people who sell on water to low-income consumers to pay for all their water on the lowest block on the tariff structure in defined areas; and

- improving performance measurement of user perceptions and utility services in low-income areas, in order to track service improvements. This is discussed further in Chapter 6.

By selling more water by providing an increased number of yard or house connections there are good opportunities for the operator's running costs to be met from water sales in those areas.

The process of becoming involved with potential customers in their own environment will involve skills, knowledge and experience that the utility may not have. This need not be a prohibiting factor as a number of options exist to bring such attributes in to the utility. For example collaboration can be explored with local NGOs, civil society groups and social development specialists in universities and so on. Such collaboration has value added benefits for all stakeholders and contributes to the development, expertise and breadth of knowledge of existing utility staff. Investment in informal settlements requires time and commitment. Utilities may consider the setting up of an inter-disciplinary team or an inter-departmental unit within the utility that can focus solely on services for informal settlements. This has been done in the Lusaka Water Company and in municipal corporations in India.

The next sections demonstrate how partnerships with NGOs, local civil society groups, large and small-scale private sector groups, water vendors, etc. can draw on an improved understanding of the communities existing and preferred services and payment regimes. New management regimes become the tools - or the means - to ensure that improved, sustainable services are sold successfully to low-income groups. Integrated within the new management regimes should be a range of policies and mechanisms to ensure that all stakeholders involved in the management and supply of improved water supplies have the appropriate incentives to serve the poor.

4.4 Partners for improving services to the poor

There are usually a number of stakeholders already working in slums or unplanned areas, such as local government, NGOs, CBOs, small water enterprises, etc. A key question for a utility is how could they best work with such organizations, taking advantage of their particular strengths to improve services. Utilities tend not to have staff with the right skills to work in informal settlements and with participatory approaches, etc., so working with other sector stakeholders is a sensible strategy.

Potential partners
Local authorities

Municipal officials often interact with local communities when dealing with a variety of services. In some cases municipal officers may have some responsibilities for improving sanitation or even water services in their area of jurisdiction. Local authorities will also usually have established structures for mobilizing communities.

Local authorities may, in conjunction with the water utilities, also act as regulators of water vendors and other delegated enterprises, particularly if the municipality has a clear environmental health responsibility which relates to issues of water quality and sanitation. Municipalities dealing with the promotion of on-plot sanitation are also important partners for utilities who are contemplating extending service options such as sewerage and disposal facilities for suction trucks.

Small water enterprises or vendors

These are individual people or groups who collect and sell water to households or other establishments in poorly served areas. Small water enterprises or small-scale providers have a number of positive impacts, including those listed in Box 4.2.

Examples of the different types of small water enterprises (SWEs) or small-scale providers and the countries where they are used are listed in Table 4.2 Some SWEs are licensed while others are not.

It may be beneficial for the utility or municipality to assist in forming an association of SWEs in a city, or at least to collaborate with SWE groups, because it will be useful to:

- share experiences about service provision in poorly served areas and how they may be improved;

- explore how to remove constraints to their operations, such as legal recognition;

- provide a forum to consider how the utility could support SWEs in providing improved services (such as providing convenient water collection points for SWEs or vendors

Box 4.2. Success factors of small-scale independent providers (SSIPs)[1]

Small service providers make a difference

Studies conducted in the four East African cities of Dar Es Salaam, Kampala, Mombasa and Nairobi in 1998 and 1999 listed the following success factors of small-scale independent providers (SSIP) in the water supply and sanitation services:

- Monopolistic public enterprises are often unable to respond to the dynamics of market demand.
- SSIP can access peri-urban areas not covered by the public enterprise.
- SSIP are commercially oriented.
- SSIP respond to the needs of the market by accessing high population density communities through the provision of standpipes and water kiosks.
- SSIP operate other businesses in addition to the provision of urban environmental services.

1. Source: World Bank (2000).

Table 4.2. Examples of small water enterprises[1]

Type of small water enterprises	Examples of countries where used
Water trucks Sell water to distributing vendors or direct to consumers	Haiti, Mauritania, Tanzania and Uganda
Animal-drawn carts Vendors selling water to consumers or water carriers from donkey, camel or horse-pulled carts	Senegal, Mali, Mauritania
Water kiosk or standpipe vendors Engaged by utility, community or private owners to sell water to consumers	Kenya, Senegal, Uganda and Tanzania
Handcarts Selling water direct to consumers at or near their homes	Indonesia, Kenya, Vietnam, Burkina Faso
Water carriers by hand or cycles They sell water directly to consumers at or near their homes	Mali, Haiti, Uganda and India
Private boreholes May be connected to standpipes or house connections	Kenya and Mauritania
Small private pipe networks	Benin, Philippines, Guinea and Mali
On-selling to neighbours May be from yard taps or flexible pipe from neighbour's house	Kenya, Cote d'Ivoire, India, Uganda

1. Source: Derived from Collignon and Vezina (2000) and Lyonnaise des Eaux (1998)

who sell on water), particularly in areas where the utility is unable to serve for some time; and

- provide a forum for the utility/municipality to explore how SWEs could support utility initiatives for serving areas that do not have water mains.

Utilities or government should not, however, try to organize the informal sector.

Community-based organizations (CBOs)

To compensate for the limited capacities of municipalities and other public sector service providers in many low-income countries, civil society are forming community-based associations organized alongside various activities, such as micro-credit schemes, water and sanitation, health, church, youth, women, or neighbourhood security associations. Many of these associations are interested in getting involved in determining the community's destiny in terms of major public services such as water, education, and health. CBOs can be effective partners in shared management arrangements for water services such as those discussed in the Kibera case study summarized in Box 4.3.

Box 4.3. Co-operative management of water distribution in Kibera, Nairobi

Kibera is one of the largest informal settlements in Africa, with a population of about 500,000 people and an estimated population density of 2,000 people per hectare. According to a survey conducted by the Water and Sanitation Program in Nairobi in Laini Saba, one of the nine villages in Kibera, the residents consider sanitation and water supply to be the most crucial problems they face.

In response to the water supply problems in the area, Ushirika, a community-based organization in Laini Saba, created a partnership with a local NGO, Maji Ufanisi, to extend piped water services to the area. Maji Ufanisi provided materials and technical expertise, while the local community arranged for labour to lay the pipeline and construct the water kiosks. In collaboration with Nairobi City Council (the water utility), a new distribution pipeline was extended to Laini Saba, which was commissioned in 1998.

A bulk flow meter was installed on the main distribution network where the Ushirika pipe connected, and the Ushirika Co-operative Water Society are issued water bills on the basis of the bulk meter readings. A management committee was set up to manage the water project on behalf of Ushirika. Consumers pay for the water by volume at the new water kiosks. The tariff is higher than the bulk cost price charged by Nairobi City Council but less than other local vendors' prices. Ushirika hire staff to sell the water at KSh2 per jerrican. These staff are paid a proportion of the money they collect according to the water meter at the kiosk. The surplus funds are then invested in other projects funded by Ushirika in Kibera

---

The Kibera case in Box 4.3 provides a good example of collaboration and partnership between a CBO, an NGO and the water utility.

Water management committees

These committees are often set up during development projects to ensure sustainability through community management. The committee members could be elected by a ward council to manage water services in their area. These organizations can be useful partners if they are active and are considered reasonably representative of their community.

Non-government organizations (NGOs) and university departments

The process of becoming involved with potential customers in their own environment in informal settlements involves skills, knowledge and experience that the utility may not have. This need not be a prohibiting factor as a number of options exist to bring such attributes into the utility. For example, collaboration can be explored with local NGOs, civil society groups and social development specialists in universities. NGOs usually deal with a number of problems of concern to the community such as water, sanitation, income generation, solid waste management, etc. These organizations typically have good skills in facilitation, negotiation, and participatory planning which could be used by utilities intending to work in informal settlements.

Private consultancy companies

A wide range of consultancy companies are becoming more common in developing countries, and they are often able to offer expertise in working with community-based organizations, fulfilling similar roles to NGOs. They may also be able to provide technical expertise. People who have gained experience with either NGOs or the public sector may move on to work as private consultants.

Developing partnerships to serve low-income areas

It would be beneficial for utilities and concerned government departments to consider the merits of either collaborating with or contracting organizations such as those listed above to undertake defined roles in improving services in low-income areas. This can be a way of using the particular skills and comparative advantage of each type of organization for the benefit of people living in low-income settlements.

Establishing formal and informal partnerships between the utility and these various sector stakeholders, can enable effective collaboration, shared understanding and synergy between the different actors. Useful publications on partnerships such as Contracting NGOs are contained on the Building Partnerships for Development (BPD) web-site: www.bpd-waterandsanitation.org. By encouraging such partnerships and developing capacity the various stakeholders will have more incentives to develop joint initiatives for improving service in low-income areas.

4.5   Incentives and policies for serving the poor

Policy level initiatives

In order to improve water services in low-income communities, there is a need to have institutional and technical innovations at different levels. A key to encouraging innovations, partnerships and positive action on the ground is to create the right incentives and policies for the key stakeholders. These can be provided by both government and utilities.

At the policymaking level, there should be incentives, disincentives and supporting pro-poor policies. Examples of incentive mechanisms and supportive policies include:

- clear government policies promoting 'universal service obligations' as a primary duty and setting yearly targets for service improvements to all consumer groups, which will form the basis of monitoring progress;

- performance agreements between governments or regulators and the utilities that incorporate service improvements against agreed targets in a financially sustainable manner;

- revised mission statements that reflect improved services to all consumer groups in a financially sustainable manner;

- well-designed performance measurement arrangements that use a variety of consumer survey techniques to produce reliable data against key indicators. It should be possible to disaggregate data for individual low-income areas in order to properly plan, monitor and evaluate service improvements;

- benchmarking programmes using appropriate indicators that enable fair comparisons between utilities;

- more flexibility on human resource management issues such as appointments and staff remuneration;

- more flexible service provision standards or norms that allow more innovative service options that specifically meet the needs of low-income areas at affordable prices;

- appropriate use of private operators (national and international) with PPP contracts that have incentives for serving the poor;

- ensuring that small water enterprises and community-based organizations have the legal right to operate and manage services in low-income areas; and

- well-designed regulatory arrangements that promote improved transparency and accountability in decision-making.

For further guidance on incentives for serving the poor in PPP contracts, refer to WSP & PPIAF's publication: *New designs for water and sanitation transactions - Making private sector participation work for the poor* (2002).[put in refs] This document provides clear guidance for the various forms of PPP contracts.

Extracts from the performance contract between the Government of Uganda and the National Water and Sewerage Corporation (2000) are set out in Box 4.4. Note that there is a clear policy for serving the poor (100 per cent coverage) and an incentive in the form of potential subsidies from the GoU for 'social mission' work. But the overriding policy of financial viability and creditworthiness for NWSC is clear and justified; otherwise the utility will not be able to raise sufficient funds for sustainable service provision.

Box 4.4. Performance contract for the NWSC water utility in Uganda

Selected provisions from the performance contract between the Government of Uganda and the National Water and Sewerage Corporation (2000) are as follows:

- **Supply/customer service objective:** The original objective of the GoU national water policy was to extend the use of safe water supplies to 100 per cent of the population. It is generally expected to achieve this aim in 10 to 15 years from the present situation of 50 per cent coverage.

- **Financial objective:** It is accepted by both parties to this contract that the achievement of a financially viable and credit worthy NWSC is the overriding objective.

If investments are a 'social mission' imposed by GoU on NWSC, then the internal rate of return of the investment must be determined in order to calculate the necessary GoU subsidy, to prevent the investment being a burden to NWSC.

Potential utility initiatives and incentives for serving the poor

The service provider (utility), whether it is private or public or a combination of both, can provide incentives for low-income consumer groups and individual households. Examples of incentive mechanisms for these groups include:

- low connection fees for pipe connections in poorer communities. The processing of new connections could be done with the help of community leaders and CBOs to ensure that the subsidy reaches the people for whom it is intended;

- lower tariff levels for less convenient service options such as standposts, kiosks, shared connections, etc.;

- the provision of materials for water connection in low-income settlements at subsidized prices and/or provision for payment in instalments;

- the opening of utility liaison points in low-income settlements to provide services such as payment points, bill dispatch and technical/billing enquires;

- investment into research in innovative options, such as local water storage arrangements, suitable for serving low-income settlements;

- encouragment of local community-based labour during the process of connecting services in low-income settlements. This offer will not only reduce the costs of connections, but will also create employment for some members of the community; and

- the offer of more flexible payment options that suit the needs of low-income consumers, such as group connections and community-managed water kiosks with regulated prices.

Examples of incentives offered to people using ground tanks in poorer communities in Durban are included in Box 4.5.

Box 4.5. Incentives offered by Durban Metro Water to ground tank users

Durban Metro Water & Waste of South Africa offers the following incentives to members of low-income communities who apply for a ground tank:

- The connection fee for the ground tank is about six times smaller than that for a conventional full-pressure system.

- Unlike users of conventional water supply systems, ground tank owners are not charged a deposit for security.

- The cost of materials is paid for in six-monthly installations.

- Local private plumbers are trained at the Durban Metro Water Services Training School, and were engaged in making water service connections in the low-income settlements.

- A community liaison officer is employed to handle issues connected with service delivery to low-income settlements.

More examples of initiatives for improving incentive mechanisms and policies to support service providers and other stakeholders in serving the poor are set out in Book 1 on guidance for government's enabling role.

4.6   Piloting and scaling up

It is beneficial to pilot marketing approaches in a few low-income areas or informal settlements in order to learn lessons that are specific to the local context, with a view to scaling up the more successful approaches to larger areas. Governments who have poverty reduction policies will be pleased to see utilities actively piloting new approaches for serving the poor. In some cases further piloting may be necessary before scaling up.

If different service, payment and management options are to be provided on a reliable and sustainable basis to different market segments, then a strategic marketing approach is recommended. This is the subject of Part III of this publication.

More specific guidance on how to target, sell and provide services is provided in Part III; particularly in Chapters 7 and 8, on *Where do we want to be* and *How might we get there*, such as Section 8.2 on the 7Ps (the marketing mix).

Part III Strategic marketing for all consumers

The art of 'strategic planning' is to know where you want to be in the longer term and what you want to achieve. The underlying presumption of this research is that the goal is to achieve financially sustainable universal service, that is to ensure service to the poor. Anything less than universal service and it is always the poor who are left out.

There are a number of reasons why, after initial piloting work to develop the best tactics for serving the poor, marketing plans for urban water services need to be reasonably strategic and comprehensive, including the following:

- Utilities need to feel confident that if they offer new options and services, then they can provide them on a sustainable and reliable basis. Comprehensive investment/strategic marketing planning can increasingly contribute to this level of confidence, particularly when potential financiers agree to fund agreed investment plans.

- Precedence and equity are also important considerations. If one slum area has new service options, there will eventually be a lot of pressure to serve other slums in a similar way, so broader strategic planning is required.

- The proportion of urban residents living in informal settlements or unplanned areas is growing, hence the need to address the perception, needs and preferences of this important group in utility-wide investment planning and institutional development.

Part III consists of the following four chapters that provide the framework for the strategic marketing approach:

- Chapter 5: What is a good strategic marketing approach

- Chapter 6: Stage 1: Where are we now?

- Chapter 7: Stage 2: Where do we want to be?

- Chapter 8: Stage 3: How might we get there?

Chapter 5

What is a good strategic marketing process?

The examples given so far indicate how the demand-responsive marketing approach can be used to pilot water (and possibly sanitation) services to low-income consumers by using an innovative, creative, participatory approach. To ensure that this type of approach can be replicated across all low-income areas in a city in a way that is sustainable in the long term requires a strategic marketing approach. What can be made to work with special effort, perhaps supported by international donors, in a few low-income areas in a city, can have a different impact on a utility's operations when it has to be scaled up across the entire city, particularly when up to 70 per cent of the population may be living in the informal, low-income housing areas.

5.1   Overview

Typical key activities in the strategic marketing process for urban water services are set out in Figures 5.1 (Part A) and 5.2 (Part B). The main stages ask the questions:

- *Where are we now?*

- *Where do we want to be?*

- *How might we get there?*

- *How do we ensure success?*

Note that in these figures there are double arrows between each stage, which emphasizes that this is an iterative process, where it may be necessary to go back one or two stages at certain times.

Strategic planning logically precedes marketing planning by providing a framework within which marketing plans can be formulated (Wilson and Gilligan, 1997). An appropriate strategic marketing process is that which leads to the production of a strategic marketing plan (SMP) or detailed investment plan that is acceptable to all stakeholders.

In this study, with its focus on serving the poor, we have set out in Part II to demonstrate the viability of pricing and service differentiation to serve the poor, particularly in informal housing areas, before considering the necessary strategic planning. From our experience and research we believe that this might have to be the necessary approach, that is to demonstrate that it is possible to serve the poor effectively before considering an integrated methodology for scaling up, city-wide and long term.

This approach is made more possible in the average utility due to the availability of 'surplus water' that is lost through leakage, illegal connections and other means. Water saved through activities such as leak reduction programmes can be directed towards immediate service improvement to the poor. There does not usually have to be any parallel delivery of new water sources and treatment in order to demonstrate the viability of delivery to informal areas because of the extent of non-revenue water, which can be as high as 50-60 per cent. Indeed, the apparent reason for one water utility to serve the unplanned areas around their city was the embarrassment of surplus water achieved through a leakage reduction programme. They needed to do something with it and recognized the ready market on their doorstep (Nickson, 2001).

Having successfully undertaken the pilot projects, and having begun to control unaccounted for water, understanding the strategic situation confronting an organization is an essential starting point in developing a marketing strategy. This understanding can be derived from an assessment of:

- organizational capabilities;

- threats from environmental forces;

- competitors' strengths and weaknesses; and

- consumer needs.

Source: Wilson and Gilligan (1997)

These key areas are captured in the more specifically defined activities in Figure 5.1 and Figure 5.2. This strategic marketing process can potentially be used to determine plans that are comprehensive and viable for all substantial investments in the urban water sector that are dependent on consumer demand.

5.2 Strategic marketing plans

Planning is an activity or a process in business that provides a systematic structure and framework for considering the future, appraising options and opportunities, and then selecting and implementing the necessary activities for achieving the stated objectives efficiently and effectively.

In the context of the water sector in developing countries, the strategic marketing plan (SMP), or business plan, is a framework for the sustainable improvement of water services and mainstreaming of poverty reduction in the utility's business. A good strategic marketing plan (SMP) shows how the utility can improve services to customers and potential customers and at the same time be financially sustainable.

The strategic marketing plan provides a clear and unambiguous statement concerning what strategies and actions will be implemented, by whom, when, and with what outcomes (Brassington and Pettitt, 2000). The SMP will usually be based on reasonably accurate information about the current status of the utility (Where are we now?), the specific objectives and investment proposals of the utility (Where do we want to be?) and the activities necessary to achieve the utility's objectives (How might we get there?). These questions can form a natural structure for an SMP report. However, a utility needs to be mindful of the preferred report formats of potential financiers.

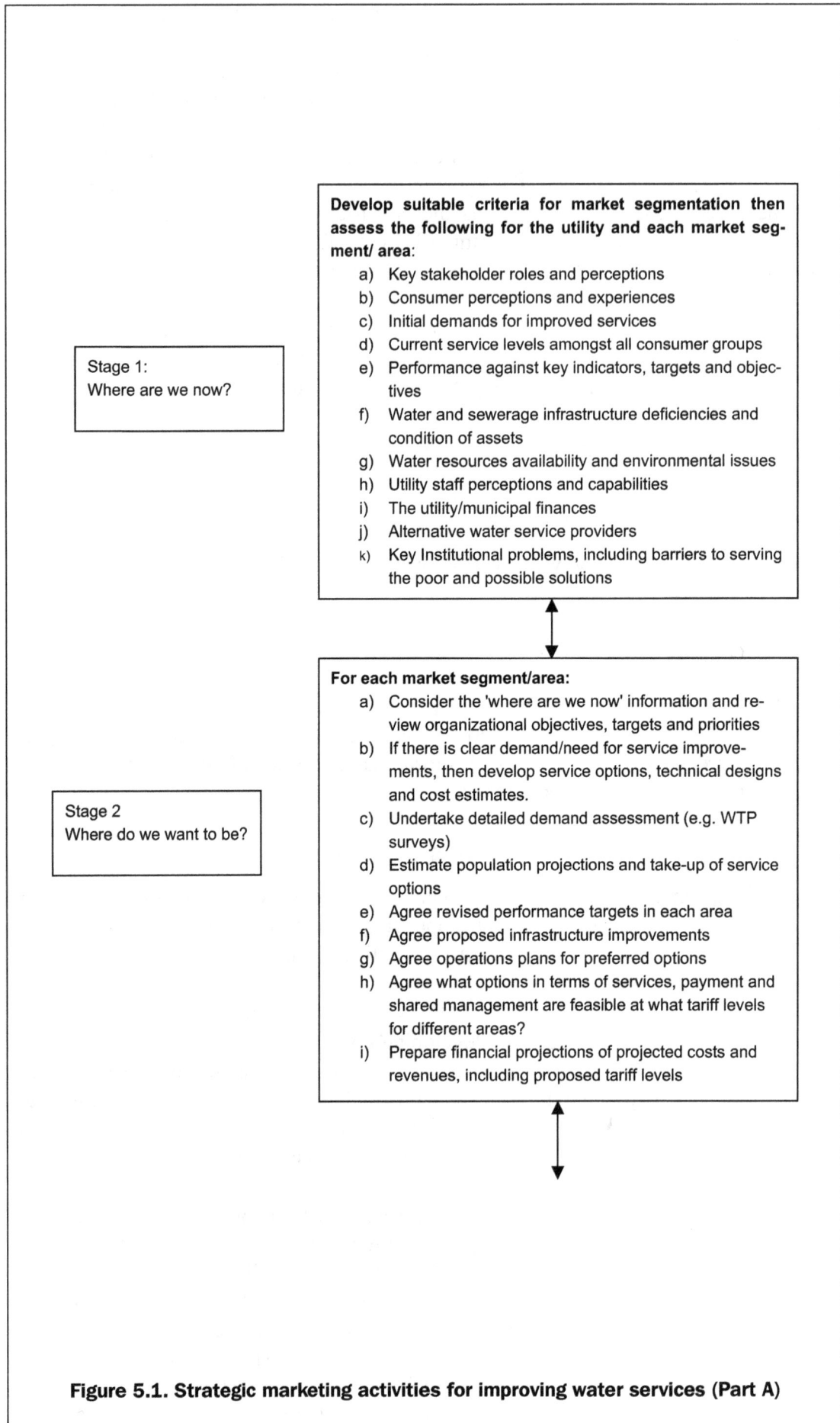

<table>
<tr>
<td>

Stage 1:
Where are we now?

</td>
<td>

Develop suitable criteria for market segmentation then assess the following for the utility and each market segment/ area:

a) Key stakeholder roles and perceptions
b) Consumer perceptions and experiences
c) Initial demands for improved services
d) Current service levels amongst all consumer groups
e) Performance against key indicators, targets and objectives
f) Water and sewerage infrastructure deficiencies and condition of assets
g) Water resources availability and environmental issues
h) Utility staff perceptions and capabilities
i) The utility/municipal finances
j) Alternative water service providers
k) Key Institutional problems, including barriers to serving the poor and possible solutions

</td>
</tr>
<tr>
<td>

Stage 2
Where do we want to be?

</td>
<td>

For each market segment/area:

a) Consider the 'where are we now' information and review organizational objectives, targets and priorities
b) If there is clear demand/need for service improvements, then develop service options, technical designs and cost estimates.
c) Undertake detailed demand assessment (e.g. WTP surveys)
d) Estimate population projections and take-up of service options
e) Agree revised performance targets in each area
f) Agree proposed infrastructure improvements
g) Agree operations plans for preferred options
h) Agree what options in terms of services, payment and shared management are feasible at what tariff levels for different areas?
i) Prepare financial projections of projected costs and revenues, including proposed tariff levels

</td>
</tr>
</table>

Figure 5.1. Strategic marketing activities for improving water services (Part A)

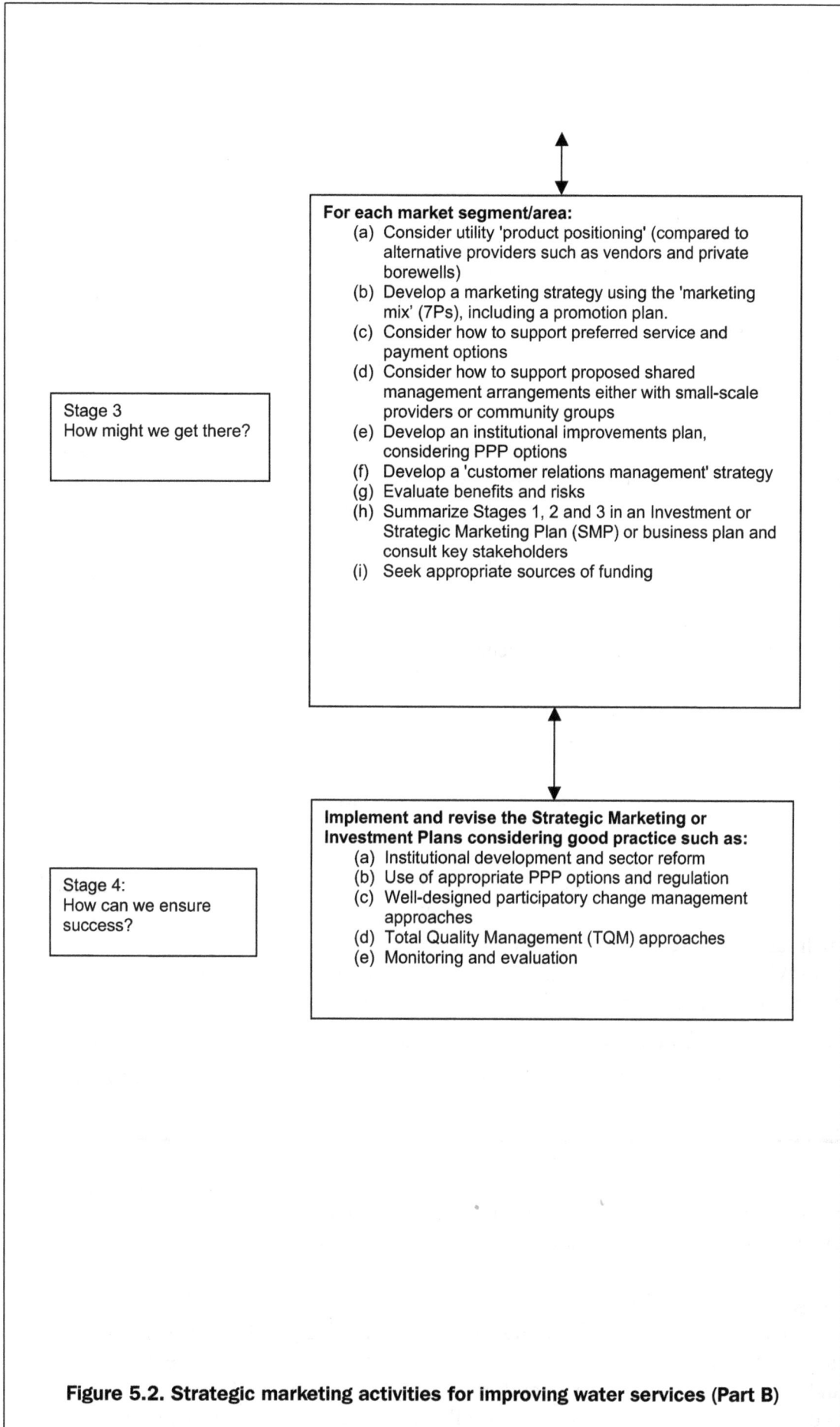

Stage 3
How might we get there?

For each market segment/area:
  (a) Consider utility 'product positioning' (compared to alternative providers such as vendors and private borewells)
  (b) Develop a marketing strategy using the 'marketing mix' (7Ps), including a promotion plan.
  (c) Consider how to support preferred service and payment options
  (d) Consider how to support proposed shared management arrangements either with small-scale providers or community groups
  (e) Develop an institutional improvements plan, considering PPP options
  (f) Develop a 'customer relations management' strategy
  (g) Evaluate benefits and risks
  (h) Summarize Stages 1, 2 and 3 in an Investment or Strategic Marketing Plan (SMP) or business plan and consult key stakeholders
  (i) Seek appropriate sources of funding

Stage 4:
How can we ensure success?

Implement and revise the Strategic Marketing or Investment Plans considering good practice such as:
  (a) Institutional development and sector reform
  (b) Use of appropriate PPP options and regulation
  (c) Well-designed participatory change management approaches
  (d) Total Quality Management (TQM) approaches
  (e) Monitoring and evaluation

Figure 5.2. Strategic marketing activities for improving water services (Part B)

It may be tempting for utility managers to complete each of the four stages of strategic marketing in very broad terms. For example at the end of the 'Where do we want to be?' stage, if the final output is just a statement of the utility's objectives, then the strategic marketing plan and process will be of only limited benefit.

This exercise is much more useful if at the end of the 'Where do we want to be?' phase there is a draft strategic marketing or business plan that includes financial projections of future costs and revenues, based on a thorough analysis of the factors listed in Stage 1. This is a key finding of research in Africa and India conducted by the research partners involved in this publication. The key elements of each stage are described below.

It is important that an element of realism is used in the planning process, as unrealistic plans tend to get ignored. In addition, it is beneficial to involve as many staff and key stakeholders in the planning process as is feasible, in a participatory manner, as this is likely to lead to better commitment at the implementation stage. Developing a shared understanding and agreement about the plans being developed can be done through small group consultations, meetings and workshops. Useful references for how to make workshops more effective is *Participatory Workshops* by Robert Chambers, 2002. and *the Participatory Learning and Action Trainer's Guide* (Jules Pretty, Ian Scoones, Irene Guijt and John Thompson, IIED London 1995)

The overall extent to which the organization is customer and commercially orientated will have a significant impact on the successful implementation of a marketing strategy.

Stage 1 - Where are we now?

It is important for an organization to objectively establish its current position. Information on 'Where are we now?' can be obtained by carrying out institutional analysis of the utility, including an assessment of the utility's existing water supply infrastructure and services.

Comprehensive consumer surveys provide a means of assessing customers' perceptions of the water utility and its services. Such studies provide useful information on the market, such as the perceptions and preferences of existing and potential customers for improvements in services. This can be done as part of a comprehensive performance measurement programme which is discussed in Chapter 6.

> Where possible, information should be based on quantitative measures using appropriate indicators - *if you cannot measure it, you cannot manage it!*

Tools such as PEST analysis (political, environmental, social and technological) and SWOT analysis (strengths, weaknesses, opportunities and threats) are useful in understanding and summarizing the institution's environment and performance.

Stage 2 - Where do we want to be?

Decisions on where the utility wants to be, in terms of targets for future investments and targets for improved performance, are best made considering the requirements of existing and potential customers. It is therefore necessary to review and agree utility objectives and targets in the light of information collected at the *'Where are we now?'* stage.

For the average utility the investment and revenue implications of achieving universal water supply might be very different from achieving universal sewerage coverage. Service options therefore have to be considered (for respective market segments) and pricing policies agreed. These should be based on reasonable projections of costs and necessary tariffs, while ensuring that the utility achieves financial sustainability at the proposed tariffs. Part of the process of selecting feasible options and determining tariffs is to ensure that the views of consumers have been taken into account, whether through customer committees, NGO representation or information derived from customer surveys and willingness to pay studies.

Projections of costs for improvements and the revenue that the utility can obtain from improvements in water services should also be carefully made. In particular, the projections should show how the utility can improve water services to existing and potential customers and achieve financial sustainability. Estimates for option take-up will therefore need to be made, and spreadsheet calculations undertaken to project future revenues.

The potential revenues are then compared with projected costs to check for financial sustainability. This is an iterative activity that may have to be carried out several times until an acceptable combination of service options, costs and prices is achieved, bearing in mind the consumers willingness to pay. When an acceptable combination is achieved, the utility should then move to the next stage of 'How might we get there?'. There may of course be more than one viable investment scenario in the financial projections, all of which might require further assessment.

The goal of financial sustainability, a return on capital invested, will place a heavy burden on customers who may have been used to receiving subsidized water (though it may deliver a dramatic reduction in prices to the poorest who have been purchasing water from vendors). This higher price burden is only fair if the water utility also bears its share through delivering services in the most efficient manner. 'Where do we want to be?' must also be answered in terms of a 'least cost provider.'

Stage 3 - How might we get there?

The financial projections for new investment programmes and the most viable investment scenarios (developed in the previous stage) need to be assessed after consideration of the marketing and institutional issues, in order to develop the final strategic marketing plan, or investment plan. It is advisable to assess the potential risks and benefits of the preferred SMP.

The development of a viable marketing strategy, perhaps using the 7Ps (product, price, promotion, place, people, process and presence) is important, as are the development of institutional development proposals, including Public-Private Partnership options.

Full consultation of the preferred strategic marketing plan among key stakeholders will assist in achieving a realistic plan and will help gain commitment. Negotiations with potential financiers are advisable, whether they be donors, banks or private operators seeking PPP arrangements. This is particularly important during the 'How might we get there?' stage, so that project proposals can be prepared in the preferred format of interested funding organizations.

Stage 4 - How do we ensure success?

The outputs from Stage 4 *(How do we ensure success?)*, will be the successful implementation of activities that have been planned in Stages 2 and 3, making any required changes to the plans in the light of experience. This publication focuses more on the first three (planning) stages. For guidance on dealing with Stage 4 we recommend publications on marketing, Public-Private Partnerships, institutional development and change management, Total Quality Management (TQM), and other conventional business manuals.

Chapter 6

Stage 1: 'Where are we now'?

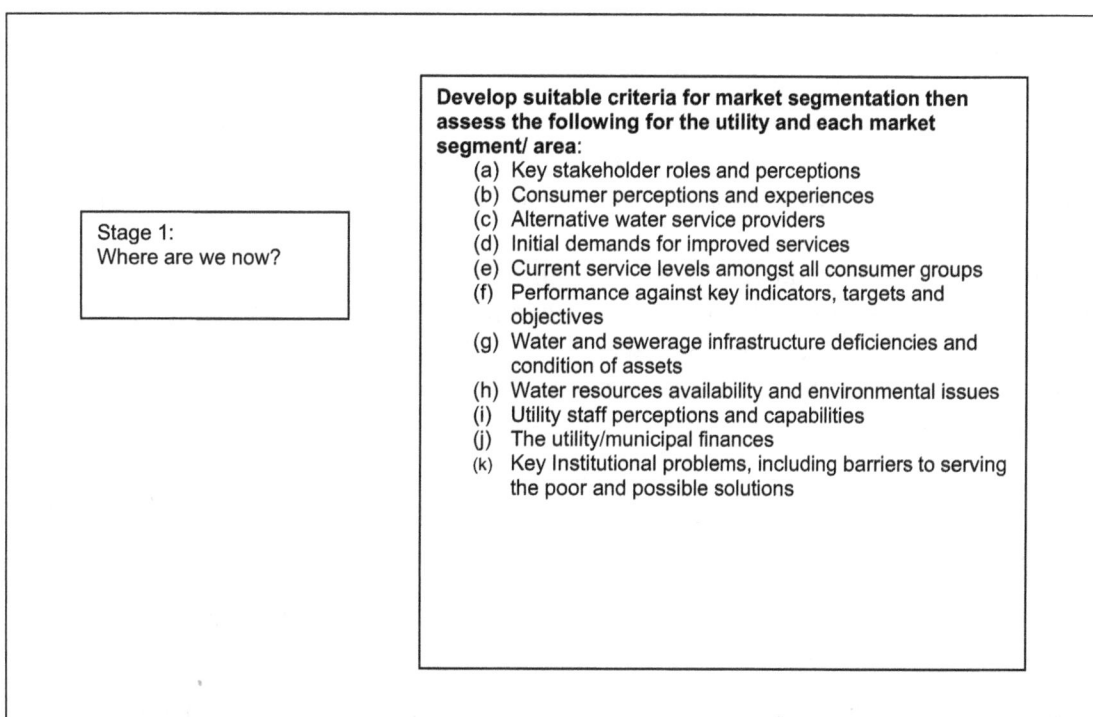

```
┌─────────────────────────────────────────────────────────────────────┐
│                                                                       │
│                              ┌───────────────────────────────────────┐│
│                              │ Develop suitable criteria for market   ││
│                              │ segmentation then assess the following ││
│                              │ for the utility and each market        ││
│                              │ segment/ area:                         ││
│    ┌──────────────────┐      │  (a) Key stakeholder roles and         ││
│    │ Stage 1:         │      │      perceptions                       ││
│    │ Where are we now?│      │  (b) Consumer perceptions and          ││
│    │                  │      │      experiences                       ││
│    └──────────────────┘      │  (c) Alternative water service         ││
│                              │      providers                         ││
│                              │  (d) Initial demands for improved      ││
│                              │      services                          ││
│                              │  (e) Current service levels amongst    ││
│                              │      all consumer groups               ││
│                              │  (f) Performance against key           ││
│                              │      indicators, targets and objectives││
│                              │  (g) Water and sewerage infrastructure ││
│                              │      deficiencies and condition of     ││
│                              │      assets                            ││
│                              │  (h) Water resources availability and  ││
│                              │      environmental issues              ││
│                              │  (i) Utility staff perceptions and     ││
│                              │      capabilities                      ││
│                              │  (j) The utility/municipal finances    ││
│                              │  (k) Key Institutional problems,       ││
│                              │      including barriers to serving the ││
│                              │      poor and possible solutions       ││
│                              └───────────────────────────────────────┘│
│                                                                       │
└───────────────────────────────────────────────────────────────────────┘
```

The typical key aspects to be examined (listed above) and that are necessary for a utility/ municipality to satisfactorily answer the question 'Where are we now' can be assessed using consumer surveys, institutional appraisal and infrastructure surveys. The adequacy of infrastructure can be assessed based on what additional infrastructure is required to meet agreed and realistic performance targets for each area.

Some of the key issues that should be examined as part of a situation analysis - and the main institutional appraisal techniques that are commonly used - are discussed in the following sections. The appraisal process should seek to integrate technical, institutional, financial, economic and social issues to ensure a thorough analysis. Many of the issues listed in the box above are important for effective utility management, but not all issues are directly related to the subject of this publication - that is marketing approaches for the urban water sector. Hence issues such as water resource availability are not dealt with in this book.

A good situation analysis looking at the issues identified above has many benefits. It can provides good data and information for much of a utility's planning activities, leading to targeted interventions and appropriate solutions.

6.1   Key consumer data

Information from consumer surveys provides the most important data for a marketing study: the experiences and perceptions of the most valuable stakeholders - existing and potential customers. Table 6.1 shows performance against key indicators for each market segment from a consumer survey conducted in Mombasa in 1999.

The difference in service levels between the different market segments are very apparent from the above table. Such consumer survey information can be compared with the utility's own system performance data to check for any anomalies. Another method of presenting data is the piechart. Figure 6.1 shows a piechart for the average water supply hours each day that was included in the Mombasa strategic marketing plan.

Another example of data collected as part of a consumer survey in Guntur, India, is shown in Table 6.2. The widely differing means of household water storage for different market segments is very apparent. The poorer households in slums and unplanned areas are clearly more vulnerable in times of water shortages.

It is important to independently survey key information such as consumption per capita per day. If you ask those responsible for service delvery they are likely to provide estimates near to the agreed norms. Table 6.3 includes survey data on water consumption per day in Lesotho's districts. This information was obtained from a marketing analysis of the water and sewerage authority in Lesotho in 2001.

In terms of selecting which consumer survey data to include in utility reports, a number of factors need to be borne in mind, including:

- The purpose of the report - different reports may require different data sets to substantiate conclusions.

- Which sets of data can best represent the experiences, perceptions and coping strategies of different market segments or groups, as part of a report describing where the consumers are now. Sometimes a number of data sets or tables, graphs, etc. are required to convey a clear picture.

- Which sets of consumer survey data support the arguments for proposed investments or options most effectively?

Table 6.1. Mombasa summary of existing services in each market segment[1]

Selected parameter	Bungalows and maisonettes	Flats	1, 2 or 3-roomed dwellings and Swahili houses	Informal settlements (slums)
Electricity supply in dwelling	100%	97%	60%	6%
Do not receive water directly from NWCPC	35%	17%	58%	96%
Receive continuous supply of water from NWCPC	30%	31%	13%	2%
Receive water once or twice a day from NWCPC	27%	40%	24%	1%
Individual house connections	94%	78%	23%	2%
Shared connections	Nil	12%	28%	4%
No piped water connection	6%	10%	49%	94%
Pays NWCPC for water directly	70%	74%	36%	1%
Obtains free water from b/hole or well	5%	3%	39%	41%
Obtains water from handcart vendors	18%	45%	57%	46%
Obtains water from kiosks	Nil	22%	56%	79%
Proportion with own b/holes/wells	39%	Nil	2%	Nil
Monthly water bill	KSh1400	KSh500	KSh450	KSh425--741
People in household	6.81	5.52	6.31	5.44
Main water source	Individual house connections (59%) and own boreholes or wells (25%)	Individual house connections (71%) and shared connections (12%)	Water kiosks (44%) and shared connections (23%)	Water kiosks (70%) and boreholes or wells (18%)

1. Source: Njiru and Sansom (2000)

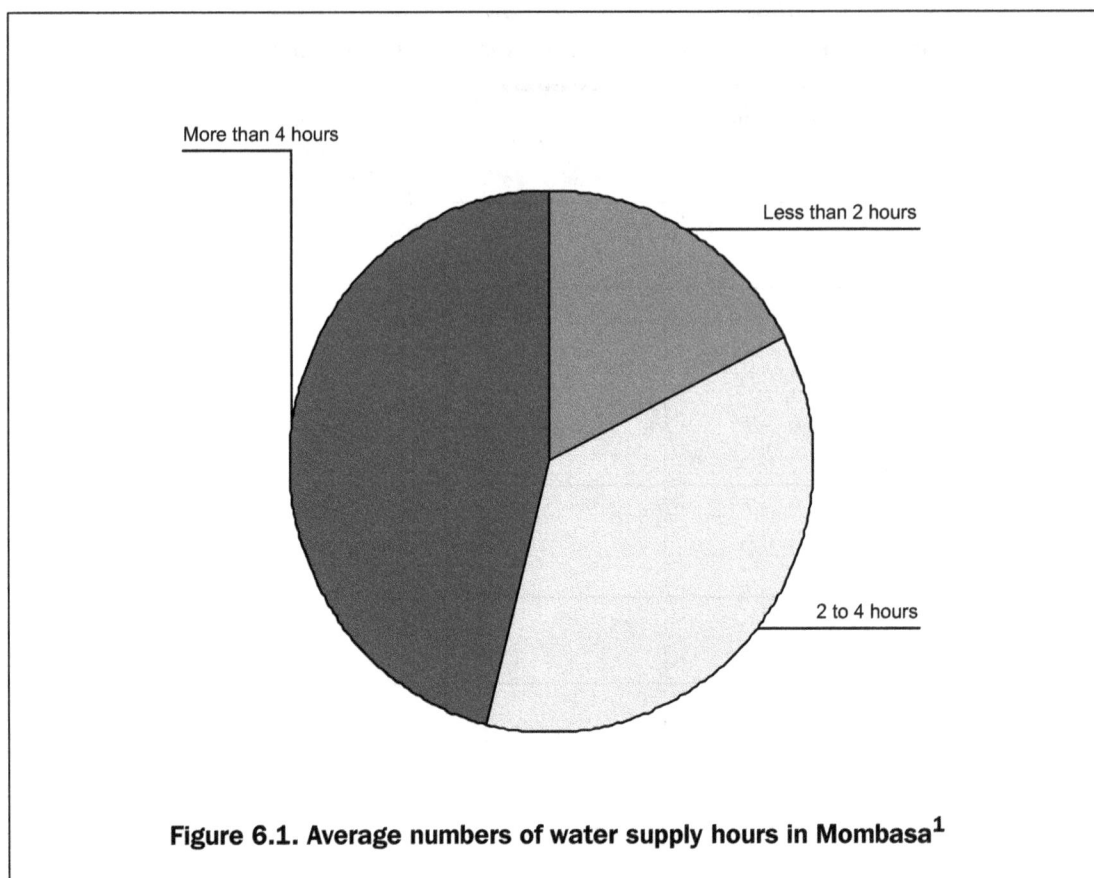

Figure 6.1. Average numbers of water supply hours in Mombasa[1]

1. Source: Njiru and Sansom (2000)

Table 6.2. Methods of water storage in Guntur, India[1]

Market segment		Percentage
Bungalows	Roof tank or ground tank or both	100
Independent houses in planned areas	Roof tank	80
Flats in planned areas	Roof tank or ground tank or both	100
Independent houses in unplanned areas	Small containers or buckets	47
Flats in unplanned areas	Roof tank or ground tank or both	97
Slums with some water supply coverage	Small containers or buckets	96
Slums with no water supply coverage	Small containers or buckets	100

1. Source: Narender and Chary (2002)

Table 6.3. Lesotho water cosumption per district[1]

District	No water	<7 litres/capita/day	7-30 litres/c/d	>30 litres/c/d
Butha-Buthe	2%	24%	42%	32%
Leribe	7%	23%	48%	22%
Berea	6%	19%	36%	39%
Maseru	4%	17%	44%	34%
Mafeteng	3%	28%	39%	30%
Mohale's Hoek	3%	23%	38%	36%
Quthing	1%	14%	57%	29%
Qacha's Nek	2%	2%	46%	51%
Mokhotlong	6%	9%	27%	58%
Thaab-Tseka	4%	35%	41%	20%
Total	**4%**	**19%**	**43%**	**35%**

1.   Source: Sechaba consultants (1996) cited in Kamalie (2001)

6.2 Perceptions and preferences of low-income groups

The PREPP methodology (mentioned in Section 2.9) provides a rapid and participatory method of assessing the perceptions and preferences of people living in informal settlements. Initial demand can be assessed with this methodology, using a costed option ranking approach. Table 6.4 shows the results of group and individual ranking of existing service options by women in five informal settlements in Guntur, India. Number 1 represents the highest rank. The preferred existing options were individual pipe connections followed by public standposts and tankers. The results for the men's group were similar. The unexpected high ranking for tankers in some areas would be worth further investigation.

Table 6.4. Guntur preferences for existing water options[1]

Existing options (women's preferences)	I K.B. Colony		II A.T. Agraharam		III Nallakunta		IV Anandpet		V Nallacheruvu	
	Group	Individual	Group	Individual	Group	Individual	Group	Individual	Group	Individual
Individual connections	-	-	1	3	1	4	-	-	1	-
Public standpost	-	-	2	2	3	4	1	-	2	7
Open well	-	-	5	-	-	-	-	-	6	-
Municipal water tanker	1	5	3	1	4	-	2	-	-	5
Fetching from public standpost in nearby slum	2	5	-	-	-	-	-	-	-	-
Public borewell (handpump)	4	-	4	-	-	-	3	-	3	-
Private vendors		-	-	-	5	-	-	-	5	-
On cycle		-	-	-	-	-	-	-	-	-
Water fetching		-	-	-	-	-	4	-	4	-
Rainwater	3	-	-	-	-	-	-	-	-	-
Pit tap	-	-	-	-	2	-	-	-	-	-

1. Source: Narender, Chary and Coates (2002)

Table 6.5 summarizes the results of group and individual rankings of proposed service options by women in six informal settlements in Guntur, India. Each of the proposed options that could be provided by the utility (Guntur Municipal Corporation) were given realistic costs by the facilitators during the option ranking process.

Table 6.5. Guntur preferences for proposed water options[1]

Proposed Options (omen)	I K.B. Colony		II A.T Agraharam		III Nallakunta		IV Anandpet		V Nallacheruvu		VI LR Colony	
	Group	Individual	Group	Individual	Group	Individual	Group	Individual	Group	Individual	Group	Individual
Community managed PSP	3	-	5	-	1	1	2	1		-	3	3
Shared connection	1		1	3	2	5	1	7	2	3	3	1
Individual connection*	2*		3	1	-		-	-	1	7	2	3
Ground tank connected to municipal line	-		2	-	-	-	-	-	-	-	-	-
Ground tank connected to bore well	-	-	-	-	-	-	-	-	-	-	-	4
Ground tank connected to water tanker	-	-	-	-	-	-	-	-	-	-	-	-
Ground tank connected to open well	-	-	-	-	-	-	-	-	-	-	-	-
Water kiosk (Municipal water)	-	-	4	-	3		-	-	-	3	-	-
Open wells	-	-	-	-	-		-	-	-	-	-	-

1. Source: Narender, Chary and Coates (2002)
   Note: *If connection fee is spread over instalments

The preferred option proposed is for shared or group connections, followed by community-managed public standposts and individual connections. This preference is probably motivated by the perceived affordability of the group connections and public standposts, compared to the individual connections.

By using a reasonably rapid demand assessment approach such as PREPP or a similar technique, a good picture emerges of intial demand in informal settlements and potentail service options for further investigation. Such data can contribute to answering the question 'Where are we now?' If necessary, more detailed demand assessment can then be carried out during the 'Where do we want to be' stage.

6.3   Alternative water service providers

Alternative water service providers or small water enterprises (SWEs) (as discussed in Section 4.4), often collectively have a substantial share of the water market in cities and towns in developing countries. It is therefore advisable for water utilities to analyse the alternative service providers in their areas of jurisdiction. The analysis will enable the utilities to make informed strategic decisions on how best to improve service provision. Some of the questions to be answered in the analysis are:

- Who are the major groups of alternative water service providers?

- What strategy are they pursuing, and how successful are they?

- What strengths and weakness do they possess in comparison with the utility?

In some cities, the service being provided by alternative water service providers is indispensable, although expensive for consumers. Box 6.1 shows an example oftheimpact of alternative water service suppliers in Nairobi.

Box 6.1. The water kiosks of Kibera, Nairobi[1]

With an estimated population of 500,000 people, Kibera is home to a quarter of the population of the City of Nairobi. Poor water supply and sanitation are among the most serious infrastructural problems. A study carried out in 1997 came up with the following major findings:

- Water kiosks that are mainly owned and operated by individual residents predominantly serve Kibera. A few kiosks are owned and operated by community groups.

- Nairobi City Council Water and Sewerage Department (WSD) licenses kiosk operators.

- The principal customers of the kiosks were neighbours and tenants. Water vendors purchase water from the kiosks in Kibera and sell it to the neighbouring areas whenever there is a water shortage.

- Only one in six kiosks have any form of superstructure, while two in? three kiosks have storage tanks.

- One of the main complaints from the kiosk operators is reliability of services from WSD pipelines.

- Water was sold at twice the price recommended by WSD during the normal supply periods. During water shortages, the price goes up.

- The kiosk owners cited delayed and irregular meter readings and bills.

- Only 10 per cent of the water consumed in Kibera was billed for. There were many instances of illegal connection, and low revenue collection efficiency

---

1.   Source: Field Note UNDP-World Bank Water and Sanitation Program, East and Southern Africa Region

Documenting the size and characteristics of the alternative water providers market in a city is important for Stage 1 as it provides valuable information for developing strategies for working with or competing against SWEs as part of Stage 2.

6.4   Institutional appraisal and development overview

Institutional appraisal and development, when practiced in a comprehensive manner, enables organizations to work systematically towards achieving their agreed objectives, provided those objectives are realistic. Unless a thorough analysis of a utility's performance is carried out, how can the utility be sure that it can sustainably and reliably extend services to new areas?

> Institutional development (ID) is 'the process of improving an institution's ability to make *effective [and efficient]* use of the human and financial re-sources available.'

Israel (1987)

The term 'effective' in the ID definition above refers to the extent to which objectives are being achieved. The term 'efficient' relates to developing improved outputs from the inputs provided. The development of organizations to carry out improvements in service provision has to come from the people involved.

Cullivan et al. (1987) point out that:

'Institutional problems are qualitatively different from specific technical or procedural problems. They affect broad areas of operational performance and therefore are "cross-cutting". Often deficiencies in an easily identifiable area of institutional output are identified as the primary problem when in reality the deficiency identified is merely a symptom of the larger problem.'

Institutional development seeks to encourage the development of the necessary spectrum of appropriate organizations to deliver services levels that customers want ('Where do we want to be?'). 'An institutional development project focuses on the development of comprehensive organizational systems and the people within the system which make them work' (Edwards, 1988). This can best be done by first analysing or undertaking an appraisal of the present situation in a systematic manner ('Where are we now?'). It is preferable that key informants including the utility staff participate in the appraisal.

Key elements of institutional analysis and development

In appraising or assessing water utilities, we also need to be aware of the potential areas and scope for institutional improvements that could be proposed in Stages 2 and 3. For comprehensive institutional development there are six key elements that need to be borne in mind. These are set out in Table 6.6 together with water sector examples of each element. Many of these examples typify good commercial approaches with a focus on serving poorer communities. If such initiatives are not currently being undertaken and they are considered sensible, this can be noted as part of the analysis during Stage 1. In order to fully ask the question 'Where are we now?' we need to consider what can be dome to make services better. Hence the need to consider issues such as those set out in Table 6.6.

Table 6.6. Key elements of institutional development

Key elements	Examples for each element
1. Structural and organizational adjustment	· Provide more organizational and financial autonomy for the water service provider organization, which provides them with the flexibility to make improvements.
	· Introduce PPP management options with well-designed contracts that include provisions for serving the poor.
	· Provide a regulatory organization for water and sewerage services, with responsibilities to ensure efficient services to all consumer groups.
	· Create a focused department or section that deals with services to informal settlements.
2. Agreeing roles, policies, objectives and performance targets	· Introduce the universal service obligation policy.
	· Agree roles amongst key stakeholders in order to improve services in poor communities.
	· Set realistic performance targets for each market segment and area served, against key indicators.
3. Human resource management	· Update recruitment policy to appoint people with the required skills for strategic marketing approaches.
	· Conduct training needs analyses amongst staff based on the organization's objectives and open staff appraisals, then implement and monitor training programme.
	· Introduce more flexibility in contracting out services, recruitment, dismissal and redundancy procedures.
	· Provide more incentives for staff and partners in terms of aspects such as more responsibility and pay for good performance.
4. Management development	· Delegate more duties and powers to staff lower down the organization and area offices.
	· Implement strategic marketing approaches throughout the organization.
	· Introduce a Total Quality Management (TQM) programme aimed at improving inter-departmental collaboration and services to all consumers.
	· Involve staff at all levels in change programmes.
5. Systems and procedures development	· Use preventative and corrective O&M management systems.
	· Introduce streamlined customer friendly procedures for bill payment, new connections, complaints redressal, etc.
	· Use flexible procedures developed for informal settlements.
	· Provide commercial double entry accounting.
	· Use well-designed computer billing systems.
6. Physical and financial resources	· Maximize revenues and control costs.
	· Construct dialogue with potential financiers and look for innovative ways to serve poorer areas.

A comprehensive strategic marketing programme would need to consider all these six institutional development areas. Previous experience has shown that institutional development programmes need to be comprehensive; deficiencies in one area can subvert the best efforts to improve one sub-system alone. Emphasis on each element would depend on the programme objectives and priority areas identified.

Tools for appraisal

For institutional appraisals, the utility's and government's policies, plans and progress against those plans provide a useful starting point. It is important to consult widely using participatory techniques such as semi-structured interviews, workshops and stakeholder analyses to develop a common understanding of the inter-linkages of problems and potential solutions.

Some of the key institutional appraisal techniques and considerations are summarized below with a brief discussion of their applicability:

Activity and responsibility analyses

An activity and responsibility matrix provides the institutional setting by specifying the degree of involvement and the roles played by stakeholders in carrying out key tasks. The matrix can be done at sector, corporate or departmental levels, depending on the objective of the analysis. Activity/responsibility matrices are a particularly useful tool in the water sector for establishing the actual allocation of responsibilities between the various institutions and highlighting problems with overlapping or fragmented responsibilities. Table 6.7 shows an example of an Activity and Responsibility Matrix for the urban water sector in Maharashtra, India.

With such a diverse spread of responsibilities there is only a limited opportunity to hold any organization accountable for service provision and implementing strategic marketing approaches. The most obvious service provider is the municipal water department, but they have very limited levels of responsibility (as of 1999). The other key stakeholders such as the state government, councillors, administrators and municipal finance departments are also concerned with many other services and are not able to devote sufficient time to water service provision. If many of these responsibilities were reallocated to one specialized service provider and one or two enabling agencies, the scope for improved accountability and services would be increased substantially.

Performance measurement

Performance measurement against key indicators is an objective means of assessing actual utility performance and services to consumers, in comparison with the agreed corporate and government objectives. Effective performance measurement is essential for city-wide service improvements on a sustainable basis, as part of a strategic marketing approach, and the benefits it offers include:

- more focused and better integrated performance data;

- easier identification of good and poor performance;

- strengthened mechanisms for identifying the causes of good or poor performance;

Table 6.7. Urban watsan services responsibilities in Maharashtra[1]

	Management of O&M	Operational investment	Capital investment	Agreeing water tariff levels	Agreeing municipal staffing levels	Human resource development
Central government			Approves some grants and loans	Sets policy guidelines	Interested	Policy and funding
State government	Involved	Some subsidies	Administrative approvals	Sets maximum and minimum limits	**Key role:** Sets limits and norms	Provides training facilities
State water board	Undertakes O&M in some towns	Interested	Technical approvals	Involved for new schemes	Involved	Provision of some training
Municipal councillors and administrators	**Key role:** Overseeing management	**Key role:** determines priorities	**Key role:** determines priorities	**Key role:** determines tariff levels	Approval role	**Key role:** determines priorities
Municipal water supply department	Day-to-day management	Puts forward proposals	Develops proposals with consultants	Involved in preparation of proposals	Puts forward proposals	Puts forward proposals
Municipal finance department	Controls cash flow	Financial approvals	Financial management	Puts forward proposals	Involved in financial implications	Involved in financial implications
Consumers	Report complaints, sometimes through Councillors			Involved through lobbying of Councillors		

1. Source: based on Franceys and Sansom (1999)

- more focused institutional roles for assessing and acting on sector performance and a framework against which capacity-building strategies and targets can potentially be developed;

- integration of all the 'tools' of performance measurement, e.g. operational monitoring, value for money review, technical audits, financial tracking studies, evaluation, etc.;

- improved information for assessing the effectiveness of water and sanitation policy and for enabling better policymaking; and

- a more credible system for arguing for more resources for the water and sanitation sector and allocating resources within the sector.

Source: Thomson (2003)

Such potential benefits are very relevant both for utilities and for government departments who are concerned with broader national economic and social objectives, such as improving services to the poor. Government departments in their enabling role should therefore promote and expect effective performance measurement of utility services. The key performance measurement steps can be broken down into five components, as shown in the Figure 6.2.

What to measure?	How to measure it?	How to collect data?	How to analyse and present data?	What to do with the data?
•Review current objectives •Identify gaps •Remove unnecessary objectives and add new ones	•Match current indicators to objectives •Agree key performance 'theme', e.g. VFM, equity, effectiveness •Identify gaps and reduce overlap of indicators •Agree a focused and balanced set of 'core' indicators •Agree definitions •Set targets	•Determine which indicators are already measured •Identify gaps in data collection •Consider scope for rationalizing data collection exercises •Reassess indicators if data collection is too costly •Agree frequency of data collection •Allocate roles for data collection	•Determine what has to be analysed •Develop data analysis systems •Develop graphical and other clear ways of presenting data •Allocate roles for data analysis and presentation	•Allocate roles for acting on the data •Inform any need for additional evaluation and audit exercises •Feed results into the budgeting and planning cycle •Assess policy implications •Adjust future objectives if necessary

Figure 6.2. General steps in performance measurement[1]

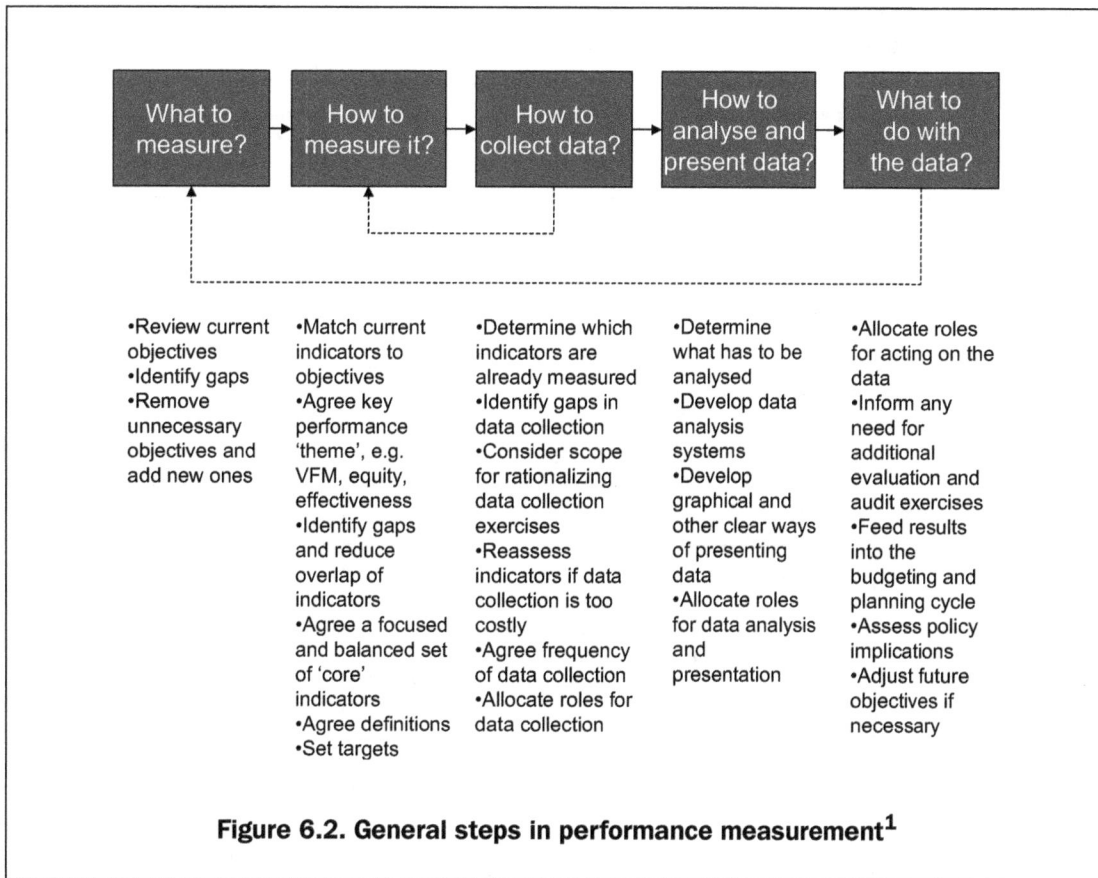

1. Source: Thomson (2003)

The key stakeholders such as government, utilities, regulator and consumer representatives have clear interests in ensuring that the performance measurement process is effective. This includes the activities listed in Figure 6.2 and the transparent exchange of information amongst the stakeholders.

Utility performance indicators and ratios

If utility performance is to be improved for all consumer groups, then we need to plan and monitor for improvements across all the utility's services using appropriate indicators. Performance should be assessed in terms of trends against key indicators over a number of years, rather than snapshots of performance. The most common performance indicators for water supply utilities relate to the themes of production, delivery, consumption, efficiency, effectiveness and finance. It is important to note that no single indicator is sufficient to provide a meaningful picture.

Table 6.8 shows examples of finance and economic indicators and ratios. Table 6.9 shows typical performance indicators and ratios that could be adapted for a given utility.

Note that there are columns in the tables for recording actual values and target values. This is a useful means of planning improvements and monitoring progress. In the third column the formulae for the relevant ratio is included. When assessing utility finances it is important to also examine any hidden subsidies.

Table 6.8. Financial indicator and ratio examples

Category	Indicator or ratio	Formulae	Actual latest value	Target for next year	Sector average
Marketing	Socio-economic GNP per capita				
	Average WTP to vendors				
Financial sustainability	Average domestic tariff				
	Comm. tariff				
	Sewerage tariff				
Profitability	Operating ratio	total cost / total revenue			
	Return on fixed assets	profit after depreciation / net fixed assets			
Liquidity	Current ratio	current assets / current liabilities			
Creditworthiness	Debt equity ratio	long term loans / equity			
Financial efficiency	Days receivable ratio	365 x accounts receivable / annual billed revenue			
	Bill collection efficiency	% of bills collected			

Those utilities who are considering a benchmarking programme should refer to the World Bank benchmarking toolkit for water and sanitation on their website. It is also beneficial to collect data per market segment or area, so that priority areas for improvement can be identified.

Potential indicators for serving all consumer groups

The United Nations Department of Economic and Social Affairs (UNDESA) estimates that by the year 2015, 88 per cent of all the increase in global population will live in urban areas of low-income countries (UNDESA Population Division, 2001.Owing to the fact that the economic growth of these countries will often not match the population increase, a larger fraction of people in urban areas of low-income countries will live in low-income settlements. There is a need, therefore, to ensure that services are delivered to these low-income communities in order to reduce human suffering.

In addition to the more general performance indicators for water utilities, indicators can be developed that specifically cater for improvements in service delivery to the different consumer groups, including low-income settlements, based on consumer surveys. These indicators can then be used to set targets and monitor trends in service levels amongst the different consumer groups. A sample format is shown in Table 6.10, which has separate columns for each market segment (based on research work in Uganda and Mombasa).

Table 6.9. Performance indicator and ratio examples

Category	Indicator or ratio	Formulae	Actual latest value	Target for next year	Sector average
Water production	Quantity of water produced	Volume treated			
	Quality of water produced	Percentage samples acceptable			
	Transmission factor	Source distance x elevation/100,000			
	Production Factor	Energy & chemicals costs as percentage of operation costs			
Water delivery (for whole city)	Target population				
	Average no. of people/ connection	Total population/no. of connections			
	Service coverage	Percentage of population served			
	Service delivery	Percentage of connections/standpipes			
Efficiency	Supply hours	Average supply hours per day at acceptable pressure			
	Non-revenue water	Percentage of water paid for/water produced			
	Maintenance	Frequency of burst/km pipes			
Consumption	Quantity of water consumed per person	Served population/water consumed			
	Working meters	Percentage of working consumption meters			
	Quality of water delivered	Percentage of samples acceptable			
Sewerage	Service coverage	Percentage of population connected to sewers			
		Percentage of population with acceptable on-site sanitation			
	Maintenance	Frequency of failure/km sewers			
	Treatment	Percentage of wastewater treated			
Effectiveness	Extent of water- related diseases	Diarrhoea /cholera/ typhoid cases per million per year			
	Customer satisfaction surveys	Proportion customers questioned expressing satisfaction			
Productivity	Staffing levels	Connections per employee			
		Population served per employee			
		Staffing costs as percentage of operation costs			

Table 6.10. Service levels indicators from consumer surveys

Example service delivery indicators	Example market segments			
	Residential houses and bungalows	Flats	One to three-room Swahili houses	Informal settlements
1. Percentage of households with their own in-house pipe connection				
2. Percentage of households with their own yard pipe connection				
3. Percentage of households who buy water from a neighbour				
4. Percentage of households using water kiosks or standposts				
5. Percentage of households who obtain water from alternative sources such as springs, wells and roof catchments				
6. Percentage of households who use more than one source				
7. Average total water consumption per person in the house - litre/person/day				
8. Average number of hours of utility water supply per day				
9. Average number of days per week that utility water is supplied				
10. Average time taken to collect all the water for the household each day from all sources (minutes)				
11. Average distance to nearest usable piped water source				
12. Average monthly household water bill				
13. Average vendor prices				
14. Percentage of both women and men satisfied with utility services				
15. Percentage of households who regularly use a functioning sanitation system within 20 metres of their residence				

Information against the indicators for the various market segments listed in Table 6.10 can be collected and updated on a regular basis, as a means of agreeing priority areas for action and setting targets for improvements in services. Note that information against all the indicators in the table should be obtained from well-designed consumer surveys. Annex 5 shows such a two-page consumer survey questionnaire that was field-tested in five towns in Uganda.

Rationale for proposed service level indicators

The rationale for the use of each consumer survey indicator in Table 6.10, in terms of benefits to consumers and the country as a whole, are as follows:

Indicators 1 to 7 relate to service levels and are important for: assessing utility progress on service improvements; checking on value for money from investments; and for setting realistic targets. The emphasis is on actual use as reported by the consumers, rather than what was planned. Such indicators can also be used to prioritize new investments.

Indicators 8 and 9 show the average number of hours and days of water supply and are important for verifying progress on utility performance in service provision.

Indicator 10 shows the average time taken to collect all the household water each day from all sources, including travel and queuing time, and is an important investment outcome indicator. This is because if time savings are achieved, then there are clear opportunities for users to spend time on more productive activities that can be beneficial to a country's economy. Where there are high water collection times it suggests that there is a high demand for piped water.

Indicator 11 illustrates the average distance to the nearest usable piped water source and is useful for prioritizing new investments on extending the pipe distribution network closer to consumers. It can also be used to assess utility progress on service improvements, to check on value for money from investments, and to set realistic targets.

Indicators 12 and 13 concerning household expenditure on water and vendor prices provide support data for assessing people's ability and willingness to pay for improved services.

Indicator 14 on levels of satisfaction with utility service it is important to assess the utility's operational performance. It is suggested that separate data is collected for both men and women, because women often have very different experiences from men in aspects such as the collection and carrying of water.

Indicator 15 on functioning sanitation is useful for stakeholders concerned with planning for improved sanitation services in low-income areas.

If such information is regularly collected using well-designed consumer surveys that are representative of each market segment or consumer group, it is very beneficial. It enables both the utility and the regulator/government department to undertake ongoing effective monitoring against targets and analysing trends. Each utility and regulator would need to review the list of indicators that are most appropriate for each city.

Such a list of indicators can also be used on an area or zonal basis, where appropriate. Using a manageable number of market segments as a means of presenting the data, however, retains a poverty focus and is clear to the reader. When utilities use these indicators and agree to work towards reasonable targets, the process can act as an incentive to serve all consumer groups.

PEST analysis

To understand the performance of any organization in serving its customers (and perhaps explaining why it is failing to serve so many prospective customers) it is necessary to understand not only the institutional context but also the wider national context. The simplified approach is to undertake what is known as a PEST analysis. This considers the key issues in the wider national, governance context or environment. Thinking through the broader Political, Economic, Social and Technical (PEST) factors or context within which a direct water provider has to operate is a useful exercise. In conventional marketing terms these factors can be considered in terms of the potential competitive threats and opportunities for the organization or sector concerned.

For the less competitive water sector, formulation of a marketing strategy is concerned with matching the capabilities of the organization with the expectations and demands of the wider socio-political environment. It is therefore necessary to carry out a periodic scanning of this environment in order to understand the extent to which it affects the strategy; and secondly the ways in which the environmental pressures can be related to the capabilities of the organization. Strategic management experts advocate a step-wise approach in analysing the environment, illustrated in Figure 6.3.

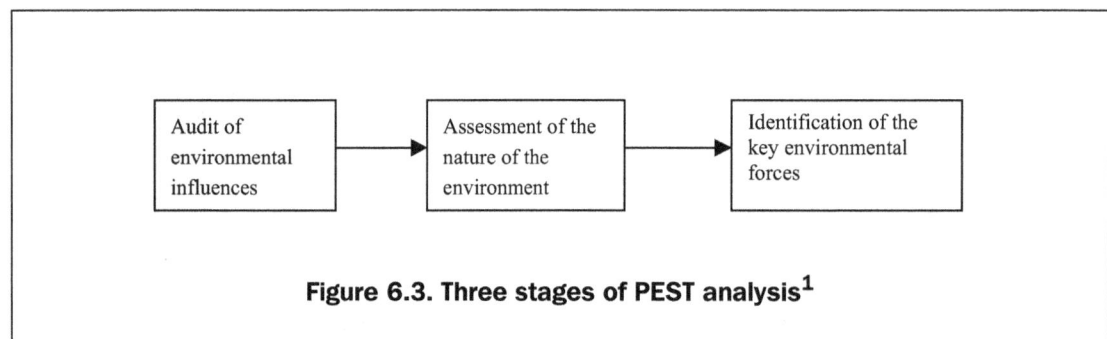

Figure 6.3. Three stages of PEST analysis[1]

1. Source: Adapted from Wilson and Gilligan (1997)

Some typical PEST factors to consider are set out in Box 6.2

The technology aspects to consider are the willingness to accept both cheaper more appropriate technologies and different non-conventional service options. Hence the need to learn about different options from elsewhere and pilot promising approaches.

It is suggested that environmental scanning should be made part of the overall process of strategic planning, and should be integrated into the duties and responsibilities of the officer in charge of corporate planning. Environmental scanning may be done in-house by a specialist organizational unit, or through outsourcing. Environmental scanning can also be participatory, whereby, periodically, senior and middle managers give their perceptions of the environment. A strategic management consultant could facilitate the process.

Subjective institutional performance descriptions

Subjective institutional performance indicators or *critical success factors* are used to analyse 'softer' issues of management that cannot be predicted from numerical objective data available in the organization. One commonly used framework for institutional analysis in water and sanitation organizations is the 'WASH' approach (Cullivan et al., 1987. The 'WASH' framework solicits the perceptions of managers, employees and

---

Box 6.2. Typical PEST factors to consider

Political/legal factors
Legislative structure
Political/government stability
Taxation policies
Employment legislation
Foreign trade regulations
Environmental protection laws
Trade union power
Donor confidence

Economic factors
GNP trends
Energy costs
Foreign exchange restrictions
Inflation rates
Investment levels
Money supply
Level of unemployment
Patterns of ownership

Socio-cultural factors
Demographics
Rural-Urban migrations
Lifestyles
Educational levels
Income levels
Attitude to work
Consumer power
Housing trends

Technological factors
Speed of technology transfer
Level of communication and IT
Level of in-country manufacturing
Availability of local expertise

Box 6.3. Categories for subjective performance descriptions[1]

Organizational autonomy

Legislative framework		**Management and administration**
Technical capability	**Leadership**	**Human resources development**
Commercial orientation		**Consumer orientation**

Organizational culture

---

1. Source: Cullivan et al., (1989)

potentially the views of external stakeholders of items categorized in nine performance dimensions.

Organizational autonomy is critical in terms of an organization's ability to manage and respond to its customers' needs. Municipality water departments, for example, which are not able to hire staff or raise tariffs to meet their projected costs, have insufficient autonomy to manage effectively. Effective organizational autonomy can be categorized by the authority to make decisions about budgets, tariffs, revenues, hiring levels, pay and incentives, control of personnel, institutional policies and systems, planning of projects, and organizational goals. There are also regulatory functions that need to be performed by governments, such as setting and monitoring objectives and targets to balance the autonomy provided.

Leadership is the capability to inspire key stakeholders to develop and understand the institution's mission/objectives, to commit themselves to that mission and to work towards its fulfilment. Effective leaders/change agents serve as positive role models and are required at all levels of an organization. Leaders are essential for agreeing and implementing institutional change programmes. Over-reliance on one leader in development projects can be a problem, particularly if they are then transferred. It is generally better to have 'Core groups' plus a Steering Committee if the long process of change is to be sustainable.

Effective management and administration is demonstrated by the capacity to get the most out of the resources available (human and other) in a deliberate or planned manner. Good managers have a clear sense of objectives and priorities; they know who to rely on to get a job done and how to delegate to them the means to do it. An effective management climate is characterized by teamwork, co-operation and good communication among staff.

To enable managers to perform effectively an efficient administrative system is required. This includes the policies and procedures which regulate, guide and facilitate the actions of managers. A mature organization has effective sub-systems such as personnel, budgeting, accounting, financial management, procurement, contracting out and management information.

Commercial orientation
Commercial orientation is the degree to which actions in an institution are driven by cost effectiveness and operating efficiency. The performance of an organization should be guided and disciplined by a strategy to achieve financial self-sufficiency at an appropriate stage of growth. This commercial orientation can be viewed at both operational and policy levels. At the policy level, commercially oriented institutions structure and stage investments, expenditures, and revenues to achieve financial equilibrium annually. At the operational level, everyday activities are guided by quality standards and by constant attention to cost factors.

The institution strives to establish a reputation as a financially well-run business in the eyes of its consumers (to promote the payment of tariffs), and in the financial and political community in order to obtain financial support for growth and to maximize financial and operating autonomy.

Customer orientation is organizing and directing the services and output of the organization towards the demands and desires of the customer. Staff of a successful water service provider organization see serving consumers as their primary function. All work, all programmes and projects are directed towards greater efficiency, effectiveness and equality of service to all consumers. Every effort is made to inform and educate customers about the role of the institution and the means it is using to achieve its (the customer's) objectives. Marketing of differentiated services to poorer communities can enable reliable service provision at affordable prices for these consumer groups.

Technical capability is the measure of the institution's competence in conducting the technical work required to carry out the responsibilities of the institution. Most of the technical work is performed directly by skilled, qualified employees, as well as outside specialists, supervised by the institution's own staff.

Human resource development (HRD): the investigation of this area includes an assessment of training needs based on organizational objectives and open staff appraisals, with a view to developing effective training or capacity development programmes. It is also necessary to examine the best means of managing and delivering the capacity development to meet those training needs.

Other key HRD areas are developing appropriate procedures for recruitment, dismissal and redundancy procedures, as well as providing more incentives for staff and partners in terms of aspects such as more responsibility and pay for good performance.

Organizational culture is the set of values and norms which inform and guide everyday actions, as part of the formal and informal work culture. An unhealthy organizational culture is likely to be highly resistant to change, protecting narrow interests (such as graft or petty bureaucratic authority). A more positive culture has a clear sense of mission and identity. In the public water sector, the institutional culture is often rather bureaucratic.

Legal framework and interactions with external institutions are the direct provider's capacity to influence positively and strategically those institutions which affect its financial, political and legal ability to perform effectively. An adequate legal and regulatory framework (both on the statute and in practice) is an enabling factor in this respect. The multiplicity of institutions in the water sector mean that positive interaction and the influencing of external institutions is generally a priority for a water institution's managers.

As an example of institutional appraisal, though restricted only to staff, managers in the National Water and Sewerage Corporation, Uganda, were asked to score their own institution according to these subjective performance descriptions, rating themselves on a scale from 1 (low or poor) to 3 (average) to 5 (high or excellent) (see Table 6.11). Started as part of a management development programme (Franceys, 1997)[, the process was continued by Mugisha (2000) to give an interesting longitudinal survey of managers' perceptions at a time of considerable institutional change in National Water.

The results show that whereas there was perceived to be a steady improvement in corporate performance indictors in terms of leadership skills, management and organization, and commercial orientation, respondents felt that there was little development in organizational culture or - most critically for a study on marketing - consumer orientation.

Swot analysis and assessment report

A SWOT analysis (Strengths/Weaknesses/Opportunities/Threats) is perhaps the most common (and most misused) mechanism for structuring information to assist in a marketing analysis. An example of a SWOT framework, adapted to meet the particular needs of a water utility, is shown in the box below.

In order to enhance the practical usefulness of the SWOT analysis, the following points should be noted:

- Better to complete once much of the data gathering from institutional and infrastructure analyses and consumer surveys has been completed.

Table 6.11. Subjective performance indicators for NWSC[1]

	1993	1996	1997	1999	
	NWSC overall score			Kampala (10)	*NWSC (24)
Leadership	2.6	2.9	3.0	2.8	3.4
Organizational autonomy	3.0	3.7	3.5	3.3	3.5
Management and organization	2.4	2.9	3.0	2.8	3.1
Commercial orientation	2.7	2.9	3.1	2.8	3.3
Consumer orientation	2.5	2.4	3.1	3.0	3.0
Legal framework	2.8	3.0	3.5	3.4	3.4
Organizational and staff culture	2.6	2.8	3.4	2.7	2.9

1. Source: Mugisha (2000)
   [1 = Poor, 3 = Medium, 5 = Excellent]
   *NWSC indicators for 1999 exclude Kampala Area

Box 6.4. Examples of items to be assessed using a SWOT analysis[1]

Internal strengths and weaknesses
Efficiency
Level of service
Assets
Buying
Employees (skills, morale, etc.)
Management
Level of technology
Information
Research and development
Utility finances

External threats and opportunities
Demands
Customer perceptions
Economic trends
Political trends
Environmental factors
Public health
Climatological
Suppliers
Contractors

---

1. Source: Adapted from Mugisha (2000)

- Keep it brief, and rank items to avoid trivia.

- SWOT statement must be 'hard' not 'soft'; objective not subjective; quantitative, not qualitative.

- Strengths and Weakness are relative to the competitor's situation.

- The SWOT analysis normally covers the whole business and not just one function.

- Use 'matching' within the SWOT to highlight strategic options.

Table 6.12 shows an example of a SWOT analysis drawn for NWSC, Uganda, in November 1999.

Table 6.12. SWOT analysis of NWSC, Kampala[1]

Opportunities	Threats
Abundant raw water sources	Raw water sources increasingly polluted
Limited political interference	Relatively poor clientele (low ability to pay)
Good and enabling water legislation	Corrupt operating environment
Relatively stable economy (low inflation rates)	Stringent environmental discharge laws have recently been introduced
More donor confidence than other utilities	Corporation tax recently introduced
Population increase, hence services expansion opportunities	Lack of in-country manufacturing of hardware inputs
Monopolistic status of NWSC	Low technological and innovative capacity
Economic liberalization allows PSP involvement	Political obligation to take on unviable towns without accompanying subsidies
Government preferential support for the water sector	Large external debt burden
Communication technology growing	
Strengths	**Weaknesses**
Knowledgeable and properly trained HR	Lack of adequate management skills
Good objectives-oriented planning	Tribalism and patronage
Willingness to change by senior management	High 'unaccounted for' water loss
Willingness to involve PSP where necessary	Reactive approach
Willingness to balance management/commercial/technical orientations	Inadequate performance measurement
Willingness and ability to curb corruption	De-motivated staff because of low pay
Better public image than other utilities	Corruption
Mindset to achieving corporation goals	Over-emphasis on technical orientation
	Imported technology
	Poor maintenance culture

1. Source: Adapted from Mugisha (2000

A thorough SWOT analysis, along with data collected using the other means discussed in this chapter, provide a good basis for a answering the question 'Where are we now?'. The key information, analyses and initial ideas for potential solutions are best captured in a utility assessment report or similar output. This document will be very useful in the next phase of strategic marketing 'Where do we want to be?'.

Chapter 7

Stage 2: 'Where do we want to be?'

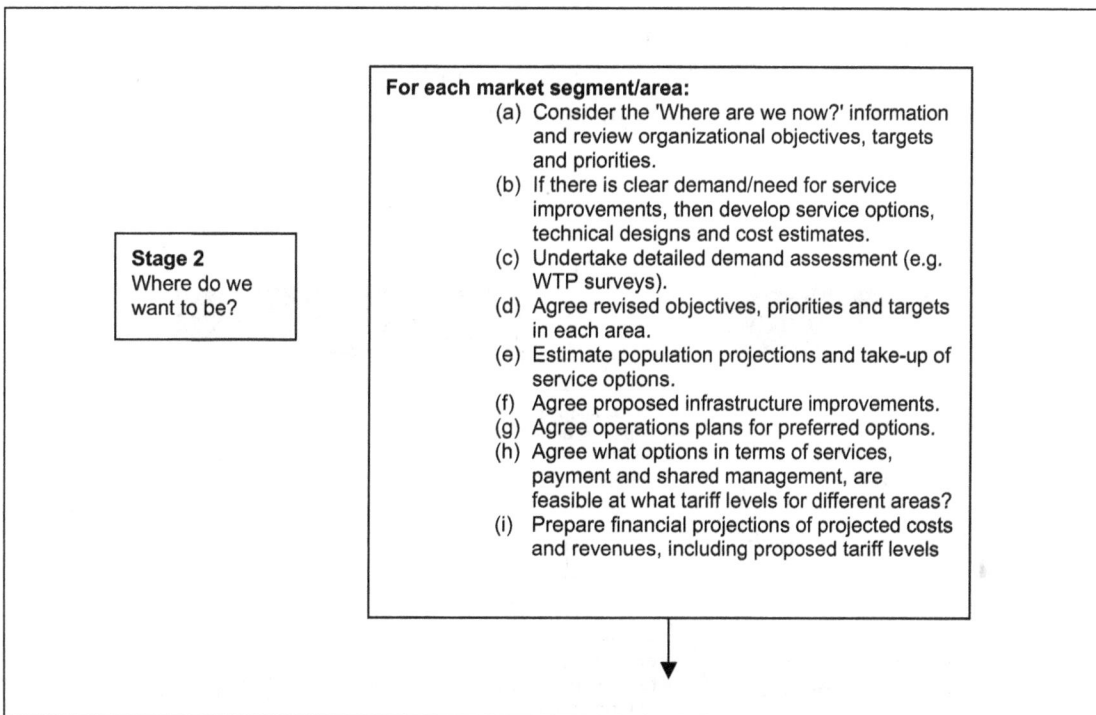

```
┌─────────────────────────────────────────────────────────────────────────┐
│                                                                           │
│                        ┌──────────────────────────────────────────────┐  │
│                        │ For each market segment/area:                │  │
│                        │   (a) Consider the 'Where are we now?'        │  │
│                        │       information and review organizational   │  │
│                        │       objectives, targets and priorities.     │  │
│                        │   (b) If there is clear demand/need for        │  │
│                        │       service improvements, then develop      │  │
│                        │       service options, technical designs      │  │
│                        │       and cost estimates.                     │  │
│   ┌──────────────┐     │   (c) Undertake detailed demand assessment    │  │
│   │ Stage 2      │     │       (e.g. WTP surveys).                     │  │
│   │ Where do we  │     │   (d) Agree revised objectives, priorities    │  │
│   │ want to be?  │     │       and targets in each area.               │  │
│   └──────────────┘     │   (e) Estimate population projections and     │  │
│                        │       take-up of service options.            │  │
│                        │   (f) Agree proposed infrastructure           │  │
│                        │       improvements.                           │  │
│                        │   (g) Agree operations plans for preferred    │  │
│                        │       options.                                │  │
│                        │   (h) Agree what options in terms of          │  │
│                        │       services, payment and shared            │  │
│                        │       management, are feasible at what        │  │
│                        │       tariff levels for different areas?      │  │
│                        │   (i) Prepare financial projections of        │  │
│                        │       projected costs and revenues,          │  │
│                        │       including proposed tariff levels        │  │
│                        └──────────────────────────────────────────────┘  │
│                                              │                            │
│                                              ▼                            │
│                                                                           │
└─────────────────────────────────────────────────────────────────────────┘
```

7.1   Overview

The completion of a thorough situation analysis (Stage 1) of the utility, and its services, consumer groups and working environment, provides a good basis for beginning to answer the question *'Where do we want to be?'* The typical key activities in Stage 2 are listed in the figure above.

Suggested outputs from Stage 2, assuming an investment plan for service improvement is being developed, are:

- outline design options and proposals;

- a review of utility objectives, targets and priorities;

- a detailed demand assessment (e.g. WTP survey report) for target areas;

- proposed service/payment and management options to be offered for each market segment or area; and

- financial projections of cost and revenues as part of an investment plan, including different investment scenarios.

As the ultimate aim in the process is to develop viable and comprehensive investment or strategic marketing plans, it is useful to think about a typical investment planning process and the inter-linkages between the various key activities. An outline process showing such inter-linkages is shown in Figure 7.1. The process begins with Box 1 - an assessment of current service levels and operations which should reveal key problems and any need for service improvements. It is also important to regularly conduct consumer surveys (Box 2) to find out consumers' (existing and potential customers) perceptions about both the service provision and the utility. Activities in Boxes 1 to 3 help answer the question 'Where are we now?'.

The key stage in the 'Where we want to be?' section of the flowchart in Figure 7.1 is Box 4 - 'Review objectives, targets, priorities and investment plans'. This should be done with the best available information, such as the data from the 'assessment of current service levels and operations (Box 1) and well-designed consumer surveys (Box 2), as well as the issues in Box 3.

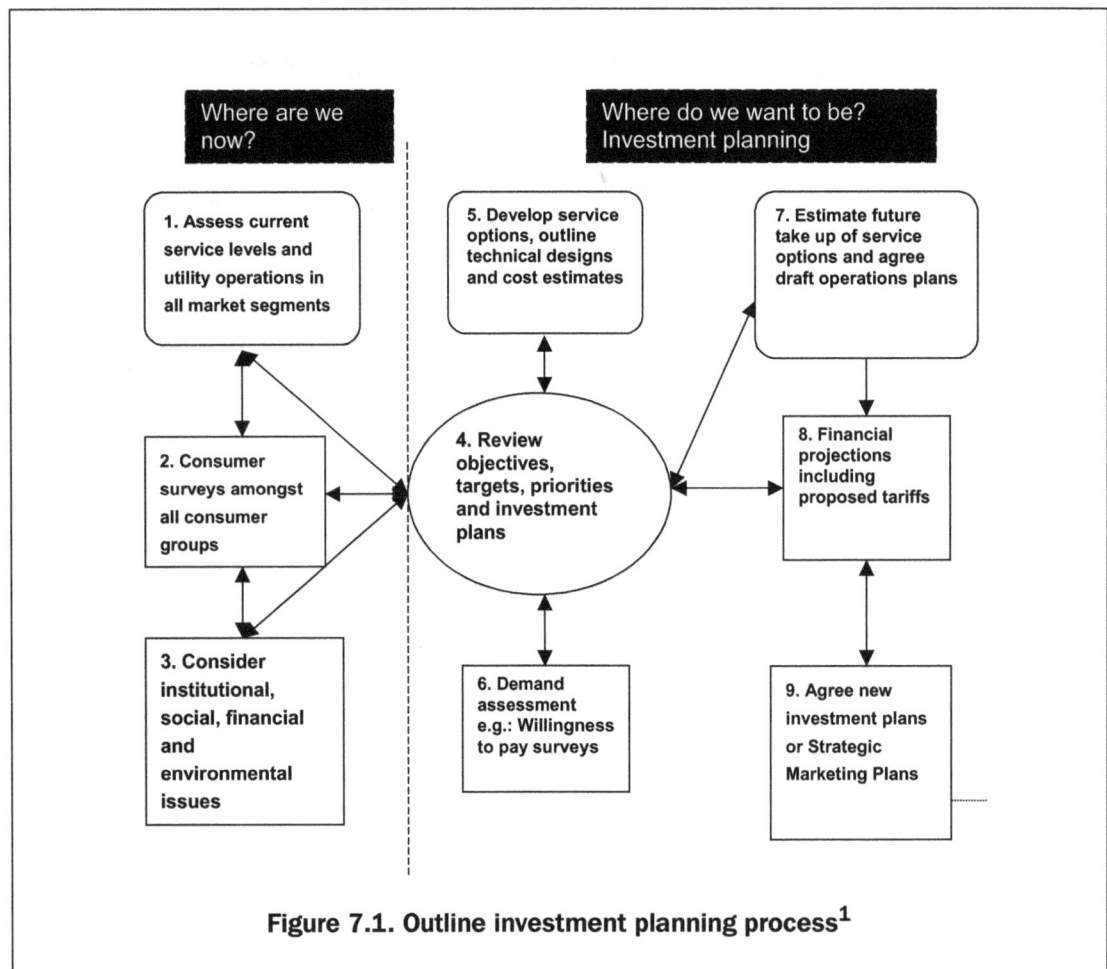

Figure 7.1. Outline investment planning process[1]

1. Source: Sansom, adapted from Revels (2002)

140

If significant new or revised investments are proposed, then it is worthwhile developing 'service options, outline technical designs and cost estimates' (Figure 7.1 Box 5) and conducting ''demand assessment (Box 6). Both these activities provide valuable information for developing the 'financial projections including proposed tariffs' (Box 8), as well as the 'operations plans for preferred options' (Figure 7.1 Box 7). The willingness to pay survey results not only provide useful data on consumer preferences, but also the average maximum willingness to pay data is valuable in determining tariff policies.

The financial projections are best done on computer spreadsheet programmes, such as Excel over a 10 to 20 year period, using a number of investment scenarios. An example financial projection sheet is shown in Annex 4. The preferred investment scenario can then form the basis of the agreed investment plan that needs to be discussed with key stakeholders. Note that many of the arrows in the outline investment planning process figure point in both directionsñ this emphasizes that the process is both iterative and ongoing.

7.2   Review priorities and objectives

In many developing countries the water utility's financial positions are often problematic. There are many reform initiatives taking place, such as decentralization, creating more autonomous utilities, embarking on various PPP contracts and regulation, developing poverty reduction strategy plans (PRSPs), as well as the continuing process of subsidy reductions. In this changing environment it is beneficial for utilities, government departments and regulators to regularly review their objectives and priorities. The situation analysis from Stage 1 provides a good basis to review broader objectives as well as specific targets.

Lack of customer orientation has contributed to the low levels of revenue in many water utilities. A more proactive consumer orientated marketing approach can substantially improve the utilities' financial position, whilst improving water services to existing and potential customers.

For most progressive water utilities, the key priorities are likely to cover:

- improvement in service provision to customers, including customer services such as billing and dealing with requests and complaints;

- improvement in the utility's financial position;

- expansion of the revenue base by capturing more of the water market (expansion of services to those people who may not be currently served and who rely on alternative sources); and

- achievement of equity in service provision by improving services to the poor.

One key area of improvement is likely to be customer services such as billing, revenue collection and general customer relations. These 'software' issues ought to go hand-in-hand with the 'hardware' issues such as infrastructure improvements and O&M that together constitute service quality. Improvements in service quality can result in the enhancement of customers' perception of the value of the service. Customers are often willing to pay more for a perceived increase in service quality, so the scope for increasing water tariffs increases. Increased revenues are required for investment in new infrastructure for bulk supply, treatment, transmission and distribution to meet both current and future needs.

Broader utility objectives are generally captured in mission statements, policy documents, customer charters, etc. Examples of mission statements for some water utilities in Africa are provided in Box 7.1.

Box 7.1. Utility mission statements

The mission statement for the National Water Conservation and Pipeline Corporation (NWCPC) in Kenya (NWCPC, 1999) is:

'The corporation is committed to providing high quality water to its customers at an affordable price and at a reasonable profit to the corporation.'

The mission statement for the National Water and Sewerage Corporation (NWSC) in Uganda is (Kayaga and Sansom, 2001):

'To be financially a self-sufficient organization developing and providing water supply and sewerage to customers at an affordable price.'

It is interesting to note from the mission statements from utilities in Kenya and Uganda that both of them only refer to their customers. But what about the people who are not their customers, people that do not have their own piped connection? Potential objectives that could be used for mission statements are set out in Box 7.2. Mission statements will also need to take account of current government policies and the current state of services in the utility's service area.

Box 7.2. Potential utility objectives

Key strategic marketing objectives for progressive water utilities :

• Provide adequate and reliable water and sewerage services whilst improving customer satisfaction through continuous service enhancements to all consumer groups.
• Through the development of cost-reflective tariffs and targeted subsidies achieve a reasonable return on the capital employed as an efficient provider.

Successful improvements in service delivery are also dependent on the utility's pricing policies, which are discussed in the next section.

7.3   Proposed tariff policies

Water utilities in many low-income countries are often unable to collect enough revenue to cover both operation and maintenance costs and the capital funds required to improve the system. The level of water tariffs are often too low to meet all the utility's full costs. Another common problem is that tariff structures penalize some consumer groups unfairly.

Approval of the water tariff is generally the responsibility of the central or state governments. This responsibility is also being transferred to regulators in some countries as a means of achieving more objective assessments. The onus is on governments to encourage regulation of water utilities to improve revenue collection through viable water tariffs. Increasingly, efficient urban water utilities in low-income countries are applying tariffs designed to cover return on investments and major capital expenses. The following text provides guidance on tariff setting and the provision of subsidies.

General principles

The determination of tariff policies should seek to address both commercial and social welfare concerns. It is beneficial if revised tariff levels can be finalized based on mutually agreeable principles. The simple but comprehensive 'AESCE' principles (which we pronounce 'ace') are outlined in Box 7.3.

Box 7.3. Developing tariff policies using the 'AESCE' principles

When considering appropriate tariff policies, AESCE is a useful memory aid:

Adequate. The average tariff should be cost reflective, which means it should cover the cost of 'OPEX' - operating costs; 'CAPEX' - capital maintenance (infrastructure renewals and depreciation); and the cost of capital - to ensure that loans can be repaid and future investment financed whilst the existing system is maintained.

Equitable. The required level of revenue should be allocated between customer groups in a fair and equitable manner for both the poorer members of the community and the different levels of service options, relative to the costs they impose on the system and to reflect social welfare objectives to achieve public health.

Simple. The tariff structure should be simple for the utility to administer and easy for customers to understand. Customers usually display greater willingness to sustain payment of water bills when they understand the bills.

Conserving. The tariff structure should influence consumption in such a way that customers are able to purchase enough water to meet their needs without being wasteful.

Enforceable. The utility should be able to enforce the tariff through viable sanctions such as court action, disconnections, etc. Tariffs that cannot be enforced are unlikely to be sustainable.

To ensure that adequate tariff levels are achieved, calculations need to include proposed future loans and investments. Section 7.4 provides some guidance on calculating tariffs using the Average Incremental Costs (AIC) approach based on future investment proposals.

In many countries rising block tariffs have been introduced to try to ensure that consumers of small amounts pay less per kilolitre than larger consumers, as well as to encourage the conservation of water. In practice problems have emerged with this system, as is described in Box 7.4

Box 7.4. Block tariffs to subsidize the poor?[1]

Many urban water utilities use a block system of tariffs for metered households. The principle is that families using less water pay less per kilolitre up to a threshold consumption per month. More affluent households who use more than the threshold pay more per kilolitre of water consumed above that threshold, in accordance with the next tariff 'slab'. This is in recognition of the fact that water is a social as well as an economic good.

Problems can arise in developing countries where a number of poor families use the same metered connection, illegally or otherwise, and they use more than the threshold amount, thus paying more for their water. Under such circumstances poor families can pay more with a block tariff system than if there was a flat tariff per kilolitre consumed. Such disparities can encourage a climate of not paying.

In Santiago, Chile they have dealt with this problem by not subsidizing the poor through lower water charges, e.g. with block tariffs, but providing separate well-targeted subsidies. Other cities that suffer water shortage problems will wish to retain the block tariff system to send economic signals to consumers to conserve water. In which case they will need to carefully design and market service options and tariff levels to ensure equity for multi-family pipe connections.

---

1. Source: DFID (1998)

So rising block tariffs do not always achieve the 'equitable' component of the 'AESCES' principles, as described in Box 7.4. Some more specific ideas for tariff setting and subsidies are:

a) Getting the tariff level and the tariff structure right helps all consumers, including the poor.

b) Subsidize access (and lack of access), not consumption.

c) Subsidized delivery mechanisms should be targeted, transparent and triggered by household indications of demand.

d) New information is often required to evaluate whether a proposed tariff or subsidy will hurt or help poor households.

e) Because tariffs and subsidies require modifications over time, decisions that must be made about social equity concerns should be incorporated into the tariff and subsidy revision process.

Source: WSP & PPIAF (2002) and Whittington (1992)

When negotiating tariff levels there are a number of key issues to be borne in mind, which are summarized in Table 7.1.

Table 7.1. Key issues for setting tariffs

Issue	Potential impact on tariff policy
National policy priorities	National or state policy might impact on tariff setting. For example, if government policy is to move to full cost recovery, including capital costs, this should impact on tariff increases.
Cross subsidization of poorer communities	If an aim is to improve equity, tariffs can be set at different levels for different user groups and service options.
Consideration of the cost of water supply and sewerage	As populations and demands increase, utilities invariably have to consider using more distant water sources. The full costs of using such sources as well as the bulk water supply and distribution networks need to be included in the tariff calculation. Sewerage and appropriate wastewater treatment is invariably higher in cost than water supply. Where sewerage programmes are envisaged the full costs should be considered in determining tariff levels.
Willingness to pay of communities	This is an important factor and is becoming increasingly accepted as a key element of tariff setting. Tariffs can be raised for those individuals / communities who are willing to pay more for water supply.
Willingness to charge	Policymakers/politicians may often be unwilling to increase water charges because they perceive that tariff increases are likely to be unpopular with the public. Orientation of policymakers is often required to demonstrate the benefits to all stakeholders of generating adequate funds through increased tariff levels.

Proposed tariff levels in the medium term are likely to be considered when doing financial projections for future investments. Where substantial tariff increases are required, they should preferably be within the willingness to pay levels that are derived from surveys. Increases are best done on an incremental basis that is acceptable to key stakeholders. Addressing the 'willingness to charge' issue mentioned in the above table is critical, so careful thought is required in developing a strategy for advocating tariff increases.

Agreeing tariffs for different service levels

By offering different options to different customer groups, there are opportunities for setting lower water prices for options that are less convenient to consumers, or where options cost the utility less to provide, or where subsidies to the poor are proposed. For example, a water kiosk that is managed by a community group will have lower operational costs for a utility than a kiosk managed by the utility itself. Trickle feed supplies are cheaper than full water pressure, so tariffs can be lowered accordingly to capture people's willingness to pay.

A simplified calculation for balancing projected income for each service option with utility costs is set out below:

If we assume that the average calculated tariff for financial sustainability for a city is, say, US$1.0 per cubic metre, and that the average consumption per household is 10 cubic metres a month, then for 50,000 paying households in a city, the total domestic water income for the utility will be:

$1.00 x 10 cubic metres x 12 months x 50,000 households = $6 million

(Average tariff x Volume of water sold = Total domestic water sales income)
(excluding connection charges, etc.)

If the total expected income from commercial/industrial and other institutions in the city is $2 million at the same tariff level, then the total projected yearly income for financial sustainability is:

$6 million + $2 million = $8 million

The tariff levels for each service option offered will need to be adapted to generate this same level of income ($8 million) as is shown in the simplified calculation in Table 7.2 below. Note the tariffs can be adjusted to match the WTP of customers for each option offered, as well as reflecting the reduced costs of provision for the different service levels offered to poor or unserved communities.

Table 7.2. Balancing service option tariffs with income

Service option	Proposed option tariff ($ per cubic metre)	Projected sales volume (cubic metres of water)	Projected income from each option
Utility-managed water kiosks	$0.8 X	300,000 =	$0.24 million
Community-managed water kiosks	$0.6 X	400,000 =	$0.24 million
Yard connection in informal settlements where customers sell on to neighbours	$0.8 X	500,000 =	$0.4 million
Individual house connection with 12 hours supply to roof tank at full pressure	$1.0 X	4.8 million =	$4.8 million
Commercial/ industrial users	$1.16 X	2 million =	$2.32 million
		Total Income	$8.0 million

The figures in Table 7.2 do not include sewerage charges, which would need to be added for household supplies where sewerage service are provided. The calculation is rather simplified, as demand for water will vary with price, but it offers the basic approach of differentiating service options at appropriate prices in order to maximize both income and the numbers of satisfied customers. The key principle behind this approach is subsidizing 'access', or options that have less access, rather than consumption. In a similar way private sector companies in general charge more for better services than they would for less convenient options.

A tariff balancing exercise such as the one shown in Table 7.2 can form the basis of a future utility tariff structure that reflects both commercial and equity objectives.

7.4 Projected costs

Achievements of financial sustainability by water utilities require that sufficient attention be given to the costs of water provision.

Cost concepts

The economic cost refers to the benefits foregone elsewhere in the economy by using scarce resources for a given purpose. In terms of providing water services, the economic cost has three components:

- the cost of raw water;

- the investment cost; and

- the operation cost.

Together, the three components constitute what is commonly referred to as the total costs. The cost of raw water consists of drawing related charges, which are important, especially with increasing scarcity of water resources. The investment cost refers to the amount spent during the planning and implementation phase of the project. This is essentially the cost of installing the water supply infrastructure, and includes financing costs. The operation cost (or recurrent cost) refers to the amount spent during the operations and maintenance phase of the project.

Total costs = cost of raw water + capital cost +recurrent cost

The average cost is determined by the total costs divided by the water production.

Average cost = Total costs/water production

The average cost starts at a very high level and falls rapidly with increasing volume. It is at a minimum at the optimum production level. With higher production, the average cost rises again. Thus, the first cubic metre is very expensive to produce, but thereafter total costs increase only slowly. Costs will rise faster as production approaches capacity.

Marginal Costs are the additional operating costs for an additional unit of output (short run). Where extensions of capacity are required to allow for increasing consumption, marginal costs includes the necessary investment costs (long run). There are two distinct situations under which marginal costs can be determined. In the first case, the average costs of service are decreasing for a certain range of output. This can happen particularly in large urban schemes where economies of scale apply. In this case, marginal costs are below average costs. The opposite is the case where the average cost is increasing. This can be the result of, for instance, expansion of the service area, development of more remote water sources or more cases of peak demand. Thus the marginal cost is above the average cost. In this case average cost pricing results in inefficiency.

On the basis of efficiency, marginal cost pricing is the most optimum. It is however difficult to apply in practice for two main reasons:

- Strict application of marginal costing can cause large and sudden fluctuations in price. The marginal cost price should change continuously according to production, which is difficult to manage in practice.

- Water supply investments are usually large and often vary substantially from year to year.

A special feature of the water sector, like other infrastructure, is that it is typically capital intensive. This feature and other difficulties in the application of marginal cost pricing have resulted in its limited use in charging for water. It is rare that one encounters any reference to marginal cost pricing in practice, since even economists do not agree on the details of its practical implementation. Due to these difficulties, the concept of average incremental cost has been introduced. To overcome the constraints of marginal cost pricing, it is assumed that average incremental cost equals marginal costs.

The average incremental cost is obtained by dividing the project's incremental costs by the incremental water sales of the same project. The cost and sales over the economic life of the project are discounted by applying the present value method. This is discussed further in the section on average incremental costs.

Estimates of costs for water supply components

Where detailed costings are not available, cost formula are a useful means of developing water supply component cost estimates. Examples of such formulae are shown below using cost functions produced by the Water Research Centre and presented in their Technical Report TR61 on 'Cost Information for Water Supply and Sewage Disposal, and Cost Index Value' published in June 1995. The figure derived from the formula is then multiplied by a suitable index also provided in TR61.

Box 7.5. Estimation of water treatment plant costs[1]

Total cost of installation ('000 British £) = $0.160*NORMCAP^{0.77}$

Where NORMCAP is the normal total installed capacity in m^3/hour.

---

1. Source: Water Research Centre (1977, page 116)

Box 7.6. Estimation for transmission mains[1]

Total cost ('000 British £) = $0.0702*LEN^{0.73}*DIAM^{0.91*(DIAM/(1000+DIAM))}$

Where LEN is total length of pipe network in metres

DIAM is mean diameter of pipe work in millimetres

---

1. Source: Water Research Centre (1977, page 90)

Box 7.7. Estimate of construction costs of concrete reservoir tanks[1]

Total cost of concrete covered tank (million UK £) = $0.0726*CAP^{0.62}$

Where CAP is the capacity of tank in thousands of cubic meters.

---

1. Source: Water Research Centre (1977, page 353)

When using such formulae it is preferable to cross check the results with the actual costs from similar local projects, in order to determine the applicability of the formulae to the local situation.

Determination of Average Incremental Cost (AIC)

The AIC represents the average or long run marginal cost over a long period of time. The Average Incremental Cost (AIC) is determined by assuming that the most economic output is where long run marginal costs equal long run marginal revenue.

AIC is calculated by dividing the present value (PV) of all incremental capital, operating and maintenance costs (C) by the present value (PV) of the incremental consumption (W) over the design life of the facilities to be constructed.

$$AIC = PV\ C\ (\$) / PV\ W\ (m^3)$$

The present values are determined by discounting the cash flows and consumption quantities at a discount rate that equals the opportunity cost of capital to the national economy. The opportunity cost is taken to be the real value of resources used in the most desirable alternative. This formula can be used to determine the AIC for different development scenarios for a water utility.

An example of determination of projected costs for Mombasa and the coastal area using the AIC method is presented in the Annexes. The calculation of accurate projected costs is important for determining tariffs that are at adequate levels for the sustainable management of services.

7.5   Selecting water service options

The range of different service options such as: house connections, yard connections, water kiosks, standposts, etc. are discussed in Chapter 3. Different service options are appropriate in different situations depending on the existing water supply infrastructure, utility finances and the perceptions of consumers. The consumer surveys and focus group discussions should provide indications of what are likely to be the type of options that people will prefer in the various market segments.

Table 7.3 and Table 7.4 show examples of service options offered to different market segments in Mombasa, as part of a willingness to pay survey and strategic marketing research. The willingness to pay survey form that was used is in Annexe 2.

Table 7.3. Service options offered for 1 to 3-roomed dwellings in Mombasa

Service level (option)	Brief description of service option
Service level 4	Continuous supply at yard connection
Service level 5	Continuous supply with storage tank at shared yard connection
Service level 6	12-hr supply at shared yard connection
Service level 7	4-hr supply at shared yard connection

Table 7.4. Service options offered to people in informal settlements in Mombasa[1]

Service level	Brief description of service option
Service level 8	Continuous supply with storage tank at shared yard connection (about 10 dwellings)
Service level 9	12-hr supply at shared yard connection (about 10 dwellings)
Service level 10	Ditto but 4-hr supply
Service level 11	Privately managed kiosk with shelter and tank
Service level 12	Community-managed kiosk with shelter and tank
Service level 13	Privately managed kiosk without shelter or tank

1. Source: Njiru and Sansom, 2001

Note that six options were offered to respondents in informal settlements (Table 7.4). It is usually preferable to offer between three and five options to any group, as this has been found to be a practical range, both from the perspective of having a manageable survey and during the analysis phase.

There are also different criteria for segmenting consumers. In the Kampala marketing research, the market was segmented based on income levels. The service options offered to low-income areas are shown in Table 7.5.

Table 7.5. Service options offered in low-income areas in Kampala[1]

Service level	Brief description of service option
Service level 5	Individual house connection through ground tank (trickle feed)
Service level 6	Community-managed water kiosk
Service level 7	Privately operated water kiosk
Service level 8	Utility-supported water vending
Service level 9	Smart token operated water kiosks (pre-paid meters installed in kiosks, then operated by smart tokens)

1. Source: Kayaga and Sansom, May 2001

Apart from the service options presented here, others can be developed depending on the particular circumstances faced by respective water utilities and the preferences of consumers. Once the service options have been developed and costed, the demand assessment can proceed.

7.6 Willingness to pay for selected options

The contingent valuation method

In the context of the water sector, a key feature of the marketing methodology is to offer feasible service options, to learn how much people are willing to pay for each service option and to select the most popular options.

The contingent valuation method (CVM) is widely used to estimate how much households are willing to pay (WTP) for various service options. (Refer to Part II for an explanation of the key concepts.) The bidding ranges and approaches used are evident from the sample willingness to pay format in Annexe 2.

One of the most common techniques for eliciting respondents' maximum willingness to pay is the *bidding game*, which requires the respondent to either go through a series of bids for each option until a negative response is generated and a threshold established or to select from a range of values. The last accepted bid is the maximum willingness to pay. This method provides the respondent with time to respond and the opportunity to develop an opinion about the payment for the improved water supply.

In general, the amount that two-thirds of the market segment are willing to pay for a service option is a reasonable figure to use in reporting the willingness to pay for the particular market segment. An example of willingness to pay results for different service options in different market segments is presented in the tables below.

Table 7.6. WTP results for people in 1,2 or 3-roomed dwellings in Mombasa[1]

Service level (option)	Brief description of service option	Market segment	Percentage of respondents within market segments who bid for the stated service option	Weighted mean WTP (KSh)	Amount which two-thirds of respondents are WTP (KSh)
Service level 4	Continuous supply at yard connection	People in 1, 2 or 3-roomed dwellings and Swahili houses	100%	1124	834
Service level 5	Continuous supply with storage tank at shared yard connection	Ditto	100%	1023	800
Service level 6	12-hr supply at shared yard connection, rationing	Ditto	62%	537	447
Service level 7	4-hr supply at shared yard connection	Ditto	54%	395	336

1. (Exchange rate is KSh73 = US$1)

Table 7.7. WTP results for people in informal settlements in Mombasa[1]

Service level (option)	Brief description of service option	Market segment	Percentage of respondents within market segment who bid for the stated service option	Weighted mean WTP (KSh)	Amount which two-thirds of respondents are WTP (KSh)
Service level 8	Continuous supply with storage tank at shared yard connection (about 10 dwellings)	People living in dwellings in informal settlements (slums)	98%	1103	592
Service level 9	12-hr supply at shared yard connection (about 10 dwellings), rationing	Ditto	95%	610	500
Service level 10	Ditto but 4-hr supply	Ditto	63%	302	236
Service level 11	Privately managed kiosk with shelter and tank	Ditto	54%	3.50 per 20-litre container	3.25 per 20-litre container
Service level 12	Community-managed kiosk with shelter and tank	Ditto	48%	3 per 20-litre container	2.65 per 20-litre container
Service level 13	Privately managed kiosk, no shelter or tank	Ditto	10%	1.50per 20-litre container	1.60 per 20-litre container

1. (Exchange rate is KSh73= US$1)

Note that both the weighted mean willingness to pay results and the 2/3 values given in Table 7.6 and Table 7.7 reveal a WTP that is much higher than the current tariff level in Mombasa. These results, along with the consumer survey information, can therefore be used to advocate for increases in tariff levels and flexible service options amongst key decision-makers.

Alternative methods of demand assessment

Apart from conducting a willingness to pay study using the contingent valuation method, focus group discussions (FGDs) can be used to obtain customer perceptions of existing water services and their preferences for improved service options. FGDs using approaches such as PREPP (which is described in Section 2.9) are particularly useful as an initial demand assessment or where a conventional willingness to pay study is not feasible due to factors such as lack of skills or resources (time or cost).

As part of PREPP a costed option ranking is done by the group and also individually by secret ballot. Table 7.8 shows individual ranking results of service options by participants in three informal settlements in Mombasa. The lower values (1 and 2) show the preferred options.

Table 7.8. Individual ranking of options in Mombasa informal settlements[1]

Service option	Kisumu Ndogo (by men)	Kisumu Ndogo (by women)	Muoroto Paradise (by men)	Muoroto paradise (by women)	VOK(by men)	VOK(by women)	Overall ranking of option
Service level 8: Shared yard connection with storage, 18-24 hrs of supply; KSh1200 per month	4	5	4	6	3	5	5
Service level 9: Shared yard connection, no storage, 12-hr of supply; KSh800 per month	5	4	5	5	6	6	6
Service level 10: Shared yard connection, no storage, 4 hrs of supply; KSh500 per month	5	2	6	3	4	4	4
Service level 11: Privately managed kiosk with storage; KSh3 per 20 litres	2	6	1	4	2	3	3
Service level 12: Community-managed kiosk with storage; KSh2 per 20 litres	1	1	3	1	1	1	1
Service level 13: Privately managed kiosk; KSh2.50 per 20 litre	3	3	2	2	5	2	2

1. (Exchange rate is KSh73 = US$1)

Table 7.8 shows that community and privately managed kiosks are in higher demand than shared yard connections. It is interesting to note that respondents in the informal settlements in Mombasa generally preferred water kiosks to shared connections, even though water would be cheaper in terms of cost per jerrican from a shared connection than a water kiosk. These results contrasted with India, where there was a good demand for shared or group connections.

The reason group members gave for preferring kiosks in Mombasa was that there would be less potential conflict with their neighbours with water kiosks than with shared connections. Whereas surveyed communities in Guntur in India and small towns in Uganda seemed willing to co-operate with their neighbours on cheaper more convenient shared connections. Such differing perceptions between consumers in different cities, highlights the need to conduct surveys to find out local community perspectives, rather than just make assumptions about people's demands.

The results of the ranking of priced options by FGDs can be used to inform selection of options and design of tariffs. However, it should be noted that this approach provides information on the relative demand for different options at the stated prices, which should be carefully determined to correspond to proposed tariff levels. But it does not provide values for the maximum willingness to pay for each option and the results are not, therefore, so valuable in determining future tariff levels as well designed WTP surveys. The FGDs do, however, provide a good basis for ongoing dialogue between the utility and community groups.

7.7   Population projections

Population growths in cities and towns in developing countries can range from 1 to 7 per cent% per annum. It is important that an accurate estimate of growth in particular towns and cities is obtained in order to inform the planning of future infrastructure and services. It is beneficial to use a 20 to 30 -year planning horizon and prepare population projections on that basis. This information can usually be obtained from census data or planning departments.

There may also be differential growth rates between market segments. Informal settlements, for example, typically grow faster than other parts of cities because of factors such as the rural - urban drift of poor people in search of income- generating opportunities. The use of recent aerial photographs and GIS can assist in monitoring the erection of new dwellings and current growth rates in informal settlements.

7.8   Estimates for service option take- up

Estimates for take- up of service options are made for each option that is to be offered in future, on the basis of the results of the demand assessment. Results of willingness to pay studies can be used to estimate the proportion of consumers within each market segment who demonstrate effective demand for each respective service option.

Knowledge of how many people live in a city and how that population and its distributed in respective market segments is also important. Water utilities can obtain population and its distribution information from census data, which provides an important source of information, especially on residential water users. By knowing the population and its distribution within each market segment, the total number of people who might population who takes up the different respective options can be estimated.

Apart from willingness to pay studies, infrastructure deficiencies should be taken into account. This is particularly important in low-income settlements where willingness to pay for higher levels of service may exist, but basic infrastructure to support high levels of service is lacking. In such an area, a gradual take- up of service options or the use of intermediate service levels such as shared connections and kiosks may be more feasible in the shorter term in order to allow time for the development of infrastructure to support the desired higher levels of service.

Social issues can also influence take- up of options. For instance, the social dynamics of an urban community might be conducive for community management of water kiosks, in which case the take- up of such an option could be high. A community that is not cohesive may not wish to have community- managed kiosks, in which case privately managed kiosks may be preferable. Focus group discussions can provide key information in this respect.

An example of estimates for the take- up of service options in the Mombasa research are summarized in Table 7.9, based on survey data and knowledge of what is feasible. Note that the suggested number of options to be offered to each market segment is less than was originally offered to respondents in the willingness to pay survey (refer to Annexe 2.). This refinement in the number of options is based on selecting which options have the highest demand and what are the most feasible for the utility to deliver. It may be necessary to further reduce or adapt the options in the light of experience in promoting the options and witnessing the level of take-up of each option, during implementation phases.

Table 7.9. Take-up of service options by Market segment in Mombasa[1]

Market segment by type of dwelling	Estimated Population in market segment	Service options and estimated proportion of option take-up
Bungalows and maisonettes	175,000	12-24hr supply at individual house connection (100%)
Flats	105,000	1. 12-24hr supply at individual connection (80%) 2. 12-24hr supply through shared connection (20%)
1, 2 or 3-roomed dwellings and and Swahili houses	280,000	1. 12-24hr supply at individual connection (25%) 2. 12-24hr supply at shared yard connection (30%) 3. 12-24hr supply at shared yard connection with storage tank (30%) 4. Privately managed kiosks with storage (10%) 5. Community-managed kiosks with storage (5%)
Informal settlements (slums)	140,000	1. 12-24hr supply at shared yard connection (10%) 2. 12-24hr supply at shared yard connection with storage tank (10%) 3. Privately managed kiosks with storage (40%) 4. Community-managed kiosks with storage (40%)

1. Source: Njiru and Sansom (2001)

Note that where there are alternative non-utility water supplies such as wells or springs, these options need to be taken into consideration when estimating the take-up of utility service options.

7.9 Estimating water consumption

There are no universally accepted levels of water consumption. Engineers and planners often use their own figures for project design, basing them on local circumstances.

Water consumption is the amount of water consumed by one person in one unit of time, and is expressed in litres per capita per day (lpcd). Consumption levels vary from place to place depending on factors such as:

- location of the area (climate, culture, etc.;)

- availability of water (method of supply/delivery/service option);

- time and distance to collect water;

- reliability of water services;

- whether internal plumbing in the house is provided;

- level of income;

- presence or absence of water borne sewerage;

- cost of water and method of payment; and

- whether water is metered or not.

Water consumption and health risks

The quantity of water delivered and used for households is an important aspect of domestic water supplies, and is one which influences hygiene and therefore public health. Based on estimates of requirements of lactating women who engage in moderate physical activity in above-average temperatures, a minimum of 7.5 litres per capita per day will meet the requirements of most people under most conditions. This water needs to be of a quality that represents a tolerable level of risk. This water volume does not account for health and well-being-related demands outside normal domestic use, such as water use in health care facilities, food production, economic activity or amenity use. (Howard and Bartram, 2002).

Accessibility to water can be categorized in terms of service level. A summary of both the degree to which different levels of service will meet requirements to sustain good health and the interventions required to ensure health gains are maximized is shown in Table 7.10 below.

Table 7.10. Water service levels and health concerns

Service level	Access measure	Needs met	Level of health concern
No access (quantity collected often below 5 l/c/d)	More than 1000m or 30 minutes total collection time	Consumption - cannot be assured Hygiene - not possible (unless practised at source)	Very high
Basic access (average quantity unlikely to exceed 20 l/c/d)	Between 100 and 1000m or 5 to 30 minutes total collection time	Consumption - should be assured Hygiene - handwashing and basic food hygiene possible; laundry/ bathing difficult to assure unless carried out at source	High
Intermediate access (average quantity about 50 l/c/d)	Water delivered through one tap on-plot (or within 100m or 5 minutes total collection time	Consumption - assured Hygiene - all basic personal and food hygiene assured; laundry and bathing should also be assured	Low
Optimal access (average quantity 100 l/c/d and above)	Water supplied through multiple taps continuously	Consumption - all needs met Hygiene - all needs should be met	Very low

The estimated quantities of water at each level may reduce where water supplies are intermittent and the risks of ingress of contaminated water into domestic water supplies will increase. (Howard and Bartram, 2002). To minimize health risks, governments and utilities should be seeking to reduce water collection times so that increased household water volumes increase. This essentially means that on-plot service options are most preferable, and water points should at least be nearby, such as buying water from neighbours. Where these options are not feasible for the time being, water kiosks or standposts can be provided.

Estimating consumption

Engineers typically use conventional methods of estimating water consumption using design standards, where specific consumption is assumed based on the type of water supply. In the context of a commercial approach to management of water services and, project design should be based on effective demand (demonstrated by willingness to pay) rather than perceived levels of consumption.

The relevant consumption figure is the minimum necessary for health and well being (say 20 lpcd). Any amount above the minimum for health (and thus required for convenience) should be provided on the basis of supply and demand. It is therefore recommended that consumption should be estimated on the basis of willingness to pay and the likely water availability.

Estimating the water consumption in a particular city requires consideration of the service option, the market segment and willingness to pay. Assuming that billing is based on metered consumption, the water tariff will also influence the actual consumption. Table 7.11 shows estimated water consumption per market segment and service options used in the Mombasa research.

Table 7.11. Estimated water consumption for service options in Mombasa

Market segment by type of dwelling	Service option	Estimated consumption (litres/capita per day)
Bungalows and maisonettes	12-24hr supply at individual house connection	· 150
Flats	3. 12-24hr supply at individual house connection 4. 12-24hr supply through shared yard connection	· 100 · 100
1, 2 or 3- roomed dwellings and Swahili houses	6. 12-24hr supply at individual house connection 7. 12-24hr supply at shared yard connection 8. 12-24hr supply at shared yard connection with tank 9. Privately managed kiosks with storage tank 10. Community- managed kiosks with storage	· 100 · 60 · 60 · 20 · 20
Informal settlements	12-24hr supply at shared yard connection 12-24hr supply at shared yard connection with tank Privately managed kiosks with storage tank Community-managed kiosks with storage tank	· 60 · 60 · 20 · 20

If the assumed consumption figures for the design of new schemes are a little high, it should not present a problem, because the spare capacity generated can be used when there is increased demand for water in that particular area, as a result of the population growing or as people can pay more for water. However, if the assumed consumption figures are much higher than the quantities customers want, then there is a clear risk of too much spare capacity in the water supply infrastructure, which represents wasted investments. Hence it is important to only promote viable service options and respond to consumer demand for services.

Once consumption estimates have been made for each service option and market segment, the volume of water sold through each of the service options to different market segments can be calculated using the population distribution and the assumed option take up. The calculation should be done bearing in mind the results of the demand assessment.

7.10 Infrastructure improvements

.Many water utilities need to invest in new infrastructure and/or rehabilitate the existing networks, in order to provide services adequately and reliably, to more consumers and attain financial sustainability.

It may be necessary to invest in new sources of water, and to increase the capacity of treatment works and also water transmission to meet future demands. The distribution network often requires expansion in order to extend services to un-served areas and to meet the utility's equity objectives of serving those who are currently not served. In the Mombasa strategic marketing study (2001), the following broad areas of investments were envisaged in order to achieve the projected water consumption rates:

- the development of a new distant water source and 220km- long transmission main, with an abstraction rate of 1.0M3/sec;

- an expansion of the distribution network to meet demands up to the year 2020;

- reduction of water losses; and

- provision of sewerage to some areas.

Network extension also improves the utility's customer base with potential for improvement in revenue. Some old sections of the network may require replacement in order to reduce leakage and improve the quality of water supplied to customers.

Infrastructure improvements, however, need to be well planned, as they are typically capital intensive. Water utilities can define infrastructure improvements either by using their own (in-house) capacity or commissioning private engineering consultancy firms to undertake engineering studies and define the most feasible investment option. The detailed designs for infrastructure improvements should be based on precisely defined performance targets for each element of the water supply system.

The estimates of option take- up with an allowance for future population projections and demand for options should inform the design of the infrastructure. Several alternative project scenarios are usually identified and compared. Selection of the most feasible infrastructure development scenario is done on the basis of technical, environmental and financial considerations. The choice of technology is particularly important in developing countries. Technology that is simple to operate is preferable to sophisticated technology that may be easy or cheaper to install but poses problems during the operation and maintenance phase. Availability of technology back-up and spares should be considered in selecting the technology to be adopted. For instance, gravity systems (that are often more expensive to install) are preferable to pumping systems wherever possible. It is particularly important to consider both the capital costs and the life- cycle costs.

Water requirements should be considered for both the short/medium term and the long term, in order to discover the most feasible solution, in terms of reliability and simplicity of operation. In particular, selection of water sources requires meeting not only technical and economic considerations but also environmental criteria.

The design of all components should include costings to determine the unit cost of water provision. If the projected revenues cannot meet the projected costs with tariffs set at acceptable levels (bearing in mind willingness to pay and willingness to charge levels), then alternative project components or concepts should be considered.

Selection of the infrastructure improvement scenario should also take into account the sources and cost of finance. The final selection of which infrastructure improvement scenario should be implemented should be made on the basis of technical, environmental and financial viability. These factors have implications for the options that the utility can reliably provide to customers in a financially sustainable manner.

7.11 Agreeing tariff levels

The utility's financial objectives and the projected costs of service provision ought to be the main determinants of the criteria for tariff design. In practice, however, setting and implementing water tariffs is a contentious issue in most countries and will depend on the 'willingness to charge' of policymakers and the 'willingness to pay' of water users. The AESCE principles (adequate, equitable, simple, conserving and enforceable), as outlined in Section 7.3, provides a good basis for agreeing both the tariff structures and the tariff levels. Experiences in setting tariffs as part of a marketing analysis for Mombasa are outlined in Box 7.8.

Box 7.8. Matching tariffs with projected costs and willingness to pay[1]

In the Mombasa strategic marketing analysis, the full costs of acceptable water services were estimated at US$1.21 (KSsh88./30) per m^3 using the average incremental cost method (AIC). The tariff was designed in such a way that customers' willingness to pay amounts for each service option and respective customer market were not exceeded. This resulted into an average tariff of KSsh89./20 (US$1.20) per m^3, which was sufficient for the utility to meet all its costs and record a modest profit.

---

1. Source: Njiru and Sansom (2001)

In order for water services to be provided in a financially sustainable manner, utilities should be committed to setting tariff structures that fully cover the costs of efficiently managed water operations. Tariffs can be designed using the principles of flat rate, declining block rate, and increasing block tariffs, although block tariffs reduce the simplicity of the tariff structure and can affect equity considerations (as is discussed in Section 7.3). An example of a proposed tariff structure is provided in Table 7.12. The basic principle used in this example is that the tariff is set depending on the level of service provided, i.e. subsidizing those options that are less convenient for users.

Table 7.12. Proposed tariff structure for Mombasa[1]

Proposed water supply options	Proposed water tariffs based on WTP survey (KSh/m^3)
12-24h Hour supply at individual house connection	60
12-24h Hour supply at shared house (flat) connection	55
12-24h Hour supply at yard connection with a utility storage tank	50
12-24h Hour supply at yard connection without a utility tank	45
12-24h Hour supply at privately managed water kiosks with storage and structure	25
12-24h Hour supply at community- managed water kiosks with storage and structure	25
12-24h Hour supply to commercial, industrial or institutional customers	120
Proposed average tariff	KSh89.20 per m^3

1. (Exchange rate is KSh73/ = to the US$1)

In the Mombasa study, the proposed tariff of KSh 89/ per m^3 to pay for the proposed investments is substantially more than the current equivalent tariff (in 2000) of about KSh 21/m3. A carefully organized promotion campaign would be required for the proposed tariff increases to be accepted. Incremental increases over a number of years are likely to be necessary.

The final agreed tariff levels may of course need to be adjusted in the light of an assessment of the projected revenues and the overall financial projections, which are considered in the following sections.

7.12 Projected revenue

Projected revenues can be calculated for respective service options on the basis of the consumption estimates, assumed take- up of options and proposed tariffs. Revenues are estimated with proposed tariffs set at levels that are adequate for full cost recovery and within willingness to pay levels for each service option and market segment of the population. Calculations for projected revenue also require consideration of unaccounted for water (water that is produced but not sold) and bill collection efficiency.

The calculation is iterative and aims to balance projected costs with projected revenues. The calculation is repeated until the projected revenue exceeds (or equals) the projected costs of providing the required services. An example of results of a sample calculation for Mombasa is shown in the Table 7.13 below.

Table 7.13 shows that the total projected revenue for the utility is KSh 3, 906, 704, 500 per annum, with an average water tariff of KSh 89.20 (about US$1.20) per m3. Assuming that the total annual costs to cover both capital and recurrent expenditure (including loan repayments) remains at the estimated amount of KSh3, 854,400,000, then the utility can make a modest profit of KSh52, 304, 500 (about US$716, 500) per annum. This means that the utility can meet both social and financial objectives and still make a profit. This profit could be used to improve water services in other un-served areas.

Table 7.13. Projected revenues in Mombasa[1]

Proposed water supply options	Expected volume of water sold and paid for (m³/yr)	Proposed water tariffs based on WTP survey (KSh/m³)	Projected income from each option (KSh)
12-24 Hour supply at individual house connection	14 691 250	60	881 475 000
12-24h Hour supply at shared house (flat) connection	766 500	55	42 157 500
12-24h Hour supply at yard connection with utility storage tank	2 146 200	50	107 310 000
12-24h Hour supply at yard connection (no utility tank)	2 146 200	45	96, 579, 000
12-24h Hour supply at water kiosks with storage and structure (privately or community-managed)	1,124,200	25	28, 105, 000
12-24h Hour supply to commercial, industrial and institutional customers	22 925 650	120	2, 751, 078, 000
Total	43,800,000m³	Average tariff is KSh89.20/m³	3, 906, 704, 500

1. (Exchange rate is KSh73/ = to the US$1)

7.13   Financial projections and investment scenarios

Financial projections that cover the loan period will be needed, as has been done for in the Kampala marketing study (refer to Annexe 4) so that incremental tariff and revenue collection increases can be balanced with loan repayments and other costs. A major responsibility for a water utility is maintaining an adequate level of revenue, which is collected equitably from all consumer groups. Total revenues should be sufficient in order to:

• provide adequate customer service to maintain and sustain the water supply services;

• to pay government taxes;

• to earn an appropriate return; and

• to ensure a secure financial status necessary to obtain credit at reasonable rates from lending institutions for any system expansion or improvement.

To ensure availability of funds on a day-to-day basis, water utilities need to plan and manage cash flows over the project period. Cash-flow planning assures that sufficient cash is available when it is required, and minimizes the need for short-term borrowing. Excess cash, if any, may be temporarily invested. Cash-flow management involves synchronizing cash inflows with outflows. Operating revenue accounts inform management decisions regarding amount and type of capital expenditures that is variable. An iterative solution could then be sought to find out what tariff structure is feasible in order to carry out service coverage expansion and service quality improvements according to the strategic marketing plan.

Each water utility has different objectives and operates under different conditions, and therefore has different cash requirements and needs. It is important that the tariff structure reflects the objectives and needs of the utility. If the cash flow is not planned for and properly managed, the corporate objectives may not be fulfilled. In planning for appropriate cash flows over the project period, the specific financial objectives of the utility must be considered. The financial objectives can be examined by answering the following:

- Is the utility fully self financing or does it receive any form of subvention from the state?

- Does the utility cater for amortizsation? Does it cater for depreciation?

- Does the utility keep depreciation and amortizsation expense accounts?

- Is the utility servicing any loans? How is the loan repayment scheduled?

- Does the utility subsidize any other entity or other departments?

A case study conducted in 2000, in Kampala, Uganda came up with a strategic marketing plan for water services for a 25- year project period. As an example, Box 7.9 shows highlights of scenarios considered in computing cash flow projections for the Kampala water supply service area. Note that different investment scenarios have been considered, in order to develop the optimum investment plan.

A summary financial projection can be seen in Annexe 4 with a planned increase in coverage from 31% to 100 per cent%. Note that the financial projections include different service options in each market segment (high, middle and low-income) and show incremental tariff increases and the cumulated surplus/deficit.

The investment scenarios should reflect the investment choices that seem most viable. These choices could be technical, such as the choice between developing different water sources. Or the choice could be between different tariff levels that are linked to different service levels. High, medium and low- cost scenarios would be examples of such choices. In determining the preferred investment scenario(s) it is useful to do sensitivity analyses by experimenting with key variables using the spreadsheet financial model to develop the option that is preferred by the key stakeholders. The final projections must include achievable infrastructure improvements and be affordable.

Box 7.9. Example financial projections for investments in Kampala[1]

During the dictatorship regime in Uganda in the 1970-1980 decade, the service coverage of corporatized urban water utility, the National Water & Sewerage Corporation (NWSC), suffered in two major ways: there was virtually no investment into expanding the water service coverage; and the existing infrastructure deteriorated because of poor O&M practices. Consequently, since 1986, NWSC has injected substantial investment funds into the infrastructure, using grants and loans sourced by the government from bilateral and multi-lateral financing institutions, with a loan repayment period ranging between 10 and 30 years. Since the early 1990s, the loan portfolio for the Kampala water supply service area has grown to about US$64 million.

Scrutiny of the investments carried out shows that expansion of water treatment plants was not matched by extension and rehabilitation of NWSC's water reticulation network, a situation that has resulted into low service coverage of about 40 per cent of the total population in Kampala. On top of the high level of un-accounted-for -water and low collection efficiency, the low coverage contributed to low revenue collection. Subsequently, NWSC asked for a reschedule of loan repayments as follows:

US $ 7.5 million in 2002/2003
US $ 8.3 million in 2003/2004
US $ 8.8 million in 2004/2005, leaving a principal balance of US $ 14.45 million on the historical loansAnalysis carried out shows that it is not possible to comply with this loan repayment schedule, and also be able to use internal sours to capitalize the infrastructure expansion projects that are critical for growth of NWSC. Consequently, to illustrate how to derive a 25-year strategic marketing plan for NWSC Kampala supply area, four scenarios were considered as follows:

- *Scenario 1:* Assumptions were made that the central government will take on payment of historical loans, and treat them as equity contributions. In this case, revenue collection would fully cater for operation and maintenance costs, as well as service expansion to cover 100% of the projected population by the 25th year of the project. The average tariff would be 0.67 US $ per cubic metre.

- *Scenario 2:* Assumptions were that revenue collection would cater for historical loans and service expansion to enable 100% population coverage by the 25th year of the project cycle. However, NWSC would have to negotiate for loan rescheduling for the last 10 years of the 25-year project cycle. The average tariff would be US $ 0.76 per cubic meter.

- *Scenario 3:* Assumptions were that the Central Government will take on payment of historical loans, and revenue collection would cater for service expansion to enable 100% population coverage by the 25th year of the project cycle. Kampala Area could also provide cross-subsidies of US$ 8 million in the first six years and step it up appropriately thereafter, to cater for operation and maintenance of other secondary towns under NWSC. The average tariff would be US $ 0.76 per cubic meter.

- *Scenario 4:* Revenue collection to cater for both historical loan repayment and subsidies specified in Scenario 3. The major assumption is that NWSC would negotiate for rescheduling of loan repayment to after the 15th year of the project, to enable capitalisation of service expansion in the early period of the project. The tariff would be US $ 0.78 per cubic meter.

All the above scenarios ensured that there are no cash-flow problems in the daily operations of NWSC.

1. Source: Kayaga and Sansom, 2001

Chapter 8

Stage 3: 'How we might get there?'

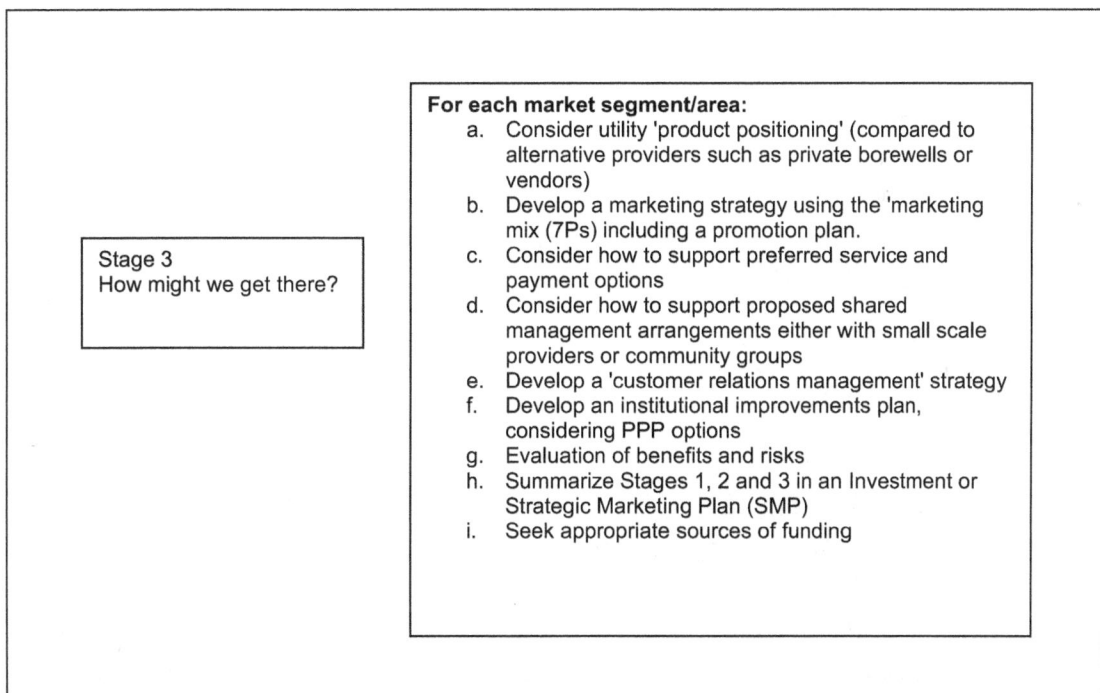

Stage 3 How might we get there?	**For each market segment/area:** a. Consider utility 'product positioning' (compared to alternative providers such as private borewells or vendors) b. Develop a marketing strategy using the 'marketing mix (7Ps) including a promotion plan. c. Consider how to support preferred service and payment options d. Consider how to support proposed shared management arrangements either with small scale providers or community groups e. Develop a 'customer relations management' strategy f. Develop an institutional improvements plan, considering PPP options g. Evaluation of benefits and risks h. Summarize Stages 1, 2 and 3 in an Investment or Strategic Marketing Plan (SMP) i. Seek appropriate sources of funding

It is assumed that draft financial projections for proposed new investments have been completed based on estimated future take up of service options and reasonable tariff policies, as discussed in the *'Where do we want to be?'* section. There may of course be one or more preferred investment scenarios still under consideration. We shall now consider how the preferred scenario might be achieved as part of a marketing strategy, considering the 'marketing mix - 7Ps', which provides a useful planning framework. Other key aspects that contribute to answering the question *'How we might get there'*, are improving 'customer relations management' and utility institutional improvements.

8.1   Product positioning

When a utility is considering a significant expansion of its services in a particular area, it needs to consider advantages/disadvantages of its service options compared to other service providers already being used in that area such as: vendors, private borewells, dug wells etc.

A utility should seek to ensure that it achieves its projected take up of its service options in the market segments chosen. Product positioning is the process of designing an image and value so that people in the target market segments appreciate the comparative benefits between what the utility offers compared to the alternative water service providers.

The process of product positioning involves three steps (Wilson and Gilligan, 1997):

- Identifying the possible competitive advantage of the organization's services;

- Deciding on those aspects to be emphasized

- Implement the positioning concept.

Many water utilities assume that it is obvious to everybody how their water quality is superior. This is not the case, as many water utilities operate in a macro-environment where literacy rates may be low and misinformation can spread. Furthermore the utilities often underestimate the impact of negative propaganda carried out by alternative water supply providers. It is important that water utilities adopt a suitable positioning strategy to assert themselves in the market. Water utilities can design their positioning strategies along the following lines:

- Positioning by attribute:

- Positioning by price

- Positioning by quality

- Positioning by application

At Durban Metro Water in South Africa a dedicated R&D department was established to develop and promote new water supply options, refer to Box 8.1. The people working in this department promoted the new options pointing out the relative merits of each option in comparison with alternatives.

Box 8.1. Community mobilisation at Durban Metro Water

The Research and Development Department of Durban Metro Water Services is mandated to maintain effective communication with low-income communities in Durban Metro. The Utility employs full time Community Liaison Officers, who are social development professionals, to keep constant contact with low-income communities. The Community Liaison officers get involved in identification of new water projects, mobilisation of communities, cultivating a willingness-to-pay among members of the communities, community involvement in the project implementation, project commissioning, and ensuring cost recovery.

There has been heightened interest in the water and sanitation sector to assist in the promotion of hygiene education to water users. Research has shown that hygiene education and promotion influences health benefits. A lot of progress in promotion of good hygiene has been made in the rural water sector. However, many water utilities have not taken on hygiene education as a vital tool for product positioning. Various NGOs/CBOs are doing the little work on hygiene education in urban areas. There would be a bigger impact if water utilities got involved in hygiene promotion. Box 8.2 gives an example of how Umgeni Water handles hygiene promotion:

Box 8.2. External education services unit of Umgeni water, S. Africa

The External Education Services (EES) Unit is of Umgeni Water, South Africa specializes in promoting hygiene education to communities and schools. The Unit disseminates this information through workshops, and through a number of other educational tools such as videos, material suitable for teaching aids, puzzles and information booklets People are also taught how to monitor their water supplies using low-cost water test kits, and also how to treat contaminated water.

Such activities can assist in generating demand amongst consumers for utility supported water service options that present less risks of contamination than alternative unprotected sources. Another example of the benefits of promotion activities in India is given in Box 8.3

Box 8.3. Marketing Sanitation in Rural India[1]

WaterAid-India's rural sanitation program was making slow progress in 1995-96. A lack of demand from households meant that partner NGOs had constructed only 460 out of 1,100 latrines planned for the 12-month period. WaterAid-India decided it was time to reformulate its strategy and focus on marketing sanitation. As a result of this change in approach, by the first six months of 1997-98, partner NGOs had achieved a dramatic turnaround in demand and constructed 5,000 latrines but were still unable to meet the spiralling demand from rural households in the project areas. WaterAid stimulated demand for sanitation through social marketing and hygiene promotion.

---

1. Source: World Bank Water and Sanitation Program South East Asia (2000)

8.2 The marketing mix - the seven P's

A useful tool for an organization wishing to ensure that it is comprehensive in it is approach to marketing and its' interactions with customers is the 7P's which are listed in Figure 8.1. This figure includes typical key issues for a water utility to consider for each of the 7Ps.

Typical questions that may arise for a utility that is developing investment plans and marketing implementation strategies are set out below for each of the 7 Ps. It is assumed that the utility has already completed the development of feasible options, demand assessment and financial projections, although the development of detailed marketing implementation strategies, are also likely to have implications for the financial projections.

Product	• Offer options menu (including technology, service level, price, management arrangements, payment choices based on consumer preferences and utility ability to deliver)

Price	• Tariff structure • Discounts for shared management schemes • Profitability • Competitiveness • Price incentives • Willingness and ability to sustain payment

Promotion	• Advertising (paper based, loudspeaker, radio, press releases) • Word-of-mouth (through front office and field staff; other customers) • Community meetings, focus groups • Sales promotion e.g. new technology demonstrations • Public Relations, planned visits to water works

Place	• Market segmentation plan • Ability to supply target group • Local external influences and/or political dynamics • Local competitive advantage • Local logistical support (decentralized O&M, payment schemes and customer services) • Different products in different market segments

People	• Quality of customer relationship • Two-way communication structures and mechanisms • Development of trust • Understanding perceptions and expectations • Loyalty to existing / potential service provider • Customer feedback • HRD/capacity building • Liaison and partnerships with civil society, NGO's, donors

Processes	• Complaint/compliments monitoring systems • Quality control for technical and billing systems • Service delivery reliability and consistency • Streamlined service procedures (connections, customer inquiries, re-connection, service recovery systems)

Presence	• Premises (decentralized/centralised) • Accessibility of utility to customers • Customer service office (location, atmosphere, image, accessibility, ease of use) • Local liaison teams/officers • Corporate image; corporate identity

Figure 8.1. Marketing mix issues for water utilities[1]

1. (Figure adapted from Brassington & Pettitt, 2000).

Products or options

• Is any further product/option development required (refer to section 3.6)

• Will the utility sell or provide new options (eg ground tanks or kiosks), or are they readily available from the open market, in which case are negotiations with suppliers necessary?

• Is any further demand assessment for the option required?

- If a new option is being piloted in a certain area, how will its viability be assessed and reported on?

- Is the utility in the position to deliver the proposed range of options? If not what needs to be in place in order to achieve sustainable management of services?

Price

- Is the proposed tariff structure consistent with the results of willingness to pay surveys and government policies?

- Does the proposed tariff structure for different service options and consumption levels follow the 'AESCE' principles (Adequate, Equitable, Simple, Conserving and Enforceable? Are the tariffs consistent with the level of service being offered?

- Do key stakeholders need to be consulted and agree on the tariff structure and policies?

- If subsidies are being offered, do they provide appropriate incentives and disincentives for customers and are the subsidies sustainable?

Promotion

- What are the most suitable options for promoting new services and options? (see Box 8.4 on Durban experiences)

- Does the promotion plan take into account the typical steps towards a purchase? (Refer to Figure 8.2)

- How can the relative advantages of the proposed improved utility services compared to alternative water service providers be emphasized in the promotion plan? (refer to the section on product positioning)

- What is a suitable range of promotional material for the utility to develop?

- How will the various utility departments be involved in promotion of new options?

- How will the utility promote its' corporate image and new simplified procedures?

What are appropriate promotional channels? For each message or piece of material what channel should be used such as: direct mailing, posters, radio, television, meetings, internet, phone book etc.

Place

- Is there an agreed market segmentation plan of the city/town that clearly shows where the different market segments (consumer groups) are located?

- Have some informal areas been missed out in the segmentation plan or in consumer surveys, could these be included in the next surveys?

- Has it been agreed which service/payment options are to be offered in which market segments and areas? Perhaps piloting in some areas is necessary?

- In some poorly served areas is it appropriate to support and regulate local water vendors by providing good water collection points and publicizing the price that the vendors pay the utility for water?

People

- Who within the utility will be responsible for service option development and approval?

Box 8.4. Durban Metro Water's promotion of service options[1]

Durban Metro Water have promoted their service options, including individual ground tanks and overhead tanks by a number of means including:

- Taking a demonstration model of the ground tank to different poorer communities around the city.

- Production and distribution of clear and concise leaflets explaining each option with drawings of each service level offered.

- Utility staff attended community meetings in the poorer areas to discuss the advantages and disadvantages of their service options and their implications.

- Production of a video dealing with the merits of ground tanks and the process of obtaining one.

- Community representatives invited to utility offices for further discussions and video shows.

- Negotiations with community groups to finally agree on their preferred options and the management arrangements.

Extensive use of the promoted service options was apparent in visits to poorer communities in Durban.

1. Source: Durban Metro Water visit by K. Sansom, 1998.

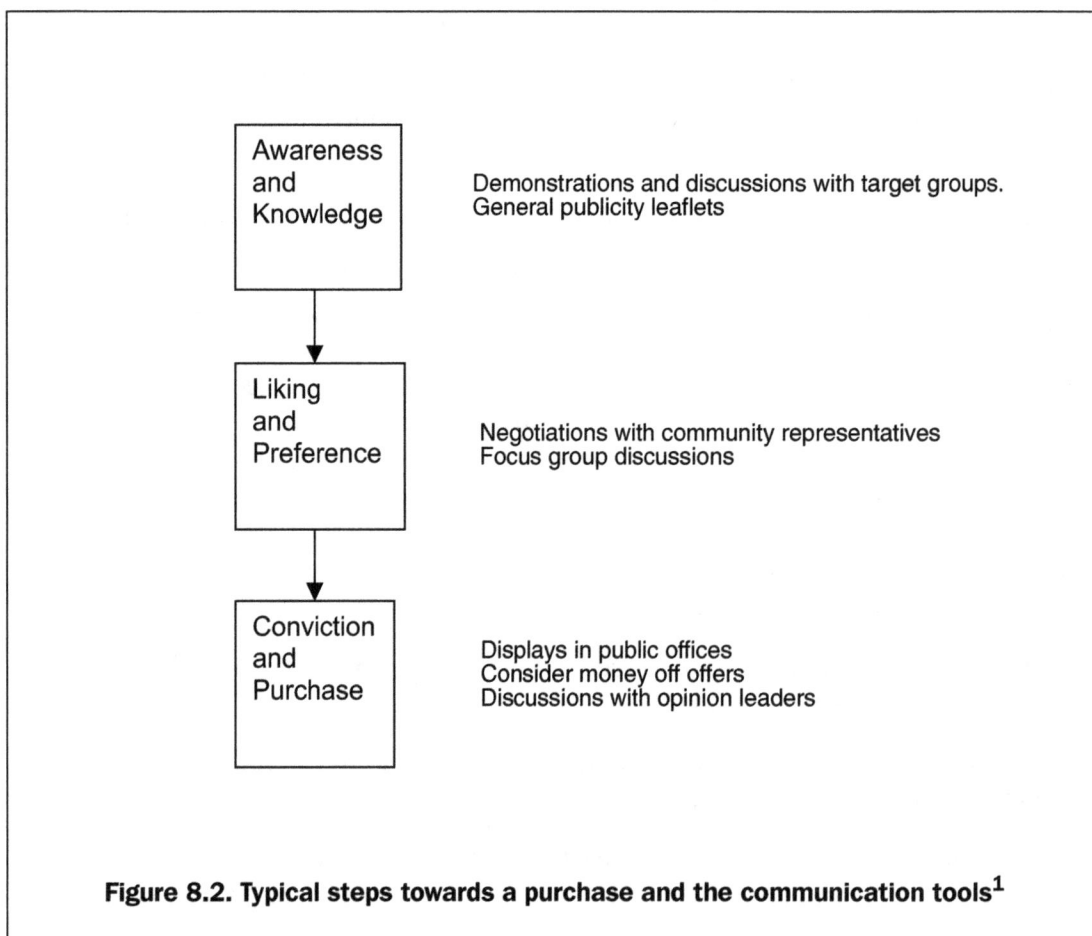

Awareness and Knowledge	Demonstrations and discussions with target groups. General publicity leaflets
Liking and Preference	Negotiations with community representatives Focus group discussions
Conviction and Purchase	Displays in public offices Consider money off offers Discussions with opinion leaders

Figure 8.2. Typical steps towards a purchase and the communication tools[1]

1. Source: Adapted from Wilson and Gilligan p 463 (1997)

- Who within the utility will be responsible for communications with community groups in poorly served areas? Will community liaison officers be appointed?

- Is there good potential for some form of shared management of services together with community groups or small scale private providers? How will this be taken forward? (Refer to chapter 4).

- How will the utility develop a good understanding of the perceptions and preferences people in the different market segments? Which combination of consumer surveys, focus group discussions and meetings is appropriate in each area? The PREPP approach to utility consultation with the poor that is described in book 3, provides a good basis for commencing ongoing dialogue.

- How will staff in the different utility departments be involved in implementing the marketing strategy and improving customer relations? (Refer to section 8.3 for references on improving customer services and relations.)

- What human resource development programme is required to develop the capacities of utility staff and other stakeholders to successfully implement the marketing strategy?

Processes

- Are the key steps in the 'customer value chain' being followed?

- Can key processes be streamlined, particularly those involving existing and potential customers? Examples of such processes could include procedures for:

a) obtaining a new connection

b) obtaining new service options offered

c) disconnections and reconnections

d) bill payment options and billing systems

e) customer complaints and complaint redressal

f) maintaining effective dialogue with community groups or small scale providers, where there is some form of shared management

g) preventive and corrective maintenance

h) updating utility asset and connection records

- Has sufficient data been collected for comprehensive investment planning?

- Can service delivery and interaction with customers be improved using approaches such as TQM (Total Quality Management).

Presence

When a utility is seeking to improve services and raise tariffs to move towards recovering all costs, it needs to develop trust amongst customers and other key stakeholders. One means of doing this is to improve its' corporate image and presence in the community. Some issues to consider in this regard are as follows:

- Should more local decentralized offices be provided in different parts of the city to make it easy for customers to make requests, enquiries and complaints?

- Should customer services offices be designed to be 'one-stop' offices so that customers do not need to go to a number of offices for different issues?

- How can a utility develop a better understanding with customers about what services the utility should provide and what are the customer's obligations? For example, should a customer charter and be developed or improved?

- Can the utility's image and presence be enhanced by having a clear logo and utility name on vehicles, letter heads, uniforms etc?

Many of these issues need to be addressed in an integrated way and are discussed further in the next section on Customer Relations Management. Box 8.5 highlights some of the customer care initiatives introduced by Hyderabad Metro Water and Sanitation Board in India that have led to an enhancement in its' corporate image and presence, despite severe water resource problems in the city.

Box 8.5. Hyderabad Metro Water Board's Customer Care Initiatives

There has been continuing improvement in Hyderabad Metro Water and Sanitation Board's customer care arrangements over a number of years, that have led to an enhancement in its corporate image, despite severe water resource problems in the city. Examples of customer care initiatives include:

a. Development of the Metro Customer Care Centre which includes:
- phone hotline that can be dialled from anywhere in the city,
- speedy complaint redressal with problems referred to the appropriate general manager,
- integration and co-ordination with revenue and billing departments,
- developing and distributing promotional material explaining the Merto Customer Care system,
- informing the customer after suitable action is taken.

b. The creation of 'one stop' or 'single window' customer care centres so that all customer enquiries, complaints and requests can be dealt with at the same locations.

c. Sanctions of new connections within 15 days. What does sanctions mean in this context?

d. The development of a customer charter that explains; what services the utility should provide; what are its key procedures and what are the customer's obligations.

e. Encouraging rainwater harvesting measures for buildings, in order to recharge groundwater levels in the city.

f. Participation in joint utility computerised payment centres, where people can go along and pay a number of utility bills at the same time.

g. The utility has held regular consultation meetings, particularly in poorly served areas, to discuss issues such as piped water supply timings and the timing of the arrival of watertankers, in order to minimize inconvenience.

h. Slum residents are given the option of paying connection charges by instalments, and standposts are being converted to group connections (5 households).

In developing the marketing strategies through frameworks such as the 7 P's, it is important for a utility to create a competitive advantage within the target market segments, compared with alternative suppliers such as vendors or consumer organized options such as individual borewells.

8.3   Improved Customer Relations Management

Developing CRM strategies

Successful companies, including those in the water sector, have found that a key to success is having a clear customer focus and by striving to provide good quality services. In the urban water sector, good customer relations management has even more relevance in developing countries, than in richer countries, because there are more alternative water supply providers within their urban areas.

Paying attention to improved customer relations is particularly important where new areas are being served or new water service/payment options are being offered as part of a marketing approach. Unless these issues are dealt with comprehensively, there may be only limited take up of service options and the predicted revenues will not be forthcoming. Serving unplanned areas and poorer communities requires a utility to be more flexible in response to problems and preferences expressed by such consumer groups.

One of the major reasons why a water utility should improve its customer relations management is to increase customer satisfaction. Satisfied customers become more loyal to the water utility. The customer loyalty creates a 'ripple effect' in the utility's revenue collection. Figure 8.3 illustrates the power of existing satisfied customers and the positive feedback loop that it generates.

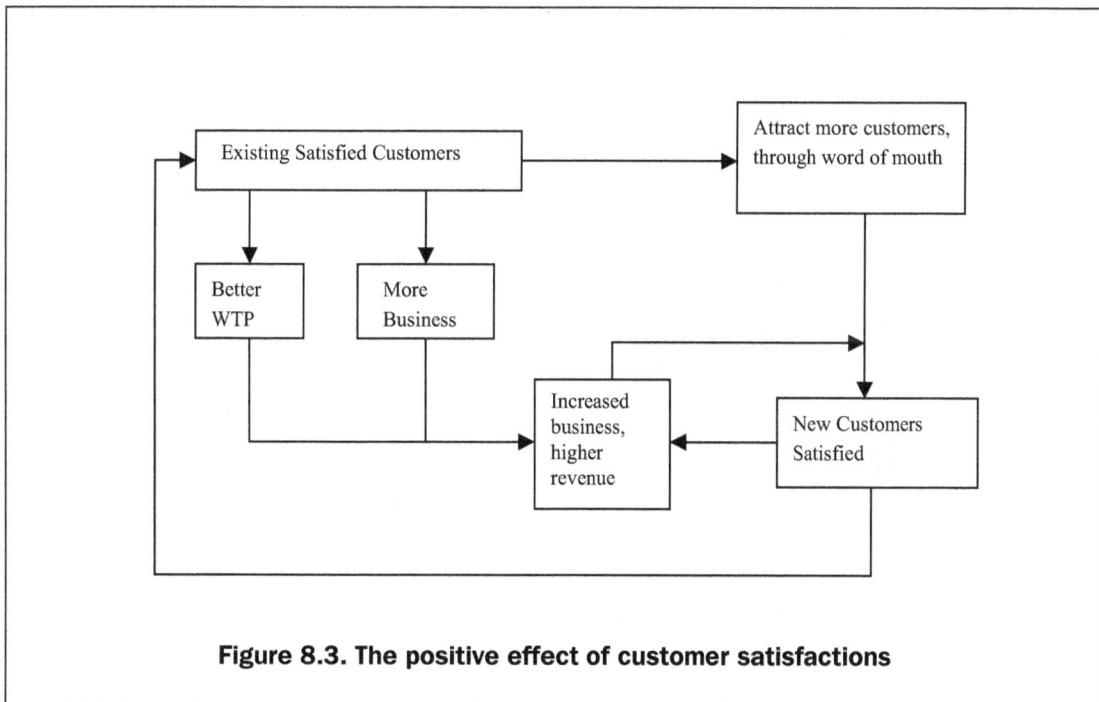

Figure 8.3. The positive effect of customer satisfactions

More satisfied customers also means that a greater willingness to sustain payment exists amongst those customers, which amounts to greater income potential for the utility. A win-win situation, satisfying both the needs of the utility and the demands of the customer, can then develop.

In order to cultivate customer orientation within the organizational culture, senior management should take the lead, by demonstrating their involvement in terms of time, effort, commitment, persistence and visibility. Senior management should ensure that improvement of customer relations management is part of the corporate mission. The staff should be involved in the formulation of the mission statement and CRM strategy. Box 8.6 shows an example of a mission statement for a water utility where a customer-focused philosophy is being emphasized.

Box 8.6. Durban Metro Water Department Mission Statement[1]

To provide a constant supply of water, and services related to provision of that water to the satisfaction of consumers in the Durban Metropolitan Area.

PHILOSOPHIES

- Good governance and honest administration is the foundation of Metro Water.Customer care is the cornerstone of our organization.

- We provide a service that is central to every household and therefore go to great lengths to solve problems speedily and effectively.

- Our staff members are central to our organization and it is our responsibility to train, motivate and challenge them, so that each realizes their full potential.

- We promote innovation by continually questioning what we do with a view to improving our service.

---

1. Source: http://www.durban.gov.za/water/index.htm

The CRM strategy should encompass all areas of the organization's activities that impact on the customer, such as the following issues:

- Creation of a customer-focused organizational structure with a given level of delegation, responsiveness, and flexibility.

- Redesign of job descriptions that ensure customer satisfaction at the primary customer interface.

- Instituting customer-focused systems that rely, to a great extent, on the decision-making capacity of the staff at the primary customer interface.

- Taking advantage of advancements in information technology, for the benefit of improved customer relations.

- Simple, short and positively-worded operating procedures that are focused on the priorities.

- A staff recruitment system that recognizes individual differences in people's skills and personality characteristics, and therefore be able to identify people who have a high customer service orientation.

- A system that recognizes and rewards staff based on their contribution to customer satisfaction.

- A staff development program geared towards improved customer relations management.

- Establishment of one-stop customer centres with a pleasant environment.

- Development of a communication strategy that encompasses a service orientation message into all organizational activities.

- Engendering the internal customer philosophy within the organization, to ensure that staff at each level are motivated and customer conscious.

Box 8.7 and Box 8.8 show examples of elements of CRM strategies undertaken by some water utilities.

Box 8.7. Simplifying procedures in Chennai to improve CRM[1]

CHENNAI METROPOLITAN WATER SUPPLY AND SEWERAGE BOARD

INTRODUCTION OF SIMPLIFIED PROCEDURE FOR OBTAINING WATER AND SEWER HOUSE SERVICE CONNECTIONS

Through introduction of a free, simple two page water and sewer connection application forms in which the applicant himself [or herself] can calculate the charges to be paid (similar to Income Tax return), the entire complicated procedures were straightened and simplified. This exercise, although, resulted in a direct loss of Rs. 6 lakhs, it was decided to follow this procedure since it introduces greater transparency in operations and greatly simplifies the existing procedures.

---

1. Source: Chennai Metropolitan Water Supply & Sewerage Board Annual Report, 1997-98

Box 8.8. Investing in technology in order to improve CRM

NWSC, Uganda have introduced the 'Custima' system, a powerful computerized programme that streamlines customer billing

Bangalore Water Supply and Sewerage Board (BWSSB), India, promotes its activities on the web (www.virtualbangalore.com).

Hyderabad Metro Water & Sewerage Board in India invested in modern technology to improve the speed of response to customer complaints in the Metro Customer Care (MCC) Centre.

RAND Water, South Africa, is preparing for involvement in management contracts with local authorities by adopting a more customer orientated approach. Investment in state of the art technology will link phones, voice mail, e-mail, faxes and the internet together, to provide residents with a single point of contact into the organization.

The internal customer and interdepartmental collaboration

The internal marketing concept holds that the employees are the first market of the organization. The main objective of the internal marketing function is to ensure motivated and customer conscious staff at each level (Ewing & Caruana, 1999). In internal marketing, staff are viewed as internal customers and jobs as internal products. Similarly, Kotler (1994) defined internal marketing as the task of successfully hiring, training, and motivating staff in order for them to serve external customers well. The quality of customer care delivered to external customers is often determined by the quality of service that internal customers, i.e. employees, provide each other.

'If the company doesn't care about me, why should I care about the customer?'
- Employee

If the quality of internal customer service is poor, the collaboration between various departments will be low. Research carried out in services management (Jaworski and Kohli, 1993; Slater and Narver, 1994; found that increased collaboration between various departments increased the level of customer service offered by an organization.

In a water utility, there is need for the following departments or sections to collaborate closely, in order for the staff at the primary customer interface to provide quality customer services:

- Customer relations and complaints

- Billing, collection and connection fees

- Meter reading

- Financial management

- Operation, and maintenance

- Major repairs

- New water and sewerage connections

- Illegal connections

- Water conservation, etc.

Achieving improvements in the management of the above utility functions, and the subsequent services provided to the customer, involves more than one department or section in a utility. Traditionally incremental improvements and cross-departmental collaboration is determined through referral to senior management. However this results in top heavy management. Those at the top invest more time on operational issues and less on strategic management. Increasingly in modern utilities, there is a greater emphasis on delegating more responsibilities and authority to lower levels and encouraging inter-departmental collaboration as part of a Total Quality Management (TQM) approach. Flatter styles of communication are preferred so that decisions can be made closer to the issue. Prevailing 'vertical hold' practices concerned with 'keeping the boss happy' are replaced by an emphasis on 'horizontal hold' that maximizes co-operation between different sections in an organization. This involves repeatedly asking two questions of employees from other departments:

- What can I do for you to improve customer services and services to the poor?

- What can you do for me to improve customer services and services to the poor?

Joint planning and implementation of viable solutions to these questions can then take place. This 'internal customer' approach requires more flexibility, good staff communication skills and effective planning; but it has demonstrated significant cost effective service improvements. Internal customers are therefore as valuable as external customers.

The 'horizontal hold' concept is particularly relevant when dealing with services in poorer communities, where greater flexibility is required. It will not be practical to refer every decision up to senior management. This implies that authority to make decisions is delegated down to people in the utility who are interacting with community groups and other stakeholders.

Customer charters

A water utility should introduce a water charter that explains in simple language what the customers should expect from the utility, and what the utility expects in return. Typical aspects to be covered in the charter are:

- The objectives of the water authority

- The service and payment options offered by the utility

- A description of procedures for matters such as new connections, payment of bills, provision of meters and complaints

- The customer's obligations

- Details of any compensation entitlements for the affected customers, where the authority does not meet its obligations for certain aspects, including the associated procedures.

In developing a customer charter a utility should seek to be informative but it needs to feel confident that it can meet its committments. By clearly describing the roles, obligations and entitlements of utility and customers in such a document and publicizing it widely, it offers a number of potential benefits:

- there is a reduced risk of misunderstandings and dissatisfaction arising

- the utility obligations can act as targets and motivating factors for their staff

- the relationship with the customer can become more of a 'beneficial exchange relationship' where mutual respect can develop.

It is worth consulting with key stakeholders such as customer representative committees, before finalizing the charter. For further information on improving customer services for water utilities refer to Coates S., Sansom K.R. and Kayaga S.M, *'Customer relations management: Part A: Introduction for urban water and sewerage authorities in developing countries'*, WELL paper, (task no. 514a), WEDC, 2001.

8.4   Supporting service, payment and management options

In order for the strategic marketing plans to take effect, the utility needs to institute systems that will support the various options of service, management and bill payment. The nature and extent of support mechanism depends on the type of options being offered to the consumers. There are however some basic systems that should be in place. The systems could be to support all the marketing systems, or to support service, payment or management options individually. Some typical examples are set out below:

General Support

1. A section of the utility should be designated the responsibility of customer satisfaction management by carrying out periodic research on customer satisfaction,

analysing the data, making recommendations, and evaluating the impact of improvements.

2. Services should be decentralized as much as possible. In big cities, zone offices should be set up in different locations, in order to provide services as close to the consumers as possible. The zones should have responsible officers who have delegated authority and responsibilities in their zones. This requires empowerment of the responsible officers. Different functions should be reflected at zone levels. This is particularly helpful for working in informal settlements.

3. A quality assurance system should be put in place to evaluate the level of service based on consumer surveys, and identify gaps for further improvement.

4. A community liaison section can be set up in the water utility to spearhead partnerships with different stakeholders for better service provision.

5. Standards and regulations may need to be amended to allow for more flexibility in service options.

6. The tariff structure should be reviewed by concerned authorities to enable pricing differentiation, depending on the different service levels.

7. Utilities should improve the office environment such as office location, space, accessibility, parking etc.

8. A training program should be instituted for all staff, specifically for those at the customer interface, in customer relations management.

9. Where resources allow, there should be a customer relations management (CRM) team that works on a 24-hour basis to provide customer care to consumers and manage the complaint monitoring system. The CRM should have computerised information systems preferably linked up with other major service units.

10. The water utility should put in place a technical emergency team to support the CRM team in handling complaints concerned with technical issues.

Support for Service Options

The same section responsible for customer satisfaction management should take responsibility of mapping out the appropriate market segmentation, in conjunction with other departments. In addition a selected team or working group can be established to look at service options that are suitable in the various market segments. This section should be responsible for identifying, piloting, developing, testing and commissioning the new or adapted service options, based on consumer surveys and demand assessment and ongoing dialogue with community groups.

Support for Payment Options

Some ideas for potential payment options are included in section 3.3. The basic aim of introducing payment options is to make it easier and more convenient for customers to pay, fitting in with their lifestyles, so that people pay more promptly and regularly. For middle and high income households, innovative payment options can be explored such as:

- At a bank

- By direct debit

- At a payment point

- At a post office

- By post

- At a building society

- Telephone banking

- Via the utility web-site

- Or a Watercard

- Joint utility internet payment centres

The selection of appropriate options for specific cities and towns will be dependent on trends in other sectors and available information technology support.

A well designed computerised billing management and payments has many advantages, including: speed, less staff required and instantaneous updates of payment records at customer service desks. It can be introduced through a local network system to all the zones. Box 8.9 illustrates a good example.

Box 8.9. Computer billing systems

Prior to the use of CUSTIMA in its billing database, National Water & Sewerage Corporation (NWSC) of Uganda used to experience many complaints from customers whose accounts were not being reconciled in time. This resulted into double-billing of the customers. Since the introduction of CUSTIMA software in the billing section, complaints have dramatically reduced, as the billing database is linked up with cash payment points, through computer local area networking.

Currently, NWSC is planning to extend the sphere of CUSTIMA software to customer relations management and network maintenance

---

For lower income consumers, ideas for potential payment options should come from the problems and coping strategies that emerged from consumer surveys and focus group discussions. A common problem for people who work in the informal economy is they have very limited savings and their preference for paying for small amounts by containers, or they seek free water sources that may have questionable water quality. Potential options to assist people in these circumstances are:

- Group connections where people can develop their own payment mechanisms, such as one household pays the water bills and then on-sells water per container to their neighbours;

- Community managed water kiosks or regulated private kiosks that ensure kiosk water prices do not fluctuate too much;

- Local utility payment and customer service offices near to poorer communities, perhaps offering more flexible payment terms;

- Smart card prepayment systems that ensure people never spend more than they can afford;

179

- Offer gradual payment mechanisms for new connections;

- Allow people to contribute their labour to reduce costs for new connections.

Whatever potential options emerge it is important to maintain dialogue especially with poorer community representatives. It may be necessary to use NGOs or consultants to facilitate this process, or capable in-house staff. New options should be piloted in some areas to check for feasibility and the need to adapt the payment system before scaling up to larger areas.

Support for shared management options

Following the consumer surveys and discussions with various partners in stages 1 and 2, the best possibilities for developing shared management arrangements either with community groups or small scale providers should emerge. Examples of successful cases of such collaborations are given in section 4.4. Such arrangements are likely to be more beneficial in areas where the utility is not able to provide services in the short to medium term.

The water utility should provide a conducive environment for creating equitable partnerships in order to enhance such shared management arrangements. This is likely to entail having full time utility staff with good communication skills who can collaborate with the various partners such as CBOs and small scale provider associations. NGOs who are active in the city can play a useful role as facilitators in the process of partnership development. Training should be provided to utility staff on how best to communicate and collaborate with community groups.

Again piloting these approaches in a few areas is probably the best strategy, in order to learn lessons before any scaling up.

8.5 Utility institutional improvements

The utility will need to develop institutional development plans based on the areas for improvement identified in the stage 1 situation analysis. It will also need to consider what are the institutional requirements that are necessary to provide the target service levels for all market segments that are set out in the proposed investment/marketing plan. The plans should be comprehensive including all the key elements of institutional development (ID), that were mentioned in section 6.4 and are:

- Structural and Organizational Adjustment

- Agreeing roles, policies, objectives and performance targets

- Human Resource Management

- Management Development

- Systems and Procedures Development

- Physical and Financial Resources

It may be necessary to consider fundamental organizational changes such as providing the utility with more autonomy or using private operators, in order to achieve the proposed performance levels, particularly where there is a lack of flexibility to introduce institutional changes in the utility. All the above key elements of ID need to be considered in any service improvement programme.

A sensible starting point is developing the right policies for serving poor areas. In Lusaka a policy document for serving peri-urban areas has been developed in response to national policy. The key components of that document are set out in Box 8.10.

Box 8.10. Lusaka's evolving policy on water and sanitation in peri-urban areas

Lusaka Water and Sewerage Company (LWSC) have developed a document that sets out it's policy on water and sanitation in per-urban areas, settlements or 'compounds' which are categorized as low-income and having high density conditions. They were no doubt encouraged to do so by the agreement of the national strategy on the same subject. The stated rationale of the LWSC document is as follows:

"Due to the multiplicity of public and private agencies, as well as the presence of numerous donors and NGOs, co-ordination of water & sanitation services is required to derive the greatest benefits from limited budgets in an area where the challenges are very great. The LWSC is one of the major actors in this field, and it has therefore taken the initiative in preparing this document".

The key areas covered by the document are set out below:

Statutory legal responsibilities of LWSC - including the provision of water & sewerage services in the area of jurisdiction of Lusaka city council and to exercise control over water sources

The institutional framework - including:

- the specified wards where peri-urban informal settlements are located
- agreed ToR for resident development committees (water committees)
- listing of the peri-urban areas and their legal status
- listing of the water and sanitation service providers in Lusaka
- summary of the roles that LWSC will undertake, including: O&M of water distribution up to the meters, collaboration with community groups, bulk supply of water to edge of some peri-urban areas, training of plumbers for community management of water distribution etc
- the roles of other institutions such as the city council who deal with sanitation aspects other than sewerage
- Options for service provision

In terms of an appropriate organizational culture, water utilities need to espouse customer orientation as the guiding business philosophy. Having evolved from a traditional civil service foundation, many water utilities in low and middle-income countries are still governed by a supply driven product/production orientation. Such water utilities therefore need to change their organizational culture. This requires senior management to champion pro-active change programmes, including the need for all employees to understand and commit to a customer focused service philosophy. Basically customer care should be built into all the tasks and actions undertaken in the water utility on a day to day basis. This can only be achieved through on-going awareness raising and the use of pro-customer business strategies. Refer to boxes 8.11 and 8.12 for examples of such strategies.

**Box 8.11. Change management and customer
orientation in NWSC, Uganda[1]**

The National Water & Sewerage Corporation (NWSC), Uganda has instituted various internal change management programmes since 1999. The major objectives of these initiatives is to enhance service delivery in such a way that customers will be satisfied with the quality of services and therefore have a higher level of willingness-to-pay for the services provided.

In February 1999, NWSC instituted a programme code-named the "100-Days Programme". This programme was closely followed by a one-year programme that sought to consolidate the achievements of the "100-Days Programme", code-named "The Service and Revenue Enhancement Programme", SEREP in short.

These programmes were carried out under normal budgetary provisions. However using the tool of performance management, change was spearheaded by three-tier staff committees in the areas of water production and sewerage services, water distribution services, revenue generation, customer care and cost reduction measures. Final evaluation of the programmes showed a substantial improvement in the general performance of NWSC.

---

1. Source: NWSC (Uganda) (2000), Evaluation of SEREP.

After analysing the existing situation in the organization, senior management should set corporate objectives centred on the need for change, which will bring about ehancement of customer orientation, on a continuous basis. The objectives should be SMART: *Specific, Measurable, Achievable, Realistic and Timely*. Having SMART targets will enable management and importantly employees to measure progress. It is advisable to map out short-, medium- and long-term objectives, which can be reviewed periodically.

Box 8.12. Customer orientation at Chennai Metro Water, India[1]

In its endeavours to achieve the objectives indicated in the Mission Statement, Chennai Metro Water will be guided by the following, being customer driven:

• Feedback from customers
• Delivering excellence in products and services
• Doing business with ethics and integrity
• Continuous endeavour to improve quality of service

---

1. Source: htpp://www.tn.gov.in/citizen/metro-water.htm

Figure 8.4 contrasts a management orientated organization with customer orientated organization, where senior and middle management support front line staff in providing better services to customers.

For a water utility to carry out a strategic marketing process effectively, it needs to undergo further institutional changes as shown below:

1. Setting up an effective marketing information system to which all departments of the utility contribute and through which they share information with others. This process of sharing information will enhance departmental interconnectedness.

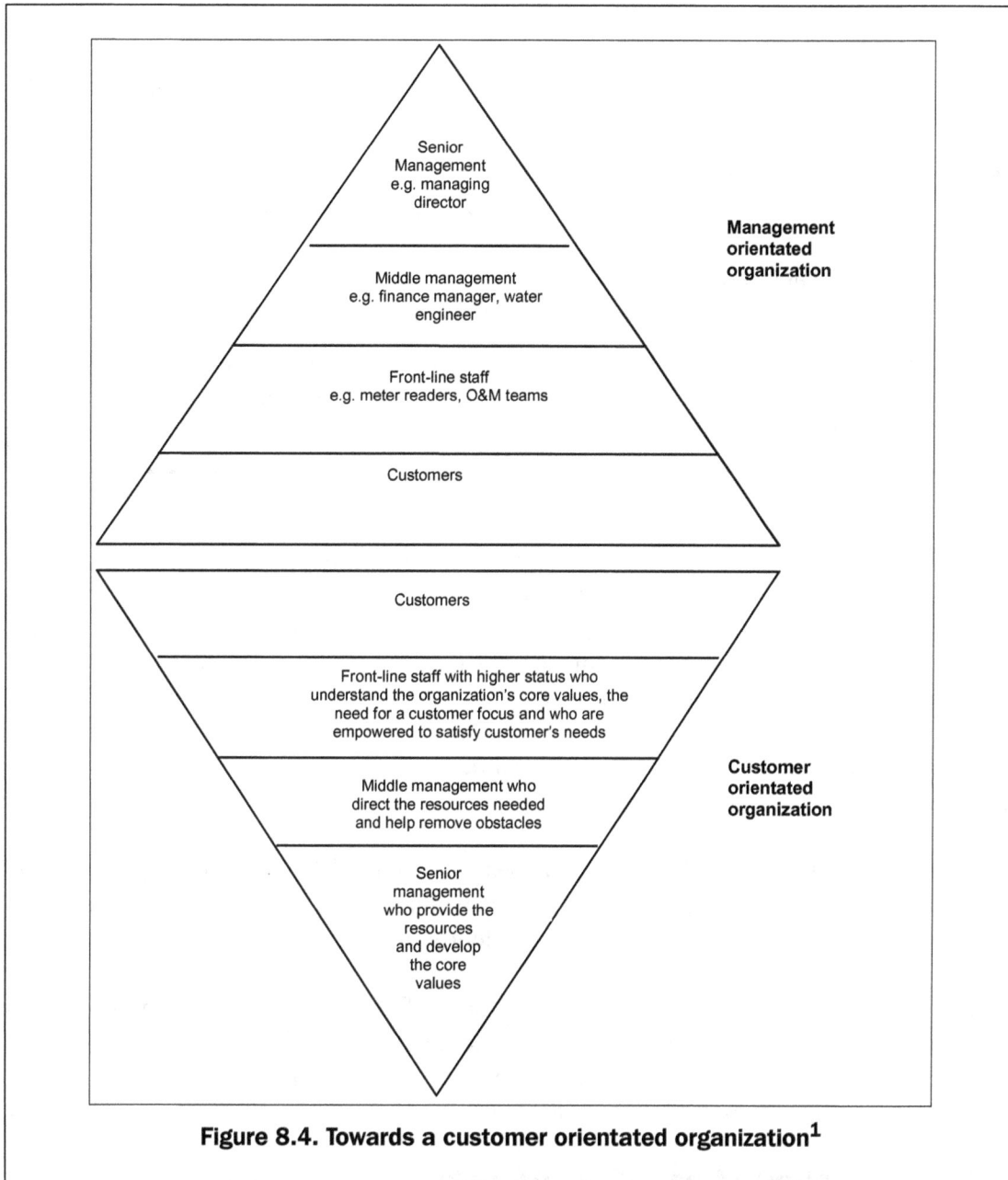

Figure 8.4. Towards a customer orientated organization[1]

1. Source: adapted from Doyle, P. (1994) p.48 cited in Wilson and Gilligan (1997) Strategic Marketing Management (2nd Edition), Butterworth Heinemann

2. Setting up a human resource development policy that is geared towards enhancing customer relations management; e.g.

- recruitment of customer interface staff basing on their interpersonal skills and ability to deliver services

- continuous training programs for all staff in customer service

- induction of new staff in customer orientation philosophy

- basing rewards/disincentives criteria on customer service enhancement

3. Setting up a section in the utility that handles issues concerned with supply of water services to low-income communities, but has good collaboration with other departments. An example of such a unit has been established in Lusaka, refer to box 8.13.

Box 8.13. Establishment of a peri-urban unit in Lusaka[1]

The Lusaka Water and Sewerage Company (LWSC) is a water company wholly owned by Lusaka City Council. In addition to the general mandate of supply water and sanitation services to residents of Lusaka, LWSC is specifically charged with supplying water to all peri-urban areas of Lusaka. To achieve its objective, LWSC has developed a peri-urban unit for serving the poor, headed by a senior manager. This unit collaborates with other stakeholders such as NGOs, in the provision of water services in the peri-urban areas.

---

1. Source: Water Utility Partnership, Project No. 5, Summary of Workshop proceedings, June 2000.

As a utility considers plans for institutional improvement it is useful to form and develop working groups from different departments (with the aid of consultants where appropriate). These groups can then develop or commission a number of proposals addressing key areas for improvement that are identified in the situation analysis. The proposals need to be costed then assessed and prioritized before moving to the implementation phase. Note the projected costs for institutional improvements need to be incorporated in to strategic marketing/ investment plans, to ensure sufficient funds are provided for these important aspects.

It is generally better to pilot new approaches or systems before scaling up across the utility. This enables staff in the organization, as well as its partners, to learn lessons from the pilots so that they can proceed more confidently in utility wide improvements.

Further guidance on institutional development can be found in Promoting institutional and organisational development, Department for International Development, London, (1998) UK and in the DFID 'Guidance Manual on Water Supply and Sanitation Programmes, (Institutional perspectives section pp 118 - 156), WELL, UK.

8.6   Evaluation of benefits and risks

Evaluation of Financial Benefits

Benefits from improved service coverage can broadly be classified into two main categories: financial benefits, and economic benefits. The financial benefits from carrying out a strategic marketing planning include improved profitability. The role of Strategic Marketing Plan can be illustrated using a flow diagram, as shown in Figure 8.5.

The financial viability of the strategic marketing plan can best be quantitatively assessed using a financial benefit cost analysis, adopted from the Asian Development Bank, as follows:

Project Revenues

Determine annual water sales revenue on a with-project and without-project basis. This could be categorized according to the different groups of users. The with-project sales should take into consideration revenues from the projected network expansion, at

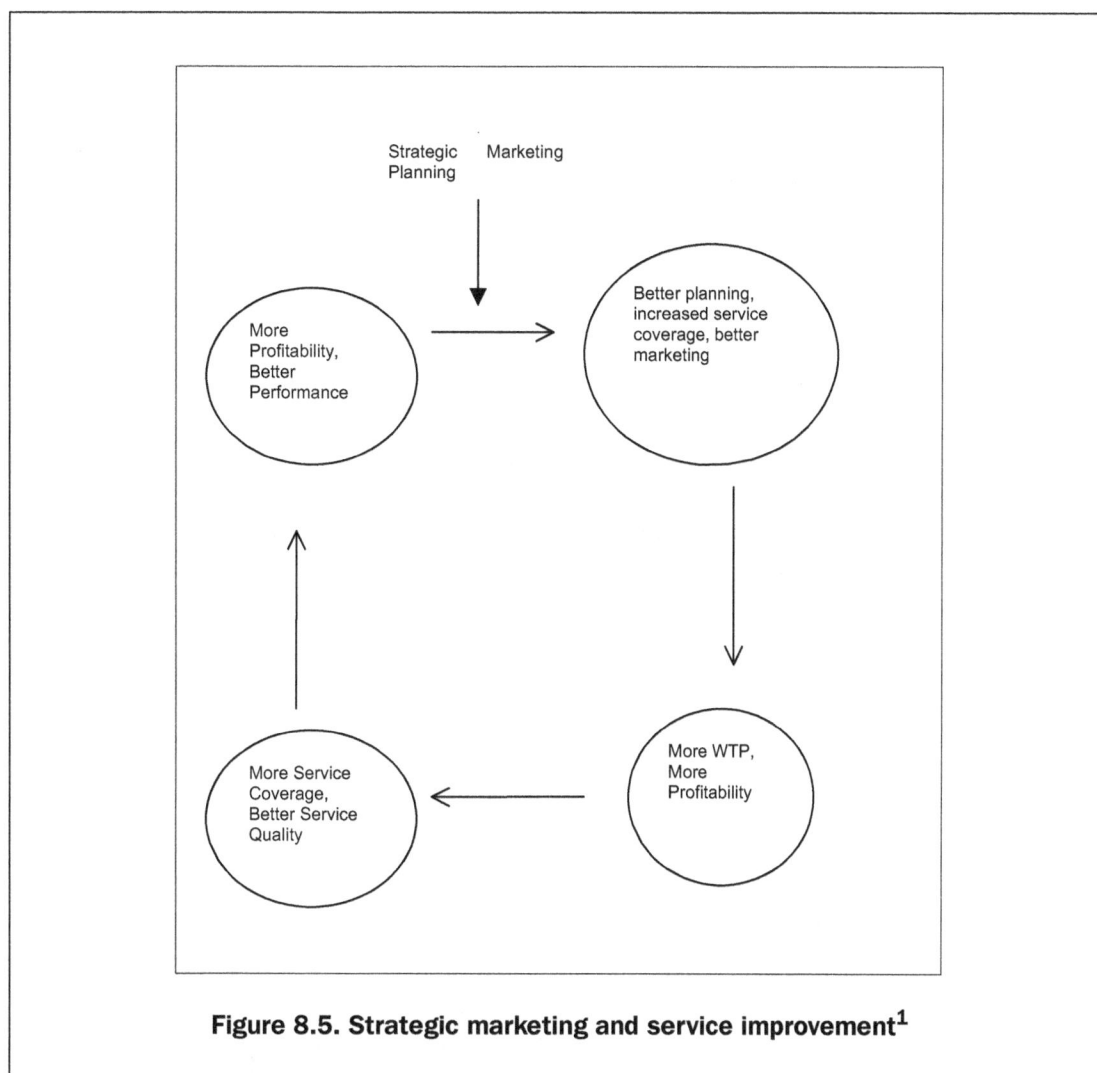

Figure 8.5. Strategic marketing and service improvement[1]

1. Source: Sample Strategic Marketing Plan for Water Services in Kampala City, Uganda, by Kayaga & Sansom (2004)

suggested tariff rates. The project revenues are the difference between revenue for the with-project and the without-project sales. These revenues should be worked out over the project period at the prevailing discount rate.

Project Costs

The project costs are worked out by computing the difference between the without-project costs and the with-project costs of the following items on a discounted basis:

*   Real investments to cater for both foreign and local costs

*   Operation and Maintenance; future O & M costs could be estimated based on the historical costs as a percentage of investment costs, or as related to the volume of water produced and/or distributed. Elements of O & M may include labour, electricity, chemicals, materials, overhead costs, raw water charges, insurance etc.

*   Reinvestments, i.e. to cater for need for replacement of different investment assets, at different times of the project cycle, depending on the lifetimes.

*   Residual values of the project assets at the end of the project life.

Net Financial Benefits

The Project Net Benefit is the difference between the project revenues and the project costs, and is sometimes referred to as Net Cash Flow. For further details on how to obtain the Financial Internal Rate of Return, refer to the Handbook for the Economic Analysis of Water Supply Projects, published by Asian Development Bank, (1999) which is available online at URL:http://www.adb.org/publications/online/water/ .

Assessment of Risks

The strategic marketing plan is based on forecasts of quantifiable variables such as demand, costs, water availability, institutional capacity, and an enabling macro-environment. The values of variables in the strategic marketing plan are estimated based on the most probable forecasts that cover a long period of time. However, a great number of factors may act to influence the outcome scenario. Risk assessment is a management tool that is used to make informed decisions about the magnitude of the risks involved, which would, if need be, lead to risk management. Figure 8.6. is a framework of steps leading to risk management.

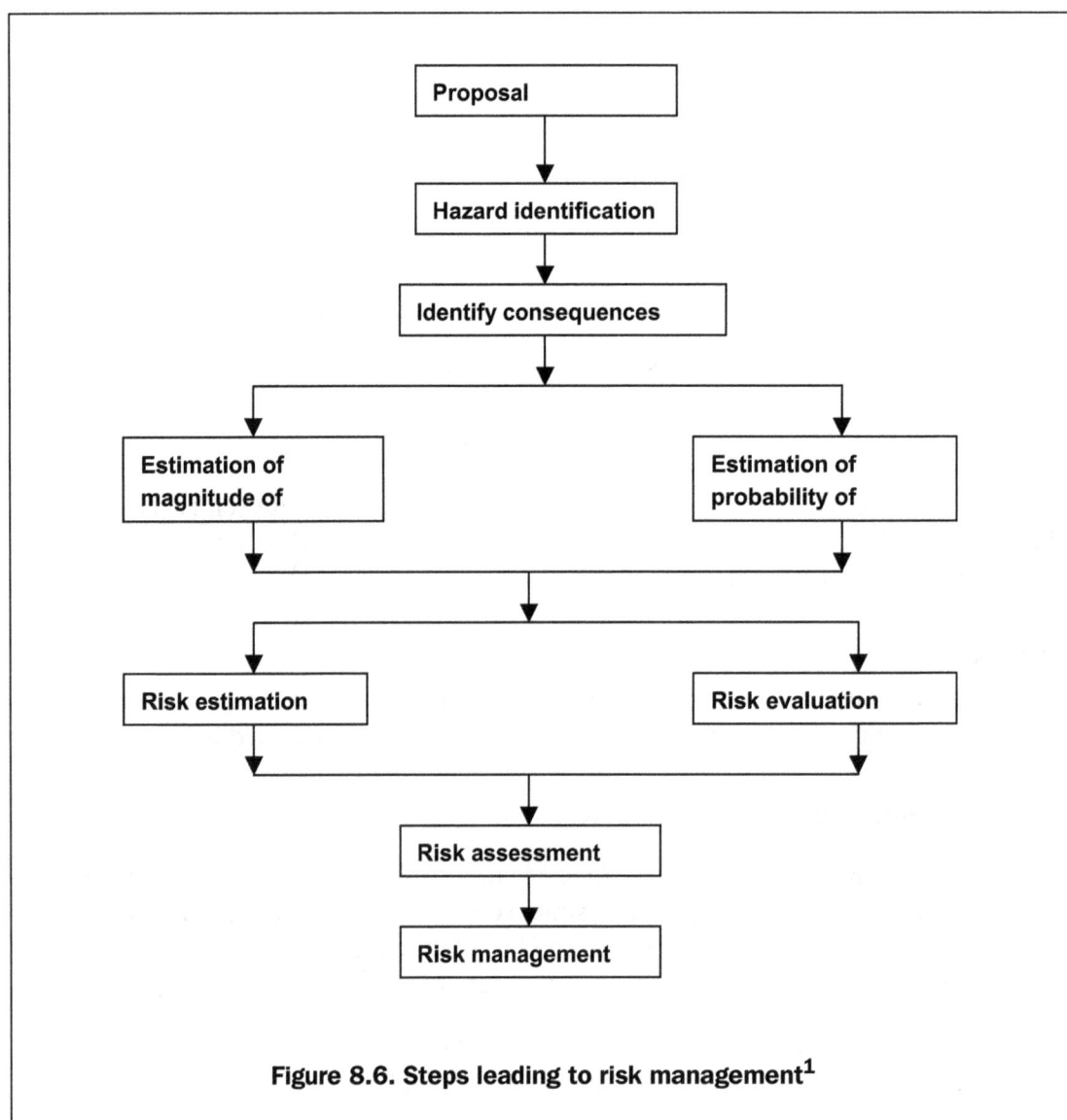

Figure 8.6. Steps leading to risk management[1]

1. Source: Skivington, P., 1997. Risk Assessment for Water Quality Management (p.7). Water Research Commission Project No. TT 90/97. Pretoria: South Africa.

Risk assessment using a framework shown in Figure 8.6. would lead to a qualitative estimation of risks into one of the categories shown in Table 8.1 .

Table 8.1. Estimation of Risk: magnitude of consequence and probabilities[1]

	Magnitude of Consequences			
Probability	Severe	Moderate	Mild	Negligible
High	High	High	Medium/low	Near zero
Medium	High	Medium	Low	Near zero
Low	High/medium	Medium/low	Low	Near zero
Negligible	High/medium/low	Medium/low	Low	Near zero

1. Source: Skivington, P., 1997. Risk Assessment for Water Quality Management (p.9). Water Research Commission Project No. TT 90/97. Pretoria: South Africa.

The variables that are considered important for consideration in risk analysis are categorized as follows:

- *Management risks.* These risks include resistance to organizational cultural change to embrace a marketing orientation; non-supportive organizational structure; inadequate technical and financial management capacity to manage the strategic marketing planning project; over-ambitious and inflexible project planning; absence of incentives for satisfactory performance; etc.

- *Financing risks,* such as failure to re-schedule loan repayment, leading to failure to liberate funds to carry out investments early in the project life.

- *Social risks,* such as low level of embracing the project and poor participation by different market segments.

- *Economic risks,* such as low economic growth; deflated income levels of consumers; high inflation rates etc.

- *Political risks;* such as political instability; delay in legislation procedures; adverse changes in legal status of the utility.

- *Construction risks,* such as delays in construction periods.

- *Environmental risks,* such as increased pollution rates of the raw water source, leading to higher production costs; drying up of raw water sources.

- *Other risks* that generally apply to institutional strengthening projects.

During the implementation of the programme, specific risks should be identified, and mitigation measures taken to reduce the extent of uncertainty surrounding these variables, wherever possible. This may require remedial action at the corporate, sector or national level. The following are some of the measures that could be taken to mitigate risks (DFID Technical Note No. 12, pp 15-16, available at http//152.60.200.132/vs3_intranet/ procedures/TN12.htm):

- Use of trials and pilot projects to test alternative approaches on a small scale before adopting them into full-scale projects.

- Use of a process approach to finding the optimum route to project implementation.

- Clear specification of objectives and of success criteria.

- Identification and assessment of all project 'stakeholders' with respect to their interests, motives, incentives, and abilities to make the project succeed or fail.

- Transferring responsibility for handling risky outcomes to agents with the greatest risk-bearing capacity.

- Building in the project design performance measures and incentives - relying where possible on market incentives - to achieve project objectives.

- Ensuring that all agents concerned with the project are thoroughly informed about the objectives and their role in fulfilling them.

8.7   PPP options and serving the poor

Many people would argue that the private sector are best placed to implement the required commercial and customer orientated approaches because they have the required autonomy, flexibility and incentives to improve services, provided the PPP contracts are well designed. But if public sector organizations are given sufficient autonomy and flexibility to manage with appropriate tariffs, there is no reason why they cannot make substantial improvements to services to all consumer groups, as many public utilities have done throughout the world.

For those organizations contemplating private sector participation, they can refer to the World Bank 'Toolkits for Private Sector Participation in Water and Sanitation', 1997, which provides comprehensive guidance on the range of PSP contracts. For those utilities or municipalities contemplating smaller Service and Management contracts, the 'Contracting Out Water and Sanitation Services - Guidance Notes for Service and Management Contracts in Developing Countries, by Sansom, K.R., Franceys, R., Njiru, C. and Morales-Reyes, J., 2003 provides practical information on contract development and monitoring.

There are four key areas where serving the poor through PPP contracts can be addressed (Brocklehurst and Evans, WSP-SA, 2001):

1.   Pay attention to process

Consultations with the poor and their representatives can be carried out to find out their preferences for service options and other aspects of the services. NGOs and CBOs who work with these groups can be useful partners in data collection, or in some cases they can represent the views of communities.

2.   Get the policy environment right

Translating government policies on serving the poor into practice requires careful policy development amending regulations where appropriate. For example dealing with issues such as flexible design standards, fair tariff policies and land tenure issues.

3. Use the contract

General targets for aspects such as increases in coverage or connections are not usually helpful, as reasons can always be found by the operator for not to include hard to reach areas. Targets for improved service levels based on geographical areas in places where many poor people live in well defined areas, can be more successful.

4. Establish robust regulatory structures that are pro-poor

Regulation can be pro-poor through such measures as not allowing private operators exclusive rights to provide water services to particular areas. Small scale providers can therefore continue to provide services to poorly served areas. Operators can also be encouraged to offer different service options in poor areas such as water kiosks, group connections and yard connections. Encouraging city-wide consultation forums can also deal with problems that arise for all consumer groups.

Selecting appropriate indicators for serving the poor is key to good performance measurement and regulation of PPP contracts. 'It is important to link incentive payments to the achievement of targets related to the provision of services to the poor, for lease and concession contracts (WSP and PPIAF, 2002)'. Specific 'serving the poor' indicators that could be used for incentive and penalty payments in comprehensive contracts such as lease and concession contracts could include:

- Increase in the number (or percentage) of active (in-house, yard and kiosk) connections in defined low income areas.

- Increase in the percentage of water sales in defined low income areas.

Unless the indicators relate to specific service levels in defined low-income areas, then it will be difficult to hold the operator accountable for service improvements. The use of such indicators does of course need to be backed up by appropriate investments and obligations in the contract for the operator. The broad aim for serving the poor should be to ensure that there are sufficient incentives in the contract for the operator to substantially improve services in informal settlements.

Refer to Table 8.2 for an example format of water supply frequency using market segments based on type of building.

The disparity in service levels between the different consumer groups is apparent from the above table. Such information can be used as a baseline for monitoring improvements in poorer areas. It is also beneficial to collect and present data by geographical area, although care is needed because there can be substantially different experiences in water services within the same area. Using such information for regulation would require regular independent consumer surveys as part of comprehensive performance measurement, which is discussed in section 6.4.

Specific guidance on how to improve service to poor communities through PPP contracts is given in the Water and Sanitation Program (WSP) and PPIAF, (2002) *New Designs for Water and Sanitation Transactions - Making Private Sector Participation Work for the Poor*, WSP, Washington D.C., USA. A series of publications on 'PPP and the Poor' that are edited by M.Sohail are available on the WEDC web-site.

Table 8.2. Water supply frequency by market segment in Mombasa[1]

Water supply frequency	Bungalows/ maisonettes	Flats	1-3 roomed houses	Dwelling in informal settlement	Average
Don't receive water from utility	34.6%	17.2%	57.7%	96.2%	54.2%
Once a day	17.9%	25.9%	19.6%		15.4%
Twice a day	9.0%	13.8%	4.1%	1.3%	6.4%
Once in 2-3 days	6.4%	8.6%	4.1%		4.5%
Once a week	1.3%				0.3%
Continuous	29.5%	31.0%	13.4%	2.5%	17.9%
Other	1.3%	3.4%	1.0%		1.3%
Total	**100%**	**100%**	**100%**	**100%**	**100%**

1. Source: Njiru and Sansom 2001

8.8   Strategic marketing or investment plans

The strategic marketing plans (SMPs) or investment plans should summarize the key aspects of data collected, analysis and proposals derived from the 3 stages described in chapters 6,7 and 8. The precise structure of the document will depend on the main areas for improvement being proposed and the requirements of potential financiers. Example draft strategic marketing plans and summaries for Mombasa, Kampala and Guntur, which were developed as part of the research programme, are provided on the WEDC web-site.

In order to benefit from the ideas and experience of key stakeholders including staff, it is beneficial to ensure that there has been adequate consultation in developing an SMP. This has the added benefit of generating more commitment for the proposals, even if it takes longer to reach agreement. It is also important that SMPs or investment plans are drafted and structured in a way that present a convincing argument for support from potential financiers.

8.9   Ensuring success

A variety of suggested frameworks, processes and principles are included in this document to aid planning for sustainable water services for all consumer groups. But utility staff and partners need to try new ideas and approaches that make sense to them, learning lessons from their own experience and elsewhere.

Adopting new approaches to serve poor areas and incorporating marketing approaches into all aspects of a utility's activities takes time, effort and good leadership, in order to overcome people's reluctance to change. Staff invariably need to experiment with new approaches before they consider them valid, adapting them to suite the local situation. This process is illustrated in Figure 8.7 and emphasizes the need to plan for sufficient time and support, so that this learning process can take place.

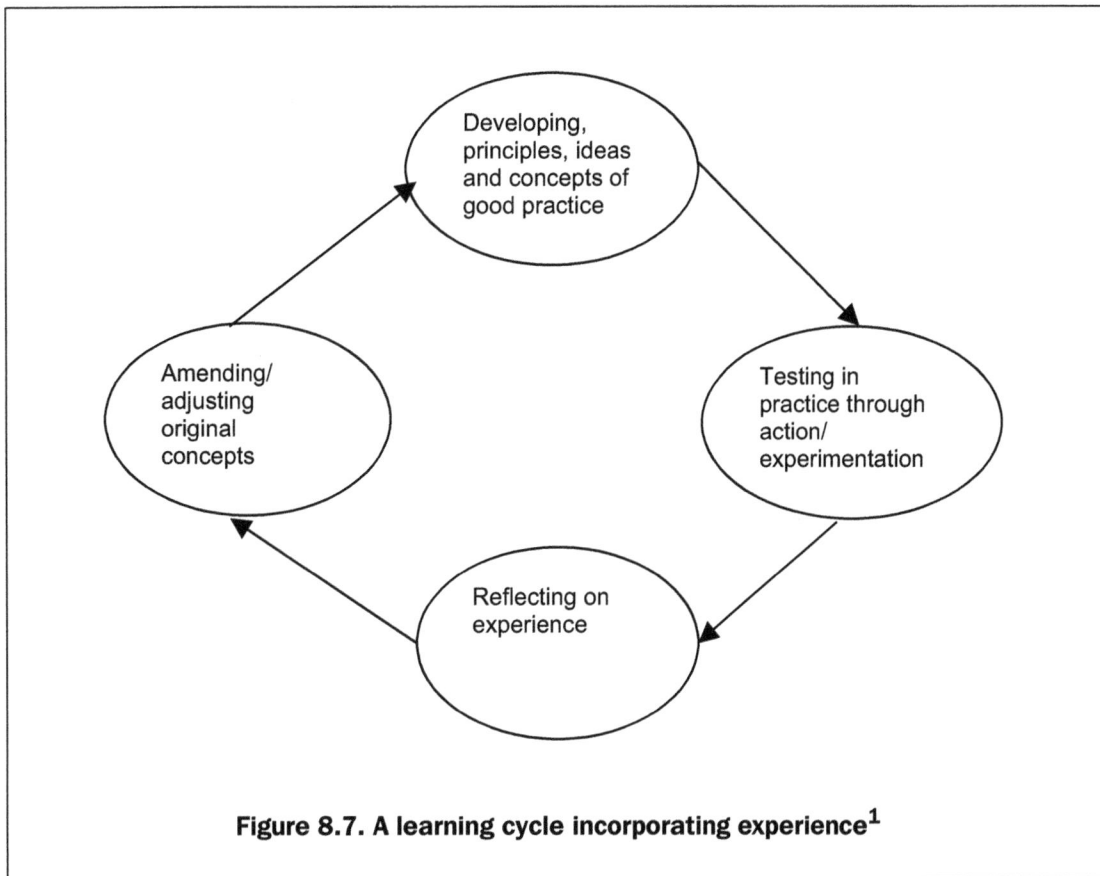

Figure 8.7. A learning cycle incorporating experience[1]

1. Source: Buckley and Caple, 1995

Staff will not always have the requisite knowledge and skills but if they have appropriate attitudes then much can be done. Examples of helpful staff attitudes include:

- A commitment to continuous improvement

- A willingness to adopt more commercial and consumer orientated approaches

- A willingness to learn from their own experiences and elsewhere

- A willingness to work in or for informal settlements

- A willingness to work productively with people from other disciplines and organizations

- A willingness to think broadly linking technical, financial, social and institutional issues.

For more information on implementing new approaches and improvement in services, refer to good publications on marketing , change management, human resources management, total quality management (TQM) and other conventional business manuals. This publication can assist in translating appropriate ideas both to the urban water sector and to the local situation in low and middle-income countries.

Chapter 9

Glossary

7ps	Product, Price, Promotion, Place, People, Process and Presence.
Buying decision process	The conscious and unconscious thinking process a consumer goes through before deciding to buy a product or service.
CBO	Community based organisations who may take an active part in decision making or management of water and sanitation services in their area.
Competition	In this document any water source or provider of supply that tempts a consumer away from using a utility provided source or which deters the consumer from buying water from the utility.
Consumer demand	An expression of desire for a particular service, assessed by the investments people are prepared to make, over the lifetime of the service to receive and sustain it.
Contingent valuation	A demand assessment technique. Several options (each associated with a range of prices) are described to a sample of potential users who then indicate their preferences. It can be used to assess people's maximum willingness to pay for services that are not currently available. The technique requires specialist skills and is more cost effective in high-density urban and peri-urban areas.
Coping strategy	A behaviour or practice used to sustain or improve a livelihood.
Customer orientation	Turning attention to the needs of the customer and using the organisations resources to satisfy those needs.
Customer value chain	The process of knowing, targeting, selling and servicing customers.

Demand	An expression of desire for a particular service, assessed by the investments people are prepared to make, over the lifetime of the service to receive and sustain it.
Effective demand	Demand for a good or service expressed by a user's willingness to pay in terms of a monetary or economic contribution.
Existing practices	How people obtain, pay and use water now.
Experiences	Accumulated knowledge, feelings and occurrences. Familiarity and know-how.
Focus group	A small group of individuals with a similar social, cultural or economic background, brought together with a facilitator to explore a particular issue.
Informal settlements	In this document it is a generic term used to describe the unplanned areas where the urban poor generally reside. It includes illegal slums, informal settlements, unplanned areas, compounds, low -income areas, townships, peri-urban areas, unplanned zones and shanty towns.
Latent demand	Demand that is only revealed after it has been stimulated (that is open to techniques that unlock demand).
Level of service	(Or service level) describes the quality of the service provided. It refers to the physical infrastructure or technology used: stand post, communal tap, a yard tap, or a house connection. It may also include other factors such as provision of a storage tank or the agreed utility water supply hours each day.
Low-income area	In this document it is a generic term used to describe where the urban poor reside. It includes illegal slums, informal settlements, compounds, townships, peri-urban areas, unplanned zones and shanty towns.
Marketing	There are a number of definitions for marketing including: 'The management process responsible for identifying, anticipating and satisfying customer requirements profitably'.
Market segmentation	The process of identifying groups of consumers in to groups defined by common characteristics, for example social status or housing type for the purposes of understanding the main consumer groups and targeting service options.

Marketing mix	The way a competitive position relative to other options is achieved.
NGOs	Non-governmental organisations typically work with community groups in low income areas, while liasing with government and service providers with a view to improving services and reducing poverty. They usually have good facilitation skills and experience of working in informal settlements.
Non-revenue water	The difference between water produced and water sold to customers expressed as a percentage of water produced.
Non-utility water sources	Including protected and unprotected springs, rainwater collected in buckets/cooking pots, shallow wells.
On-selling	Water sold from an individual house connection to neighbours. The utility charges one person only.
Perceptions	The way in which people see a situation determining how they are likely to behave.
Poverty	Poor quality of life combining low income, poor health and education, deprivation in knowledge and communications, and the inability to exercise human and political rights.
Preferences	Judgment that something is 'best for purpose' from the user's perspective.
Price and service differentiation	Process of developing appropriate service options (technology and management) at appropriate prices based on the needs of different market segments - customer groups, on a sustainable basis.
Small water enterprises	SWEs are also called small scale independent providers and are part of the informal private sector who provide water services to consumers, particularly in areas where complete water services are not provided by a utility.
Social marketing	The application of marketing techniques to stimulate demand. The underlying motivation is to reduce exposure to environmental health risks rather than a profit motive.
Strategic marketing	Marketing as a management process whereby the resources of the organization are used to satisfy the needs of selected consumer groups in order to achieve the objectives of both parties. Strategic city-wide planning is usually required in the urban water context.
Tri-sector partnership	In this document partnerships between government, the private sector and civil society.

Unplanned areas	Refer to 'informal settlements' definition.
Utility-direct sources	Including public stand post, kiosk, communal yard taps and house connections.
Utility-indirect sources	Including handcart vendors and bicycle vendors who get their water from a utility source.
Want	A desire for a good or service that goes beyond a felt need in that it may satisfy a person's longer term needs or aspirations, but may not be price sensitive, hence the need to consider consumer demand.
Willingness to charge	The low willingness of key stakeholders such as politicians to increase tariffs to adequate levels is common, hence the need to encourage an increased 'willingness to charge' using appropriate advocacy strategies.
Willingness to pay	The financial or economic contribution that people are willing to make to receive and sustain a particular service.
Willingness to pay surveys	A variety of survey techniques such as the contingent valuation method (CVM) that can be used to illicit the maximum amount that respondents are willing to pay for a given service level.

Chapter 10

References and Bibliography

Blokland, M., Saade L.and Pieter van Dijk M., (2003) *'Institutional Arrangements for Municipal Wastewater and Sanitation' with case studies from Argentina, India, Mexico, Philippines, South Africa, Switzerland and Zambia'*, IMO,

Brassington F and Pettitt S, *'Principles of Marketing'*, Second Edition, Financial Times/ Prentice Hall. 2000

Brocklehurst C., and Evans B.(2001) *'Serving Poor Consumers in South Asian Cities'*, The Water and Sanitation Program-South Asia, India

Buckley R. and Caple J. , (1995) *The Theory and Practice of Training*, Kogan Page Ltd., London, UK

Chary V.S, (2000) *Change Management Forum Background Note*, unpublished report, Administrative Staff College of India, Hyderabad.

Coates, S., Sansom, K.R., Kayaga, S.M., Chary S, Narender A. and Njiru, C., and. (2004) *Serving All Urban Consumers: A marketing approach to water services in low and middle-income countries. Book 3- PREPP - Utility consultation with the urban poor*, WEDC, Loughborough University, UK.

Coates S., Sansom K.R. and Kayaga S.M, *'Customer relations management: Part A: Introduction for urban water and sewerage authorities in developing countries'*, WELL paper, (task no. 514a), WEDC, 2001.

Coates S., Sansom K.R. and Kayaga S.M, *'Customer relations management: Part B: Draft customer services guidelines for Tanzanian Urban water utilities'*, WELL paper, (task no. 514b), WEDC, 2001

Coates S. Sansom K.R., Kayaga S. *'PREPP - improving utility watsan services to low-income communities'* , Paper presented at the 27th WEDC Conference, Lusaka, Zambia, August 2001.

Collingnon B., M.Vezina, *'Independent water and sanitation providers in African Cities'* Water and Sanitation Program, April 2000

Collingnon B. *'Restructuring the Water Services in port Au Prince Shanty Towns'* Waterfront, issue 11, UNICEF, USA

Cook, R. (1992), *'Aspects of Customer Service'* ITC magazine, March-April, pp10-12.

Cullivan, D.E. et al (1988) *Guidelines for Institutional Assessment for Water and Wastewater Institutions*, WASH Technical Report No. 37, USAID, Washington.

DFID, (1998) *'Guidance Manual on Water Supply and Sanitation Programmes, (Institutional perspectives section pp 118 - 156)*, WELL, UK

DFID (2003) *Promoting institutional and organisational development*, Department for International Development, London, UK

Economist (2002) 'How to save 1m children a year', *The Economist*, 6 July.

Farnham, David, and Horton, Sylvia; *Managing the new public services*, 2nd Edition, Macmillan Press Ltd, ISBN 0-333-66435-3; 1996

Franceys R.W.A.F and Sansom K.R (1999),*'The Role of Government in Adjusting Economies: Paper no. 35 - India Urban Water Supply'*, DFID, University of Birmingham.

Franceys, R., (1997) *Private Waters? - A Bias Towards the Poor*. Unpublished Position Paper on Private Sector Participation in the Water and Sanitation Sector: Issues for the Department for International Development, United Kingdom

Gould J. and Nissen-Peterson E., (1999), *'Rainwater catchment systems for domestic supply'*, Intermediate Technology Publications, London.

Grosh M. and P. Glewwe *Designing Household Survey Questionnaires for Developing Countries: Lessons from 15 Years of the Living Standards Measurement Study. Volumes 1, 2, and 3.*, The World Bank, Washington DC, (2000).

Heskett, James L. (1986) *Managing in the service economy*; Harvard business school press, Boston, Massachusetts, ISBN 0-87584-130-9.

Howard, A.G., (2002), *Water quality surveillance - a reference manual*, WEDC, Loughborough University, UK

Howard, G.; Bartram, J. (2003). Domestic water quantity, service level and health. Geneva, Switzerland: World Health Organisation (WHO), http://www.who.int/ water_sanitation_health/Documents/domesticwater/domestwatertoc.htm

Inocenia, A. (2002) 'Manila Water and Sewerage Concessions', in A. Weitz, and R. Franceys, *Beyond Boundaries: Extending services to the urban poor*, Asian Development Bank, 2002.

Israel A. (1987) *'Institutional Development - Incentives to Performance'* World Bank, 1987

Jones, Peter, (Ed.) (1989) *Management in service industries*, Pitman Publishing, Longman Group UK Limited, London,ISBN 0-273-02953-3, 1989.

Kamalie A. (2001), *Marketing and service differentiation of the Water and Sewerage Authority*, Lesotho, MSc thesis at IHE, Delft, The Netherlands

Katko, T S: Paying for water in developing countries, Tampere university of technology, Tampere, 1991

Kayaga, S.M., 2002. *The Influence of Customer Perceptions of Urban Utility Water Services on Bill Payment Behaviour: Findings from Uganda*, PhD Thesis, WEDC, Loughborough University.

Kayaga S. and Sansom K.R., (2004), *Serving All Urban Consumers Book 5 - Sample Strategic marketing plan for water services in Kampala city, Uganda*, WEDC, UK

Kline Weinrich N. (1999), *Hands-on social marketing - a step by step guide*, Sage Publications, London.

Lyonnais des Eaux, (now Ondeo, Suez), (1998), *'Alternative solutions for water and sanitation in areas with limited financial resources'*, Paris.

Mugisha, S., (2000) *Organisational Behaviour and Performance: PPP in Watsan Services, Uganda*. Unpublished MSc Thesis, IHE-Delft, The Netherlands.

McDonald M.(1989) *'Marketing plans: how to prepare them, how to use them'* second edition, Oxford, UK

Narender A., Chary V.S and Sansom, K.R., (2004), *Serving All Urban Consumers Book 6 - Sample Strategic Marketing Plan for Water Services in Guntur* WEDC: http://www.lboro.ac.uk/wedc/projects/psd/.

Narender A.,.Chary V.S and Coates S., (2002), *'Testing of PREPP Methodology in Guntur'*, unpublished working paper, ASCI/WEDC.

Nickson, R.A. (2001), *'Establishing and Implementing a joint venture: Water and Sanitation Services in Cartagena, Columbia. Building Municipal Capacity for Private Sector Participation'*, Working Paper No. 442 05, GHK International, London

Njiru, C. and Sansom, K.R., (2004). *Serving All Urban Consumers Book 4 - Sample Strategic Marketing Plan for Water Services in Mombasa and Coast Region of Kenya*. WEDC, UK

Obel-Lawson E., and B.K. Njoroge, (1998) *'Small Service Providers make a Big Difference' - Field Note Number 5*, UNDP-World Bank, Water and Sanitation Program, Nairobi, Kenya

Revels C., (2002) *Business planning for small town water supply*, paper presented at the Addis Ababa Conference on Water Supply and Sanitation (WSS) Services for Small Towns and Multi-Village Schemes, Ethiopia, Water and Sanitation Program, World Bank.

Sage R., (2000) *'Meaningful Relations'* Water Services, UK.

Sansom, K.R., Franceys, R., Njiru, C. and Morales-Reyes, J. (2003), *Contracting Out Water and Sanitation Services: Volume 1, Guidance Notes for Service and Management Contracts in Developing Countries*, WEDC, Loughborough University, Loughborough.

Sansom, K.R., Franceys, R., Njiru, C. and Morales-Reyes, J. (eds) (2003), *Contracting Out Water and Sanitation Services: Volume 2, Case Studies and Analysis of Service and Management Contracts in Developing Countries*, WEDC, Loughborough University, Loughborough.

Sansom, K.R., Kayaga, S.M., Franceys, R.W.A.F, Njiru, C., Coates, S. and Chary, S. (2004) *Serving All Urban Consumers: A marketing approach to water services in low and middle-income countries. Book 1 - Guidance for government's enabling role*, WEDC, Loughborough University, UK.

Sansom, K.R., Coates, S., Njiru, C. and Franceys, R., *"Strategic Marketing to Improve Both Water Utility Finances and Services to Poor Urban Water Consumers"*, Discussion Paper, WEDC, Loughborough University,1999.

Skivington, P., (1997) *Risk Assessment for Water Quality Management* (p.9). Water Research Commission Project No. TT 90/97. Pretoria: South Africa.

Sohail, M. et al (2004) Series of publication on: *PPP and the Poor*. WEDC, Loughborough University, UK.
http://www.lboro.ac.uk/wedc/projects/ppp-poor/index.htm

Thomas P. and Green G (1993), *Rainwater quality from different roof catchments*, Water, Science and Technology, Vol 28, No.3/5.

Tremolet S. and Browning, S. (2002) *The interface between regulatory frameworks and partnerships - Public, private and civil society partnerships providing water and sanitation partnerships to the poor*. Business Partners for Development - BPD (http://www.bpd-waterandsanitation.org).

Vargas, M. (2002) *'Incentives for utilities to serve the urban poor, El Alto, Bolivia'*, R. Franceys (ed). IHE for WSSCC, Geneva.

Water and Sanitation Program (WSP) and PPIAF, (2002) *New Designs for Water and Sanitation Transactions - Making Private Sector Participation Work for the Poor*, WSP, Washington D.C., USA.

Water Utilities Partnership, (2000) *Performance indicators of some African water supply and sanitation utilities*, WUP, Cote D'Ivoire.

Water Utility Partnership (WUP) Africa (2003) *Better water and sanitation for the urban poor - good practice from Sub-Saharan Africa*, WSP and WUP, Cote d'Ivoire.

Wedgwood A. and Sansom K.R. *Willingness to pay surveys - a streamlined approach - Guidance notes for small town water services*, WEDC, Loughborough University, Loughborough, 2003

Wilson, RMS & Gilligan, C; (1997), *Strategic Marketing Management:*, 2nd Edition, Butterworth-Heinemann, UK

Whittington and Swarna (1994): *"The economic benefits of potable water supply projects to households in developing countries"*, Staff paper No. 53, Department of Environmental Sciences and Engineering, University of North Carolina at Chapel Hill.

Whittington D., (1992) *'Possible adverse effects of increasing block water tariffs in developing countries'* Economic development and cultural change', USA.

Whittington, D (1997) *Administering Contingent Valuation Surveys in Developing Countries*, World Development 1997

WHO, *'Financial Management of Water Supply and Sanitation*, (1994) WHO, Geneva.

WHO and UNICEF, *'JMP Global Water and Sanitation Assessment'* (2000), WHO, Geneva.

World Bank (1997) *'Toolkits for Private Participation in Water and Sanitation',* World Bank, Washington DC.

Chapter 11

Annexes

11.1   Annex 1: Example consumer survey format

Questionnaire No:

Mombasa Customer Survey and Willingness-to-pay Questionnaire

TO THE ENUMERATOR: Please read the following statement to each customer/potential customer before you ask the questions.

My name is ……………………………………, and I am working for a Research Project being conducted …………………………………….. The Researcher is investigating how urban water utilities such as the National Water Conservation and Pipeline Corporation (NWCPC) can provide and maintain improved water services to existing and new customers in a financially sustainable manner.

We would like you to assist us by taking time to answer the following questions. If you do not wish to answer a particular question please leave it out. You have been chosen to take part in the survey on a purely random basis. Your name will not be indicated in this questionnaire and your answers will be treated confidentially.

We have received permission to conduct this study from the Permanent Secretary, Office of the President, Provincial Administration and Internal Security. Thank you for your co-operation.

The language used for the interview is ……………...Survey date ………………Time:………….

Section 1: General Details about where you live: (tick the appropriate box)

1a) Part of City where you live

A)   Mombasa Island

B) Mombasa North Mainland

C) Mombasa West Mailand

D) Mombasa South Mainland

1b) Local name of Area:……………………………………………………………………………

1c) Type of dwelling (Enumerator to indicate here the Market segment of the household)

A) Bungalows or Maisonettes -----------------------

B) Flats--

C)1, 2, or 3 roomed house or Swahili house------

D) Dwelling in an informal settlement or slum----

1d) How long have you lived in this dwelling? ……………………………………………………..

Section 2: Your current water supplies (for all water users)

**2 a) Where do you and other members of your household obtain water?
(Please tick all the water sources that you use)**

A) Your own (individual) piped water connection

B) A shared water connection next to your dwelling

C) We obtain water from the Water Kiosk

D) We obtain water from the Hand Cart Water Vendors

E) We obtain water from the Private water tanker

F) We obtain water from a public bore-hole or well

G) We obtain water from a private bore-hole or well

H) We have our own Private bore-hole or well in our compound

2b) What is your main source of water supply?

A) Your own (individual) piped water connection

B) A shared water connection next to your dwelling

C) Water purchased from a Water Kiosk

D) Water purchased from hand-cart water vendors

E) Private water tanker

F) Water obtained from a public bore-hole or well

G) Water obtained from a private bore-hole or well

H) We have our own Private bore-hole or well in our compound

2c) Do you use NWCPC water and also water from other sources?

A) YES   B) NO

2d) Water Storage: What methods of water storage do your household use?

A) Roof tank   B) Underground or ground level tank outside the house

C) Water tank in the house   D) Small containers & jerricans

2e) How many days can your water storage last when there is no water supply? (continued overleaf)

A) One day

B) Two days

C) Three days

D) Four days ☐

E) Five days ☐

F) More than five days ☐

2f) **Piped connections:** Which of the following statements best describes your household's situation with regard to piped water connections?

A) We have our own individual house connection ☐

B) We have a shared piped connection ☐

C) We do not have any piped connection. ☐

2g) Have you applied to NWCPC for a water connection?

A) Yes ☐

B) No ☐

2h) **To whom do you pay for water?** (More than one box can be ticked if applicable)

A) Water utility (NWCPC) ☐   B) water kiosk operator ☐

C) Hand cart water vendors ☐   D) private water tanker ☐

E) Landlord ☐   F) Buy from bore-hole or well ☐

G) We have our own Borehole ☐   H) Obtain free water from Borehole or well ☐

I) We do not pay for water ☐

Section 3: Piped water received directly from NWCPC's pipelines:

If your household obtains water from NWCPC through taps in the house or from a yard tap (shared water connection)- please answer the following questions from 3.1 to 3.3

NOTE FOR ENUMERATOR: IF THE RESPONDENT DOES NOT RECEIVE NWCPC PIPED WATER PLEASE MOVE TO SECTION 4.

3.1 Water service levels provided by NWCPC

a) Supply frequency - On average how frequently do you receive piped water from NWCPC?

A) Once a day ☐   B) Twice a day ☐   C) Once in 2 or 3 days ☐

D) Once a week ☐   E) Continuous ☐   F) Other ☐   (please state)...............

b) Reliability: Does the water supply reliably arrive at the frequency you have stated?

A) Yes ☐   B) No ☐   C) Sometimes ☐

---

c) Supply duration - How many hours of water supply do you usually receive on average from NWCPC each time the piped water arrives?

A) Less than 2 hours [ ]   B) 2 to 4 hours [ ]

(C) More than 4 hours each time [ ]

d) Timing- At what times of the day do you usually receive piped water from NWCPC?

A) Mornings only [ ]   B) Evenings only [ ]   C) Both Mornings & Evenings . [ ]

D) All day [ ]   E) All Night [ ]   F) All day and Night [ ]

e) Are these times convenient for you?

A) Yes [ ]   B) No [ ]

f) If NWCPC has to ration water to customers and supply water only once in a day for a few hours, at which of the following time would you wish to receive water?

A) Mornings [ ]   B) Evenings [ ]

C) Other [ ]   (Please state)…………………………..

g) Water pressure: Does the water you receive from NWCPC's connection have enough pressure to reach and enter a roof tank or elevated tank?

A) Yes [ ]   B) No [ ]   C) Sometimes [ ]

D) I am not sure [ ]

h) Quantity: - Do you receive enough (sufficient) piped water from the water utility (NWCPC) for your use?

A) Yes [ ]   B) No [ ]

C) Do not receive piped water from utility (NWCPC) directly [ ]

i) Quality: - How would you generally rate the appearance of water supplied by NWCPC?

A) Good quality water (Clear and colourless) most of the time [ ]

B) Poor quality water (Muddy/brown) most of the time [ ]

j) Water Treatment: What type of water treatment do you carry out on the water from NWCPC?
A) Do not treat [ ]   B) boil drinking water [ ]   C) use water filter or purifier [ ]

D) Other [ ]

SERVING ALL URBAN CONSUMERS - BOOK 2

k)   Overall are you satisfied with the piped water supply from NWCPC?

A) YES ☐   B) NO ☐

l) Why? Indicate below

A)   Inadequate quantity or pressure ☐

B)   Costly (too expensive) ☐

C)   Low in Quality (colour/turbidity etc) ☐

3.2 Billing and payment of Water Charges (for NWCPC customers)

a)   Do you receive a water bill from NWCPC?

A) Yes ☐   B) No ☐

b) Do you have a water meter?

A) Yes ☐   B) No ☐

c) **How are you billed for water charges?**

A) By flat rate charge because I have no water meter ☐

B) Based on meter readings since I have a meter and it is read regularly ☐

C) By meter reading estimate (because my meter is not read) ☐

D) By meter reading estimate (because my meter does not work) ☐

E) I do not know ☐

d) How much do you pay to NWCPC for water on average each month? ....

e) How much did you pay for the piped connection charges? ....

f) How often do you receive a water bill from the water utility (NWCPC)?

A) Every month ☐   B) Once in 2 or 3 months or even more ☐

C) I never receive water bills from NWCPC ☐   D) Other ☐ (Please state)...............

g) How often do NWCPC meter readers read your water meter?

A) Every month ☐   B) Once in 2 months ☐   C) Once in 3 months ☐

D) Once in 4 to 6 months ☐   E) Once a year ☐   F) Never read ☐

h) **How do you pay for your water bills?**

A) Cash or cheque to NWCPC's cashiers office ☐   B) cheque by post ☐

C) NWCPC officers collect the cheque ☐   D) I pay the meter reader ☐

E) I do not pay ☐   F) I pay the landlord. ☐

i) **Do you understand the water bills that are sent to you?**

A) Yes ☐   B) No ☐

j) **Is the water bill that you receive reasonable?**

A) Yes ☐   B) No ☐

k) **How often do you pay the water bills for your household?**

A) Every month ☐   B) Whenever I receive bills ☐

C) Once in 2 or 3 months ☐   D) Other (specify)……………………………………..

l) **Do you have any complaints about the present billing system?**

Yes ☐   No ☐

3.3 *Customer Services provided by NWCPC*

a) When you find a problem with your water services do you make a complaint to NWCPC?

A) Yes ☐   B) No ☐

b) When you have a problem with your water supply or billing etc., who do you complain to?

A) The local NWCPC area office ☐   B) The Regional NWCPC office ☐

C) Other, please specify…………………………………………………..……………..

c) When you have a complaint or query with your water supply or billing etc., how do you contact NWCPC?

A) Visit in person ☐   B) By post (letter) ☐   C) By telephone ☐

d) How many times have you or a member of your household visited the NWCPC offices to make a request or complaint over the last one year?…………..

e) Do you consider the NWCPC offices to be accessible (distance, opening times, friendly etc.) to you?

A) Yes ☐   B) No ☐

f) How would you rate the customer services provided by NWCPC for the following aspects:
(Please tick the most appropriate box from good to poor)

	Good	average	poor
i) Process for obtaining a new water connection	☐	☐	☐
ii) Complaints on over billing	☐	☐	☐
iii) Complaints on irregular delivery of bills	☐	☐	☐
iv) Complaints for service interruptions such as lack of water	☐	☐	☐

g) Overall, how would you rate the general customer service that the NWCPC representatives give you?

A) Good ☐   B) Average ☐   C) Poor ☐

Section 4: Alternative Water Sources

4.1 CUSTOMERS WHO OBTAIN WATER DIRECTLY FROM WATER KIOSKS (either always or sometimes)
If you use water directly from Water Kiosks please answer the following questions:

a) Are the water kiosks, that you use, managed by

A) A private vendor ☐   B) the NWCPC ☐   C) A community group ☐

b) Do you or members of your household collect water from the kiosk(s), or do you have it delivered to your house?

A) Collected by a member of your household ☐   B) Delivered to your house ☐

C) Some delivered and some collected ☐

If you ticked boxes A) or C) please answer questions c) and d) below

c) How far is the water kiosk (that you use) from your house?

A) Less than 100m ☐   B) Between 100 -200m ☐   C) more than 200m ☐

d) How long does it usually take to collect water from the kiosk each time (one round trip)?.............................

e) **Timing.** In general, can you obtain water from the kiosk at convenient times of the day?

A) Yes ☐   B) No ☐

f) **Supply frequency -** If you wanted, are you able to obtain water from this water kiosk?

A) Continuous (all the time) ☐   B) Once a day ☐   C) Twice a day ☐

D) Once in 2 or 3 days ☐   E) Once a week ☐

g) **Reliability:** Does this water kiosk reliably provide water at the frequency you have stated?

A) Yes ☐   B) No ☐

h) **Quantity: -** Do you receive enough (sufficient) water from the water kiosk for your use?

A) Yes ☐   B) No ☐

i) How many (20 litre) containers does your household usually use from kiosks in a day?........

j) **Quality: -** How would you generally rate the appearance of water you obtain from the water kiosk?

A) Good quality water (Clear and colourless) most of the time ☐

B) Poor quality water (Muddy/brown) most of the time ☐

k) **Water Treatment:** What type of water treatment do you carry out on the kiosk water ?

A) Do not treat ☐   B) Boil drinking water ☐   C) Use water filter or purifier ☐

l) **Costs:** How much do you pay for a **20**litre container of water obtained from the kiosk?

A) During normal time when there are no water shortages?.................................
B) When there are water shortages?..

m) Overall are you satisfied with the water supply from the water kiosk?

A) YES ☐   No ☐

n) If not satisfied, why?

A) Inadequate quantity or pressure ☐

B) Costly (too expensive) ☐

C) Low in Quality (colour/turbidity etc) ☐

o) Do you think NWCPC should provide more water kiosks in your area?

A) Yes ☐   **B)** No ☐

4.2 Alternative Water Sources: *If you use water from other sources (other than NWCPC water and kiosks) such as boreholes, open wells or from water vendors, please answer the following questions:*

a)   What alternative water sources do you use?

A) Boreholes ☐   B) Open well ☐   C) Rainwater ☐

D) Hand cart water vendors ☐   E) Water tankers ☐

F) Other ☐   (Please specify here)...

b) Is this water source that you use, managed by;

A) A private vendor ☐   B) the NWCPC ☐   C) A community group ☐

D) Your household ☐   E) Other ☐   (Please specify here)...........................

c) Do you or members of your household collect water from this source, or do you have it delivered to your house?

A) Collected by a member of household ☐   B) Delivered to your house ☐

If you ticked boxes i) or iii) please answer questions c) and d)

d) How far is the water source (that you use) from your house?

A) Less than 100m ☐   B) Between 100 -200m ☐   C) more than 200m ☐

e) How long does it take to collect water from this source each time (round trip)?...................

f) **Timing.** In general, can you obtain water from this source at convenient times of the day?

A) Yes ☐   B) No ☐

g) **Supply frequency -** If you wanted, are you able to obtain water from this source?

A) Continuous (all the time) ☐   B) Once a day ☐   C) Twice a day ☐

D) Once in 2 or 3 days ☐   E) Once a week ☐

F) Other ☐   (please describe)...

h)   **Reliability:** Does this water source reliably provide water at the frequency you have stated?

A) Yes [ ]   B) No [ ]

i) **Quantity:** - Do you receive enough (sufficient) water from this source for your use?

A) Yes [ ]   B) No [ ]

i) How many (20 litre) containers of water do you use from this source in a day?.................

k) **Quality:** - How would you generally rate the appearance of water from this source?

A) Good quality water (Clear and colourless) most of the time [ ]

B) Poor quality water (Muddy/brown) most of the time [ ]

C) Other [ ]   (Please specify) ....

l) **Water Treatment:** What type of water treatment do you carry out on this water ?

A) Do not treat [ ]   B) boil drinking water [ ]   C) use water filter or purifier [ ]

D) Other [ ]   (Please specify) ....

m) **Costs:** How much do you pay for a 20 litre container (jerrican) of water from this source during normal time when there are no water shortages?...

n) How much do you pay for a 20 litre container (jerrican) of water from this source when there are water shortages?..

o) Overall are you satisfied with the water supply from this source?

    A) YES [ ]

    B) NO [ ]

p) If not satisfied, Why?

A) Inadequate quantity or pressure [ ]   B) Costly (too expensive) [ ]

C) Low in quality (colour, turbidity, etc) [ ]   D) Opening times [ ]

E) Long queues [ ]   F) Other [ ]   (Please state).................................

q) If NWCPC could provide more water kiosks near where you live, would you buy water from the NWCPC water kiosk instead of obtaining water from this source (source indicated in question "a" above)

A) Yes [ ]   B) No [ ]

4.3 Water from Vendors: *If you use water supplied by vendors (either sometimes or always), please answer the following questions:*

a)   Do you know the sources from which Hand-cart vendors obtain water?

A) Yes [   ]   B) No [   ]

b)   If you know, where does the water vendors who supply your household obtain water from?

A) Borehole [   ]   B) Open well [   ]   C) NWCPC Water kiosk [   ]

D) Rainwater [   ]   E) Streams/Springs [   ]   F) NWCPC individual connection [   ]

G) A combination of sources [   ]   (please specify)………………………….

c) How much do you pay for a **20** litre container of water brought to you by the Hand-cart water vendor during normal time when there are no water shortages?………………………………

d) How much do you pay for a **20**litre container of water brought to you by the Hand-cart water vendor during times when there are water shortages?…………………………………………..

e) Why do you prefer to buy water from a water vendor instead of collecting the water directly from the sources where the vendor obtains water?

………………………………………………………………………………………………………
………………………………………………………………………………………………………

f) Why do you obtain water from other sources instead of using NWCPC water?

A) I do not have a water connection [   ]

B) I have a connection but NWCPC water is not enough [   ]

C) NWCPC water is costly (too expensive) compared with other sources [   ]

E) Other reasons [   ]   (Please specify)……………………………………………

d)   If NWCPC could provide a water kiosk near your area with water available most of the time, would you buy water from the NWCPC water kiosk instead of buying water from vendors?

A) Yes [   ]   B) No [   ]

Section 5 - Socio-Economic Aspects

5.1 Are you (the respondent)

A) Male ☐   B) Female ☐

5.2 Are you (the respondent)

A) Head of household ☐   B) Spouse ☐   C) Other ☐

5.3 Is the head of the Household

A) Male ☐   B) Female ☐

5.4 Please give the total number of people (including children) who live in your household (dwelling)………………..

How many rooms does your dwelling have?…………………………..

5.6 If renting, how much money is the rent for your dwelling per month? ………………

5.7 What is the ownership status of the dwelling (premises) occupied by your household?

A) Privately owned by my family ☐

B) Provided to family by Employer (e.g Government, Council or a Company) ☐

C) Privately rented to our family by a private landlord ☐

D) Other (please specify) …………………………………………………………………..

5.8 Do you have electricity in your dwelling?

A) Yes ☐   B) No ☐

If the answer is "No", then move to part B

If the answer is "Yes", continue with questions 5.9 to 5.11 and then move to part B

5.9 How much is your monthly electricity bill? KSH………………………..

5.10 Do you consider your monthly electricity bill to be reasonable?

A) Yes ☐   B) No ☐

11.2   Annex 2: Example WTP survey form

Opening statement to the bidding game

(To the enumerator: Please read this statement slowly to the respondent)

As you may know, there is a growing deficiency of clean water not only in Kenya, but in the whole world. The available surface water is often polluted and not suitable for human consumption in its present form. Water from the Indian Ocean is salty and would require a lot of money to treat it and make it suitable for human consumption. NWCPC spends a lot of money on electricity, chemicals, pipes, pumps, motors, and other equipment including staff salaries in order to purify the water, store it and transport it to your homes with pipes. Water utilities such as NWCPC should be able to cover all operation and maintenance costs with some money left to finance improvements in water supply. In the past NWCPC has not had enough funds to be able to cover all operating and maintenance costs or even to finance improvements in water supply. This is the main reason why water supply to your house may not be reliable, sometimes resulting in serious water shortages in Mombasa and the surrounding coastal areas.

I will describe the nature of different types of possible service options to you and then ask whether you would like to have the services at a suggested price. During this procedure you shall have to think about the advantages of each type of water service to your household.

NWCPC has the intention of ensuring that each household should pay for water according to the type of service they receive and the amount of water used. Those who use more should pay more. Furthermore NWCPC water tariff entails that those households that use most water pay more per quantity of water than those who use less.

Before NWCPC carries out any improvements to the water services, it is important to know what **type** of water services people want, and **how much money** people are willing to pay for each type of improved service. With this information, NWCPC can then plan to give people the type of water service that the people want and are willing to pay for.

Now I am going to ask you some questions to learn whether your household would be willing to pay more money in order to improve the water supply in Mombasa. It is important that you answer questions, as truthfully as you can so that we can know the amount you are willing to pay for an improved supply of water to your household.

Bidding game
To the enumerator:

The bidding game is targeted to three types of respondents, depending on the type and location of the house they reside in (market segment). Please decide in which category (market segment) the respondent belongs. Then under each category several service levels have been specified, starting with the highest service level.

Please guide the respondent through the bidding game, starting with the highest set price. When the respondent chooses a price please tick in the box against that bid, and stop the exercise. Otherwise go through the various service levels in the respondents' category.

Category I: Individual house connection - has three service levels but is not included here.

Catogory II: Those living in shared buildings in formal (planned) areas. This includes swahili houses, 1, 2 or 3 roomed dwellings without internal plumbing located in planned areas of the city)

(For a respondent who lives in a shared building e.g. Swahili house, constructed of permanent or semi-permanent building materials, and located in a formally planned area. The building does not have an individual water connection with internal plumbing, neither does it have capacity for a water connection with internal plumbing in the future. Instead residents will most likely have a yard tap serving a number of families who live in the shared building).

Service Level 4

Assume that you will be receiving clean piped water through a shared yard connection with adequate pressure providing enough water at the tap in the compound of the house where you stay. Assume that the water is available continuously for 24 hours every day. Assume that your household is able to obtain enough water from the tap in the compound any time of the day or night. Whenever you wish you can also carry out plumbing in your house and extend the water inside your house.

(17) Would you be willing to contribute KSh.2500/- per month towards the water bills for the tap?

If 'Yes' - Willingness to Pay is KSh.2500/- ....END ☐

If 'No' go to (18)

(18) Would you be willing to contribute KSh.2000/- per month towards the water bill for the tap?

If 'Yes' - Willingness to Pay is KSh.2000/- ....END ☐

If 'No' go to (19)

(19) Would you be willing to contribute KSh.1800/- per month towards the water bill for the tap?

If 'Yes' - Willingness to Pay is KSh.1800/- ....END ☐

If 'No' go to (20)

(20) Would you be willing to contribute KSh.1600/- per month towards the water bill for the tap?

If 'Yes' - Willingness to Pay is KSh.1600/- ....END ☐

If "No" go to (21)

(21) Would you be willing to contribute KSh.1400/- per month towards the water bill for the tap?

If "Yes" - Willingness to pay is KSh.1400/..........END

If "No" go to (22)

(22) Would you be willing to contribute KSh1200/- per month towards the water bill for the tap?

If "Yes" - Willingness to pay is KSh.1200/- ....END

If "No", go to (23)

(23) What is the maximum amount of money per month you are willing to contribute towards the water bill for the tap in your compound in order to get a continuous water supply at good pressure 24 hours every day?

I would be willing to pay a maximum of KSh...........................per month for water service level 4.

All respondents in this market segment whose willingness to pay is less than KSh.1200/- should be requested to answer questions under SERVICE LEVEL 5 below.

Now go to the Next Service Option

Service Level 5
Assume that you will be receiving clean piped water through a shared yard connection providing enough water at the tap in the compound of the house where you stay. Assume that NWCPC has provided a storage tank next to the existing connection that you share with your neighbours and that the tank receives and stores water so that you can draw the water from your yard connection continuously even during the rationing hours. Assume that because of this storage tank, your household is able to obtain enough water from the tap in the compound any time of the day or night. Whenever you wish you can also carry out plumbing in your house and extend the water inside your house.

(17) Would you be willing to contribute KSh.2500/- per month towards the water bills for the tap and the storage tank?

If 'Yes' - Willingness to Pay is KSh.2500/- ....END

If 'No' go to (18)

(18) Would you be willing to contribute KSh.2000/- per month towards the water bill for the tap and the storage tank?

If 'Yes' - Willingness to Pay is KSh2000/- ....END

If 'No' go to (19)

(19) Would you be willing to contribute KSh.1800/- per month towards the water bill for the tap and the storage tank?

If 'Yes' - Willingness to Pay is KSh.1800/- ....END   [   ]

If 'No' go to (20)

(20) Would you be willing to contribute KSh.1,600/- per month towards the water bill for the tap and the storage tank?

If 'Yes' - Willingness to Pay is KSh.1600/- ....END   [   ]

If "No" go to (21)

(21) Would you be willing to contribute KSh.1400/- per month towards the water bill for the tap and the storage tank?

If "Yes" - Willingness to pay is KSh.1400/..........END   [   ]

If "No" go to (22)

(22) Would you be willing to contribute KSh1200/- per month towards the water bill for the tap and the storage tank?

If "Yes" - Willingness to pay is KSh.1200/- ....END   [   ]

If "No", go to (23)

(23) What is the maximum amount of money per month you are willing to contribute towards the water bill for the tap and the storage tank in your compound that will enable you to get a continuous water supply at any time of the day or night?

I would be willing to pay a maximum of KSh...........................per month for water service level 5.

Now go to the Next Service Option.

Service Level 6
Assume that you will be receiving clean piped water through a shared yard connection providing enough water at the tap in the compound of the house where you stay. Assume that the water is supplied on rationing basis, but with good pressure, for 12 hours every day. Assume that your household is able to obtain enough water from the tap in the compound. Whenever you wish you can also carry out plumbing in your house and extend the water inside your house.

(24) Would you be willing to contribute KSh.1200/- per month towards the water bills for the tap?

If 'Yes' - Willingness to Pay is KSh.1200/- ....END   [   ]

If 'No' go to (25)

(25) Would you be willing to contribute KSh.1000/- per month towards the water bill for the tap?

If 'Yes' - Willingness to Pay is KSh.1000/-..........END

If 'No' go to (26)

(26) Would you be willing to contribute KSh.800/- per month towards the water bill for the tap?

If 'Yes' - Willingness to Pay is KSh.800/-..........END

If 'No' go to (27)

(27) What is the maximum amount of money per month you are willing to contribute towards the water bill for the tap in order to receive 12 hours of water supply every day (service level 5)?

I would be willing to pay a maximum of KSh....................per month for water service level 6.

All respondents in this market segment whose willingness to pay for service level (5) is less than KSh.800/- per month should be requested to answer questions under SERVICE LEVEL 7 below. These are the respondents whose answer to question number 27 is less than KSh.800/- per month.

Service Level 7

Assume that you will be receiving clean piped water through a shared yard connection providing enough water at the tap in the compound of the house where you live. Assume that the water is supplied on rationing basis, in the morning and evening for a minimum period of 4 hours every day and that your household is able to obtain water from the tap in the compound only in the mornings and evenings for a total of 4 hours. Whenever you wish you can also carry out plumbing in your house and extend the water inside your house.

(28) Would you be willing to contribute KSh800/- per month towards the water bills for the tap?

If 'Yes' - Willingness to Pay is KSh800/- ....END

If 'No' go to (29)

(29) Would you be willing to contribute KSh700/- per month towards the water bill for the tap?

If 'Yes' - Willingness to Pay is KSh700/- ....END

If 'No' go to (30)

(30) Would you be willing to contribute KSh600/- per month towards the water bill for the tap?

If 'Yes' - Willingness to Pay is KSh600/- ....END

☐

If 'No' go to (31)

(31) Would you be willing to contribute KSh500/- per month towards the water bill for the tap?

If 'Yes' - Willingness to Pay is KSh500/- ....END

☐

If "No" go to (32)

(32) What is the maximum amount of money per month are you willing to contribute towards the water bill for the tap in order to receive 4 hours of water supply every day at your compound (service level 6)? (Remember that you may also extend the water to your house when you carry out plumbing inside your house).

I would be willing to pay a maximum of KSh...................per month for water service level 7.

Category III: People living in informal settlements

(For a respondent who lives in a shared house or individual shack, constructed of semi-permanent or temporary building materials, and located in an informal area or slum. such a building will not have internal plumbing. space for a yard tap and a storage tank might be found if the slum is upgraded.

Service Level 8
Assume that you will be receiving clean piped water through a shared yard connection (shared by about 10 dwellings) providing enough water at the tap in the compound of the dwelling where you stay. Assume that NWCPC has provided a pipeline, a storage tank, and a shared connection next to your dwelling. Assume that you are sharing the connection and the storage tank with your neighbours and that the tank stores water so that you can draw the water from your yard connection continuously even during the rationing hours. Assume that because of this storage tank, your household is able to obtain enough water from the tap in the compound for 18 to 24 hours a day.

(33) Would you be willing to contribute KSh.2500/- per month towards the water bills for the tap and the storage tank?

If 'Yes' - Willingness to Pay is KSh.2500/- ....END

☐

If 'No' go to (34)

(34) Would you be willing to contribute KSh.2,000/- per month towards the water bill for the tap and the storage tank?

If 'Yes' - Willingness to Pay is KSh.2000/- ....END

☐

If 'No' go to (35)

(35) Would you be willing to contribute KSh.1800/- per month towards the water bill for the tap and the storage tank?

If 'Yes' - Willingness to Pay is KSh.1800/- ....END

If 'No' go to (36)

(36) Would you be willing to contribute KSh.1600/- per month towards the water bill for the tap and the storage tank?

If 'Yes' - Willingness to Pay is KSh.1600/- ....END

If "No" go to (37)

(37) Would you be willing to contribute KSh.1400/- per month towards the water bill for the tap and the storage tank?

If "Yes" - Willingness to pay is KSh.1400/..........END

If "No" go to (38)

(38) Would you be willing to contribute KSh1200/- per month towards the water bill for the tap and the storage tank?

If "Yes" - Willingness to pay is KSh.1200/- ....END

If "No", go to (39)

(39) What is the maximum amount of money per month you are willing to contribute towards the water bill for the tap and the storage tank in your compound that will enable you to get a continuous water supply at any time of the day or night?

I would be willing to pay a maximum of KSh.................per month for water service level 8.

All respondents in this market segment whose willingness to pay is less than KSh.1200/- should be requested to answer questions under SERVICE LEVEL 9 below.

Now go to the Next Service Option for respondents whose willingness to pay is less that KSh.1200 per month

Service Level 9
Assume that you will be receiving clean piped water through a shared yard connection (shared by about 10 dwellings) providing water at the tap in the compound of the dwelling where you stay. Assume that NWCPC does not provide a storage tank next to the connection. Assume that the water is supplied on rationing basis for about 12 hours every day. Assume that your household obtains water from the tap in the compound, that you share with about 10 other dwellings.

(40) Would you be willing to contribute KSh.1200/- per month towards the water bills for the tap?

If 'Yes' - Willingness to Pay is KSh.1200/- ....END

If 'No' go to (41)

(41) Would you be willing to contribute KSh.1000/- per month towards the water bill for the tap?

If 'Yes' - Willingness to Pay is KSh.1000/- ....END

If 'No' go to (42)

(42) Would you be willing to contribute KSh.800/- per month towards the water bill for the tap?

If 'Yes' - Willingness to Pay is KSh.800/- ....END

If 'No' go to (43)

(43) What is the maximum amount of money per month you are willing to contribute towards the water bill for the tap in order to receive 12 hours of water supply every day (service level 9)?

I would be willing to pay a maximum of KSh...................per month for water service level (9).

All respondents in this market segment whose willingness to pay for service level (9) is less than KSh.800/- per month should be requested to answer questions under SERVICE LEVEL 10 below. These are the respondents whose answer to question number 43 is less than KSh.800/- per month.

Service Level 10 (Shared yard connection without tank)

Assume that you will be receiving clean piped water through a shared yard connection (shared by about 10 dwellings) providing water at the tap in the compound of the house where you live. Assume that NWCPC does not provide a storage tank next to the connection. Assume that the water is provided on rationing basis for 2 hours in the morning and 2 hours in the evening, a maximum period of 4 hours every day. Assume that your household obtains water from the tap in the compound, that you share with about 10 other dwellings.

(44) Would you be willing to contribute KSh 800/- per month towards the water bills for the tap?

If 'Yes' - Willingness to Pay is KSh 800/- ....END

If 'No' go to (45)

(45) Would you be willing to contribute KSh 700/- per month towards the water bill for the tap?

If 'Yes' - Willingness to Pay is KSh 700/- ....END

If 'No' go to (46)

(46) Would you be willing to contribute KSh 600/- per month towards the water bill for the tap?

If 'Yes' - Willingness to Pay is KSh 600/- ....END

If 'No' go to (47)

(47) Would you be willing to contribute KSh 500/- per month towards the water bill for the tap?

If 'Yes' - Willingness to Pay is KSh 500/- ....END

If "No" go to (48)

(48) What is the maximum amount of money per month are you willing to contribute towards the water bill for the tap in order to receive 4 hours of water supply every day at your compound (service level 10)?.

I would be willing to pay a maximum of KSh.........................per month for water service level (10).

Service level 11 (Privately managed water kiosk with shelter and storage tank)

Assume that you obtain water from an Improved Water Kiosk that is provided with a shelter (suitable building), a storage tank and several taps. The improved water kiosk obtains water from NWCPC's pipelines. The kiosk is metered by NWCPC and is privately managed by an operator who pays the water bill for the water sold to NWCPC. Assume that this kiosk is open from 7 a.m. to 7 p.m. daily, and good quality water from the NWCPC pipeline is available throughout the day with adequate pressure.

(49) Would you be willing to pay KSh.7/- per 20-litre container of water bought from the improved water kiosk?

If 'Yes' - Willingness to Pay is KSh.7/- ....END

If 'No' go to (50)

(50) Would you be willing to pay KSh.6/- per 20-litre container of water bought from the improved water kiosk?

If 'Yes' - Willingness to Pay is KSh.6/- ....END

If 'No' go to (51)

ANNEXES

(51) Would you be willing to pay KSh.5/- per container of water bought from the improved water kiosk?

If 'Yes' - Willingness to Pay is KSh 5/- ....END

If "No" go to (52)

(52) Would you be willing to pay KSh 4/-per 20-litre container of water bought from the improved water kiosk?

If 'Yes' - Willingness to Pay is KSh 4/-..........END

If 'No' go to (53)

(53) Would you be willing to pay KSh 3/- per 20-litre container of water bought from the improved water kiosk?

If 'Yes' - Willingness to Pay is KSh 3/-..........END

If 'No' go to (54)

(54) What is the maximum amount of money you are willing to pay for a 20-litre container of good quality water obtained from an improved water kiosk where water is available at good pressure throughout the day?

I would be willing to pay a maximum of KSh..........................per 20-litre container of good quality water from an improved water kiosk.

All respondents in this market segment whose willingness to pay for service level (11) is less than KSh.4/- per 20 litre container should be requested to answer questions under SERVICE LEVEL 12 below. These are the respondents whose answer to question number 54 is less than KSh.4/- per 20 litre container of water.

Service level 13 (Community managed water kiosk with shelter and storage tank)
Assume that you obtain water from an Improved Water Kiosk that is provided with a shelter (suitable building), a storage tank and several taps. The improved water kiosk obtains water from NWCPC's pipelines. The kiosk is metered by NWCPC and is managed by a community group. The community group operates the kiosk and then pays water bills to NWCPC for the water consumed as measured by the water meter. Assume that this kiosk is open from 7 a.m. to 7 p.m. daily, and good quality water from the NWCPC pipeline is available throughout the day with adequate pressure. In order to make the water affordable to members of the community group, you are required to provide at least one days' of free work (without payment) per month at the water kiosk selling water to other community group members.

(55) Would you be willing to pay KSh 6/- per 20-litre container of water bought from the community managed water kiosk?

If 'Yes' - Willingness to Pay is KSh 6/- ....END

225

If 'No' go to (56)

(56) Would you be willing to pay KSh 5/- per 20-litre container of water bought from the community managed water kiosk?

If 'Yes' - Willingness to Pay is KSh 5/-..........END

If 'No' go to (57)

(57) Would you be willing to pay KSh 4/- per 20-litre container of water bought from the community managed water kiosk?

If 'Yes' - Willingness to Pay is KSh 4/-..........END

If 'No' go to (58)

(58) Would you be willing to pay KSh 3/- per 20-litre container of water bought from the community managed water kiosk?

If 'Yes' - Willingness to Pay is KSh 3/-..........END

If 'No' go to (59)

(59) Would you be willing to pay KSh 2/- per 20-litre container of water bought from a community managed water kiosk?

If 'Yes' - Willingness to Pay is KSh 2/-..........END

If "No" go to (60)

(60) Would you be willing to pay KSh 1.50 per container of water bought from a community managed water kiosk?

If 'Yes' - Willingness to Pay is KSh 1.50..........END

If "No" go to (61)

(61) Would you be willing to pay KSh 1/- per container of water bought from a community managed water kiosk?

If 'Yes' - Willingness to Pay is KSh 1/-..........END

If "No" go to (62)

(62) Would you be willing to pay K-cents 50 per 20-litre container of water bought from the community managed water kiosk?

If 'Yes' - Willingness to Pay is K-Cents 50..........END

If 'NO' go to (63)

(63) What is the maximum amount of money you are willing to pay for a 20 litre container of water obtained from a community managed water kiosk that is open from 7.00 am to 7.00 pm?

I would be willing to pay a maximum of KSh...........................per 20 litre container of water from a community managed water kiosk.

(64) In order to make the cost of water to members of the community group affordable, it is proposed that each community group member should contribute KSh200/-per month towards the cost of employing a kiosk attendant. Once each group member pays Ksh200/-per month, group members would pay reduced charges for each 20-litre container bought from the community water kiosk.

Would you be willing to contribute KSh200/- per month to the cost of employing a kiosk attendant (or alternatively contribute at least one days' free labour per month, working at the community water kiosk)?

A) Yes ☐   B) No ☐

Service level 12 (Privately managed water kiosk without shelter or storage tank, that is ordinary water tap)

Assume that you obtain water from an ordinary Water Kiosk (this is a tap without any storage tank) supplied with water by NWCPC pipeline through a water meter to record consumption. An operator, who sells water in units of 20litres and then pays water bills to NWCPC, privately manages the Water Kiosk. Assume that this kiosk is open from 7 a.m. to 7 p.m. daily. Sometimes times the pressure of water is low, as there is no storage tank next to the water kiosk.

(65) Would you be willing to pay KSh 4/- per 20-litre container of water bought from the water kiosk?

If 'Yes' - Willingness to Pay is KSh 4/- ....END ☐

If 'No' go to (66)

(66) Would you be willing to pay KSh 3/- per 20-litre container of water bought from the water kiosk?

If 'Yes' - Willingness to Pay is KSh 3/- ....END ☐

If 'No' go to (67)

(67) Would you be willing to pay KSh 2/- per container?

If 'Yes' - Willingness to Pay is KSh 2/- ....END ☐

If "No" go to (68)

(68) Would you be willing to pay KSh 1.50 per container of water bought from the privately managed water kiosk?

If 'Yes' - Willingness to Pay is KSh 1.50..........END

If "No" go to (69)

(69) Would you be willing to pay KSh 1/- per container of water bought from the privately managed water kiosk?

If 'Yes' - Willingness to Pay is KSh 1/-..........END

If "No" go to (70)

(70) What is the maximum amount of money you are willing to pay for a 20-litre container of water obtained from an ordinary privately managed water kiosk? The water kiosk is managed by a private person and is open from 7 am to 7 pm.

I would be willing to pay a maximum of KSh……………………..per 20 litre container of water from an ordinary privately managed water kiosk.

Now, the bidding game is finished.

END OF QUESTIONNAIRE. *Please thank the respondent for his/her time spent with you.*

Time questionnaire completed...

Section Seven: To help us with future questionnaires please answer the following questions.

7:a) How long did you spend completing this questionnaire?..

7:b) Did you understand all the questions?

A) Yes ☐   B) No ☐

Please make any other comments about any part of this questionnaire in the space

....

....

....

Thank you for completing this questionnaire.

Eng. Cyrus Njiru, WEDC, Loughborough University, UK. July 2000

To the Enumerator:

Your Name:...

Supervisors name:..

Supervisor checked completed form (please sign)...................................

Date completed:...

11.3   Annex 3: Calculations for Average Incremental Cost (AIC)

Determination of projected costs and tariffs require project definition and cost estimates. The following calculations are based on research findings in Mombasa.

Project definition and cost estimate
Recent engineering studies concluded that there was need to improve bulk water supply and to strengthen the distribution network in Mombasa and the coastal area. Among other outputs, the studies defined two main project components:

• Bulk water supply development for Mombasa and

• Improvements to water distribution network in Mombasa.

The total construction cost of the bulk supply component is estimated at US$223 million. The operation and maintenance costs for this component is estimated at US$1.82 million per year. It is assumed that these costs will remain constant for the life of the project since flow of water is by gravity.

The construction cost for the component to improve the distribution network is estimated at US$62 million. Assuming commercial management, the optimal operation and maintenance costs for the distribution system is estimated at about Ksh27/= (US$0.37) per m3.

The total capital costs to implement both the bulk supply component and improvements in distribution network is estimated at US$285 million.

Project Scenarios
Two different scenarios for determination of the average incremental cost (AIC) for Mombasa are considered. The scenarios are based on implementing the two project components recommended by the recent engineering studies. It is assumed that NWCPC succeeds in obtaining low interest, long term investment capital to undertake bulk supply development, transmission and distribution works. The following assumptions have been made to facilitate determination of AIC costs:

• Capital costs are only incurred at the end of construction period, after which the project starts to produce benefits.

• The only benefits delivered by the project are in form of revenue from sale of water. In practice, infrastructure projects, and more so water projects, deliver social and economic benefits, most of which cannot be easily quantified.

• Annual operation and maintenance (O & M) costs are constant. In many infrastructure projects, O & M costs increase over time as the infrastructure gets old. O & M costs could also reduce over time if management efficiency increases in the operations and maintenance phase of a project.

• The life of the project is assumed to be only 25 years for purposes of calculating the AIC. It is known that such projects have a much longer life span. In particular, most gravity based water projects deliver benefits for longer periods, sometimes as long as fifty to a hundred years. The existing Mzima pipeline water project is over 45 years old and still producing the same quantity of water it was producing 45 years ago at minimal operation and maintenance cost.

230

- The quantity of water produced by the infrastructure and sold to customers is constant throughout the life of the project. In practice, some water projects operate at a low capacity on commissioning and achieve full production capacity a few years later as population and water demand increases. Since Mombasa is a capacity constrained city with suppressed demand, high willingness to pay but with problems of obtaining investment capital, it is assumed that the project now under consideration will be operated at full capacity soon after commissioning. Other projects will come on line after a few years to help meet the water demand of the growing population.

The total capital cost for both project components is US$285 million. Provision for rehabilitation of the system is made at US$10 million. It is assumed that this amount will be spent in the 10th year after commissioning. Both scenarios 1 and 2 assume that financing will be available to finance bulk supply and improvements to the distribution network. It is assumed that the full costs of improving the water supply system will be met from water sales from the entire region.

The following further assumptions are made:

- Financing is secured at 8% per annum with a grace period equal to the construction period, so that repayments commence after commissioning when water is sold to customers.

- Management of the distribution system will be on commercial basis.

The operation and maintenance cost for Sabaki (Baricho) water source has been estimated at US$0.59 per m^3. It is assumed that Marere and Tiwi maintain production at capacities of 12,000m^3/day and 6,000m^3/day respectively and that Baricho source maintains its present contribution of 72,000m^3/day. The total amount of water distributed by the strengthened network is assumed to be 176,400m^3

Scenario 1 assumes a high level of management efficiency estimated at 15% unaccounted for water (UFW) and 90% bill collection efficiency. For this scenario, the average incremental cost of water works out as US$1.08 per m^3. With the present exchange rate of KSh73/= to the US$, the Average Incremental Cost is about Ksh78.85/= per m^3

Scenario 2 assumes a moderate level of management efficiency at 20% unaccounted for water (UFW) and 85% bill collection efficiency. For this scenario, the average incremental cost of water works out as US$1.21 per m^3. With the present exchange rate of KSh73/= to the US$, the Average Incremental Cost is about Ksh88.30/= per m^3.

Detailed calculations for each of the two scenarios are presented below.

Scenario 1: AIC calculation based on high level of management efficiency
Scenario 1 assumes a high level of management efficiency.

Further assumptions are:

- Unaccounted for water (UFW) is 15% so that 85% of water produced is sold (billed for).

- Revenue (bill) collection efficiency of the water utility is 90% (with commercial management). This means that 90% of the water sold is actually paid for.

Total Capital Cost of the second Mzima pipeline, storage, & distribution
US$285,000,000

Annual O&M cost (Mzima bulk supply, 86400m3/day) US$2,000,000/yr

Annual O&M cost (Baricho & Tiwi bulk sources, 78,000@US$0.59)US$16,797,000/yr

Annual O&M costs (distribution system with commercial management)US$8,000,000yr

Total operation and maintenance costs US$26,797,000/yr

Annual water produced 176,400m3/day $64,386,000m^3/yr$

Annual water sold (@15%UFW) $54,730,000m^3/yr$

Annual water sold and paid for (@90% bill collection efficiency) $49,260,000m^3/yr$

Discount Rate 8%

With these assumptions, the average incremental cost for the project is calculated as
shown below.

Table 11.1. Scenario 1: AIC calculation based on high level of management efficiency (15% UFW and 90% bill collection efficiency)[1]

Year	Capital Costs in '000 US$	Operation and MaintenanceCosts in '000 US$	Total Costs in '000 US$	Discount Factor at 8% Discount Rate	Present Value of Total Costs in '000 US$	Water sold and paid for in '000m^3/yr	Present Value of Water sold and paid for in '000m^3/yr
1	285,000	16,797	301,797	0.926	279,464	25,000	23,150
2		26,797	26,797	0.857	22,965	49,260	42,216
3		26,797	26,797	0.794	21,277	49,260	39,112
4		26,797	26,797	0.735	19,696	49,260	36,206
5		26,797	26,797	0.681	18,249	49,260	33,546
6		26,797	26,797	0.630	16,882	49,260	31,034
7		26,797	26,797	0.583	15,623	49,260	28,719
8		26,797	26,797	0.540	14,470	49,260	26,600
9		26,797	26,797	0.500	13,399	49,260	24,630
10	10,000	26,797	36,797	0.463	17,037	49,260	22,807
11		26,797	26,797	0.429	11,496	49,260	21,133
12		26,797	26,797	0.397	10,638	49,260	19,556
13		26,797	26,797	0.368	9,861	49,260	18,128
14		26,797	26,797	0.340	9,111	49,260	16,748
15		26,797	26,797	0.315	8,441	49,260	15,517
16		26,797	26,797	0.292	7,825	49,260	14,384
17		26,797	26,797	0.270	7,235	49,260	13,300
18		26,797	26,797	0.250	6,699	49,260	12,315
19		26,797	26,797	0.232	6,217	49,260	11,428
20		26,797	26,797	0.215	5,761	49,260	10,591
21		26,797	26,797	0.199	5,333	49,260	9,803
22		26,797	26,797	0.184	4,931	49,260	9,064
23		26,797	26,797	0.170	4,556	49,260	8,374
24		26,797	26,797	0.158	4,234	49,260	7,783
25		26,797	26,797	0.146	3,912	49,260	7,192
				TOTAL PRESENT COSTS	545,312	TOTAL PRESENT VALUE OF WATER SOLD AND PAID FOR	503,336

1. Average Incremental Cost = (Present Value of Total Costs)/(Present Value of water sold and paid for
=US$545,312,000 503,336,000m^3 = US$1.08per m^3

In this scenario, the average incremental cost of water is US$1.08 per m^3. With the present exchange rate of KSh73/= to the US$, the Average Incremental Cost is about Ksh78.85/ = per m^3

In order to break even, the average tariff would be set at US$1.08 per m^3.

Scenario 2: AIC calculation based on moderate level of management efficiency
Scenario 2 is similar to scenario 1 above but at a lower level of management efficiency. In this scenario, the AIC is calculated assuming that UFW is 20% and bill collection efficiency is 85%.

Total Capital Cost of the second Mzima pipeline, storage, & distribution	US$285,000,000
Annual O&M cost (Mzima bulk supply, 86400m^3/day)	US$2,000,000/yr
Annual O&M cost (Baricho & Tiwi bulk sources, 78,000@US$0.59)	US$16,797,000/yr
Annual O&M costs (commercial management assumed)	US$8,000,000/yr
Total operation and maintenance costs	US$26,797,000/yr
Annual water produced 176,400m^3/day	64,386,000m3/yr
Annual water sold (@ 20%UFW)	51,510,000m3/yr
Annual water sold and paid for (@ 85% bill collection efficiency)	43,800,000m3/yr
Discount Rate	8%

With these assumptions, the average incremental cost for the project is calculated as shown below.

In this scenario, the average incremental cost of water is US$1.21 per m^3. With the present exchange rate of KSh73/= to the US$, the Average Incremental Cost is about Ksh88.30/ = per m^3

In order to break even, the average tariff would be set at US$1.21 per m^3.

The above calculations show that efficient management of a water utility has the potential to lower water tariffs.

Table 11.2. Scenario 2: AIC calculation based on high level of management efficiency (15% UFW and 90% bill collection efficiency)[1]

Year	Capital Costs in '000 US$	Operation and Maintenance Costs in '000 US$	Total Costs in '000 US$	Discount Factor at 8% Discount Rate	Present Value of Total Costs in '000 US$	Water sold and paid for in '000m^3/yr	Present Value of Water sold and paid for in '000m^3/yr
1	285,000	16,797	301,797	0.926	279,464	24,000	22,224
2		26,797	26,797	0.857	22,965	43,800	37,537
3		26,797	26,797	0.794	21,277	43,800	34,777
4		26,797	26,797	0.735	19,696	43,800	32,193
5		26,797	26,797	0.681	18,249	43,800	29,828
6		26,797	26,797	0.630	16,882	43,800	27,594
7		26,797	26,797	0.583	15,623	43,800	25,535
8		26,797	26,797	0.540	14,470	43,800	23,652
9		26,797	26,797	0.500	13,399	43,800	21,900
10	10,000	26,797	36,797	0.463	17,037	43,800	20,279
11		26,797	26,797	0.429	11,496	43,800	18,790
12		26,797	26,797	0.397	10,638	43,800	17,389
13		26,797	26,797	0.368	9,861	43,800	16,118
14		26,797	26,797	0.340	9,111	43,800	14,892
15		26,797	26,797	0.315	8,441	43,800	13,797
16		26,797	26,797	0.292	7,825	43,800	12,790
17		26,797	26,797	0.270	7,235	43,800	11,826
18		26,797	26,797	0.250	6,699	43,800	10,950
19		26,797	26,797	0.232	6,217	43,800	10,162
20		26,797	26,797	0.215	5,761	43,800	9,417
21		26,797	26,797	0.199	5,333	43,800	8,716
22		26,797	26,797	0.184	4,931	43,800	8,059
23		26,797	26,797	0.170	4,556	43,800	7,446
24		26,797	26,797	0.158	4,234	43,800	6,920
25		26,797	26,797	0.146	3,912	43,800	6,395
				TOTAL PRESENT COSTS	545,312	TOTAL PRESENT VALUE OF WATER SOLD AND PAID FOR	449,186

1. Average Incremental Cost = (Present Value of Total Costs)/(Present Value of water sold and paid for)
= US$545,312,000/449,186,000m^3 = **US$1.21 per m3**

11.4   Annex 4: Example financial projections for Kampala

Year	0	5	10	15	20	25
HIGH INCOME AREAS						
Service Level 1:Full pressure						
Total Number of Accounts	13960	16460	20960	32260	56260	83260
Consumption (m3 per year)	3566780	4475029	6063627	9930720	18428554	29020381
Av. Consump. Per Account per Month	21.3	22.7	24.1	25.7	27.3	29.0
Lifeline billing		355536	452736	696816	1215216	1798416
Merit Billing		2406948	3265827	5355438	9950047	15686451
Total Billing		2762484	3718563	6052254	11165263	17484867
MIDDLE INCOME AREAS						
Service Level 1:Full pressure						
Total Number of Accounts	13960	21160	28660	48460	115460	187460
Consumption	3566780	5752832	8291200	14917629	37820137	65339426
Av. Consump. Per Account per Month	21.3	22.7	24.1	25.7	27.3	29.0
Lifeline billing		457056	619056	1046736	2493936	4049136
Merit Billing		3094230	4465582	8044778	20420057	35318066
Total Billing		3551286	5084638	9091514	22913993	39367202
Service Level 2:12-hr household supply						
Total Number of Accounts	0	6000	12000	20500	30500	40500
Consumption	0	1387559	3139791	6068659	10215463	15347320
Av. Consump. Per Account per Month	0.0	19.3	21.8	24.7	27.9	31.6
Lifeline billing		129600	259200	442800	658800	874800
Merit Billing		743357	1687285	3270112	5517854	8307376
Total Billing		872957	1946485	3712912	6176654	9182176
Service Level 3: 12-hr yard tap supply						
Total Number of Accounts	0	2500	5000	6000	7000	8000
Consumption	0	361343.5	817654	1110121	1465332.8	1894731
Av. Consump. Per Account per Month	0.0	12.0	13.6	15.4	17.4	19.7
Lifeline billing		54000	108000	129600	151200	172800
Merit Billing		190489	433210	590766	782833	1015702
Total Billing		244489	541210	720366	934033	1188502
Service Level 4:Shared connection						
Total Number of Accounts	0	2500	5000	6300	7000	7350
Consumption	0	867224.4	1962370	2797504	3516798.6	4177881.6
Av. Consump. Per Account per Month	0	28.9	32.7	37.0	41.9	47.4
Billing		260167	588711	839251	1055040	1253364
LOW INCOME AREAS						
Service Level 5:Ground tank						
Total Number of Accounts	0	4000	8800	10900	13400	18400
Consumption	0	319184	783841	1091398	1502045	2292290
Av. Consump. Per Account per Month	0	6.6	7.4	8.3	9.3	10.4
Billing		95755.2	235152.3	327419.4	450613.5	687686.9
Service Level 6:Community kiosk						
Number of Accounts	0	500	850	1060	1540	2540
Consumption	0	239388.1	456246.4	638933.4	1030586.4	1877450.2
Av. Consump. Per Account per Month	0	39.9	44.7	50.2	55.8	61.6
Billing		47877.6	91249.3	127786.7	206117.3	375490.0
Service Level 7:Public Kiosk						
Number of Accounts	545	795	1045	1165	1265	1365
Consumption	895163	1587913	2370548	2958744	3576218	4274377
Av. Consump. Per Account per Month	136.9	166.4	189.0	211.6	235.6	261.0
Billing		317582.7	474109.6	591748.7	715243.6	854875.4
Service Level 8:Utility water vending						
Number of Accounts	0	190	290	320	320	320
Consumption	0	294841.6	486644.8	598350.1	676978.26	765938.76
Av. Consump. Per Account per Month		129.3	139.8	155.8	176.3	199.5
Billing		58968.3	97329.0	119670.0	135395.7	153187.8
Service Level 9:Prepaid metered kiosk						
Number of Accounts	0	130	230	290	340	390
Consumption	0	300785.9	569899.5	783430.5	1000715.3	1246324.6
Av. Consump. Per Account per Month		192.8	206.5	225.1	245.3	266.3
Billing		60157.2	113979.9	156686.1	200143.1	249264.9
TOTAL DOMESTIC DEMAND	8028723	15586102	24941822	40895488	79232829	126236119
NON-DOMESTIC DEMAND	16439877	20981912	26778828	34177324	43619889	55671260
NON-DOMESTIC CONNECTIONS	8612	10991	14028	17904	22850	29163
Commercial/Industrial	6465	8251	10531	13440	17154	21893
Consumption upto 30m3/month.conn	775800	2970418	3791089	4838497	6175285	7881402
Revenue from 1st step consumption	465480	2079292	2653763	3386948	4322700	5516982
Revenue from 2nd step consumption	12531262	11502571	14680520	18736477	23913020	30519746
Government/Institutional	2147	2740	3497	4463	5697	7271
Revenue from Govt/Institutions	80847	4707774	6008445	7668468	9787124	12491126
TOTAL NUMBER OF ACCOUNTS	37077	65226	96863	145159	255935	378748
TOTAL REVENUE (million US$)	13.08	26.56	36.23	51.53	81.98	119.32
TOTAL EXPENDITURE (million US$)	11.42	16.82	50.77	28.42	54.60	59.20
Surplus/Deficit	1.66	9.74	-14.54	23.11	27.38	60.12
Cumulated Surplus/Deficit	1.66	34.55	30.73	85.42	44.95	283.54
TOTAL DEMAND (m3)	24468600	36568014	51720650	75072812	122852717	181907380
Average Tariff (US$/m3)		0.73	0.70	0.69	0.67	0.66
TARGET COVERAGE	31%	51%	62%	69%	87%	100%
Year	0	5	10	15	20	25

TARIFF	$/m3
Merit Billing hse conn. above 6m3 p.m.	0.55
Government/Institutional	0.6
Small Scale Ind/Comm up to 30 m3 p.m.	0.7
Commercial/Ind activities > 30 m3 p.m.	0.9
Public tap rate	0.2

11.5 Annex 5: Short questionnaire for water services in infomal settlements

1. From where do you and other members of your household obtain water?

Please indicate all the water sources that are used by the people in your household and whether you use that water for drinking and cooking or other uses. Please also estimate the average number of 20-litre jerrycans that are collected each day from each source for your household (tick boxes as necessary).

	For drinking and cooking	Other uses	Average no. of jerrycans used a day from each source for your household
i) Your own piped water connection (inside your house)	☐	☐	………
ii) Your own piped water connection (outside your house)	☐	☐	………
iii) Buy water from your neighbour	☐	☐	………
iv) A shared yard water connection	☐	☐	………
v) Private vendor	☐	☐	………
vi) Water kiosk	☐	☐	………
vii) Public standpost	☐	☐	………
viii) Water tanker	☐	☐	………

		For drinking and Cooking	Other uses	Average no. of jerrycans used a day from each for your household
ix)	Handcart /bicycle water vendor	☐	☐	…………
x)	Private open well	☐	☐	…………
xi)	Handpump	☐	☐	…………
xii)	Rainwater from roofs	☐	☐	…………
xii)	Spring water	☐	☐	………..
xiii)	From pools of water/lake or stream	☐	☐	………..

Total ………

(*Note – check where vendors obtain their water to avoid double counting)

2. What is the number of people in your household? …………………………………….

3. What is the average time to collect water for *all* the household *each day*? ……………………(minutes)

4. What is the distance to the nearest piped water source that you can use?……………..………….(metres)

5. What is the average price of water from local vendors? ……………………………..(per 20-litre jerrycan)

6. Average number of days per week that piped water is available? …………(answer if you use piped water)

7. What is the average number of hours of piped water per day?……………(answer if you use piped water)

8. Are you satisfied with the utility water services? (yes or no) ……………(answer if you use piped water)

9. What is the average total household expenditure on water? ………………(per week)

10. In you household, what percentage of water is collected by:

women: …….. children……….. men ……………..

11. How far from your house is there a functioning sanitation system such as a latrine or toilet that you regularly use?…………………………………….(metres)

12. What material are the walls of your house made from:

a) unburnt bricks………… b) burnt bricks or blocks …………… c) mud and pole ……………..

Notes from the researchers after completing this form: (e.g. was the respondent able to answer the questions that are relevant for them, and any problems encountered or suggested changes?) To be included on a separate sheet.

www.ingramcontent.com/pod-product-compliance
Lightning Source LLC
Chambersburg PA
CBHW080952050426
42334CB00057B/2603